MAKING FAILURE FEASIBLE

Working Group on Economic Policy

Many of the writings associated with this working group are published by the Hoover Institution Press or other publishers. Materials published to date, or in production, are listed below. Books that are part of the Working Group on Economic Policy's Resolution Project are marked with an asterisk.

Making Failure Feasible: How Bankruptcy Reform Can End "Too Big to Fail"*
Edited by Kenneth E. Scott, Thomas H. Jackson, and John B. Taylor

Bankruptcy Not Bailout: A Special Chapter 14*
Edited by Kenneth E. Scott and John B. Taylor

Across the Great Divide: New Perspectives on the Financial Crisis
Edited by Martin Neil Baily and John B. Taylor

Frameworks for Central Banking in the Next Century
Edited by Michael Bordo and John B. Taylor

Government Policies and the Delayed Economic Recovery
Edited by Lee E. Ohanian, John B. Taylor, and Ian J. Wright

Why Capitalism?
Allan H. Meltzer

First Principles: Five Keys to Restoring America's Prosperity
John B. Taylor

Ending Government Bailouts as We Know Them*
Edited by Kenneth E. Scott, George P. Shultz, and John B. Taylor

How Big Banks Fail: And What to Do about It*
Darrell Duffie

The Squam Lake Report: Fixing the Financial System
Darrell Duffie et al.

Getting Off Track: How Government Actions and Interventions Caused, Prolonged, and Worsened the Financial Crisis
John B. Taylor

The Road Ahead for the Fed
Edited by John B. Taylor and John D. Ciorciari

Putting Our House in Order: A Guide to Social Security and Health Care Reform
George P. Shultz and John B. Shoven

MAKING FAILURE FEASIBLE

FEASIBLE

*How Bankruptcy Reform Can
End "Too Big to Fail"*

EDITED BY

Kenneth E. Scott, Thomas H. Jackson,
and John B. Taylor

HOOVER INSTITUTION PRESS
Stanford University | Stanford, California

www.hoover.org

Hoover Institution Press Publication No. 662

Hoover Institution at Leland Stanford Junior University,
Stanford, California 94305-6003

First printing 2015
21 20 19 18 17 16 15   7 6 5 4 3 2 1

Manufactured in the United States of America

The paper used in this publication meets the minimum Requirements of the American National Standard for Information Sciences—Permanence of Paper for Printed Library Materials, ANSI/NISO Z39.48-1992. ⊚

Cataloging-in-Publication Data is available from the Library of Congress.
ISBN: 978-0-8179-1884-2 (cloth : alk. paper)
ISBN: 978-0-8179-1886-6 (epub)
ISBN: 978-0-8179-1887-3 (mobi)
ISBN: 978-0-8179-1888-0 (PDF)

The Hoover Institution gratefully acknowledges the following individuals and foundations for their significant support of the Working Group on Economic Policy:

Lynde and Harry Bradley Foundation

Preston and Carolyn Butcher

Stephen and Sarah Page Herrick

Michael and Rosalind Keiser

Koret Foundation

William E. Simon Foundation

John A. Gunn and Cynthia Fry Gunn

Contents

List of Figures and Tables   ix

Preface   xi
John B. Taylor

1 | The Context for Bankruptcy Resolutions   1
Kenneth E. Scott

2 | Building on Bankruptcy: A Revised Chapter 14 Proposal
for the Recapitalization, Reorganization, or Liquidation
of Large Financial Institutions   15
Thomas H. Jackson

3 | Financing Systemically Important Financial Institutions
in Bankruptcy   59
David A. Skeel Jr.

4 | Resolution of Failing Central Counterparties   87
Darrell Duffie

5 | The Consequences of Chapter 14 for International Recognition
of US Bank Resolution Action   111
Simon Gleeson

6 | A Resolvable Bank   129
Thomas F. Huertas

7 | The Next Lehman Bankruptcy   175
Emily Kapur

8 | Revised Chapter 14 2.0 and Living Will Requirements under the Dodd-Frank Act   243
William F. Kroener III

9 | The Cross-Border Challenge in Resolving Global Systemically Important Banks   249
Jacopo Carmassi and Richard Herring

About the Contributors   277

About the Hoover Institution's Working Group on Economic Policy   283

Index   285

List of Figures and Tables

Figures

4.1 Example of CCP Default-Management Waterfall of Recovery Resources   91

6.1 Resolution Has Three Stages   131

6.2 Unit Bank: Balance Sheet Overview   133

6.3 Determination of Reserve Capital and ALAC Requirements   135

6.4 Prompt Corrective Action Limits the Need for Reserve Capital   137

6.5 Unit Bank with Parent Holding Company   141

6.6 Parent Holding Company/Bank Sub: Balance Sheet Overview   142

6.7 Bank Subsidiary Is Safer Than Parent Holding Company   150

6.8 Resolution of Parent   152

6.9 Banking Group with Domestic and Foreign Subsidiaries   160

6.10 SPE Approach Requires Concurrence of Home and Host   163

7.1 Insolvency Event for a Dealer Bank   185

7.2 Recapitalization's Ability to Stop Runs Sparked by Insolvency   187

7.3 Lehman Stock and Bond Prices January–December 2008   189

7.4 Lehman Corporate Structure   190

7.5 Market Valuation of Lehman's Solvency Equity   193

7.6 Liquidity Losses over Lehman's Final Week   198

7.7 Only Holdings Files   211

7.8 Counterfactual Timeline of Chapter 14 Section 1405 Transfer   213

7.9 Structure of the Section 1405 Transfer 216

7.10 Recapitalizing Subsidiaries after Sale Approval 223

7.11 Post–Chapter 14 Asset Devaluations Short of Insolvency 225

7.12 G-Reliance on Fed Funding during the Financial Crisis 230

7.13 New Lehman's Initial Public Offering 234

7.14 Approving a Plan and Paying Claimants 236

9.1a Number of Subsidiaries of the Largest US Bank Holding Companies 253

9.1b Number of Countries in Which US Bank Holding Companies Have Subsidiaries 253

9.2 Evolution of Average Number of Subsidiaries and Total Assets for G-SIBs 254

Tables

6.1 Bail-In at Parent Does Not Recapitalize the Subsidiary Bank 145

6.2 Bail-In at Subsidiary Bank Recapitalizes the Subsidiary Bank 148

6.3 Decision Rights during Resolution Process 158

7.1 Lehman's and Holdings' Balance Sheets 196

7.2 Post–Chapter 14 Hypothetical Liquidity Stress Test 9/8–9/26 228

7.3 Holdings' Balance Sheet, Recoveries, and Claims 238

9.1 Profile of G-SIBs 254

9.2 Disaggregation of Subsidiaries of 13 G-SIBs by Industry Classification (May 2013) 256

Preface

John B. Taylor

Motivated by the backlash over the bailouts during the global financial crisis and concerns that a continuing bailout mentality would create grave dangers to the US and world financial systems, a group of us established the Resolution Project at the Hoover Institution in the spring of 2009. Ken Scott became the chair of the project and George Shultz wrote down what would be the mission statement:[1]

> The right question is: how do we make failure tolerable? If clear and credible measures can be put into place that convince everybody that failure will be allowed, then the expectations of bailouts will recede and perhaps even disappear. We would also get rid of the risk-inducing behavior that even implicit government guarantees bring about. "Heads, I win; tails, you lose" will always lead to excessive risk. And we would get rid of the unfair competitive advantage given to the "too big to fail" group by the implicit government guarantee behind their borrowing and other activities. At the same time, by being clear about what will happen and that failure can occur without risk to the system, we avoid the creation of a panic environment.

This book—the third in a series that has emerged from the Resolution Project—takes up that original mission statement once again. It represents a culmination of policy-directed research from the Resolution Project of the Hoover Institution's Working Group on Economic

---

1. George P. Shultz, "Make Failure Tolerable," in *Ending Government Bailouts as We Know Them*, ed. Kenneth Scott, George P. Shultz, and John B. Taylor (Stanford, CA: Hoover Press, 2010).

Policy as its members, topics, and ideas have expanded and as the legal and market environment has changed.

The first book, *Ending Government Bailouts as We Know Them,* published in 2010, proposed a modification of Chapter 11 of the bankruptcy code to permit large failing financial firms to go into bankruptcy without causing disruptive spillovers while continuing to offer their financial services—just as American Airlines planes kept flying and Kmart stores remained open when those firms went into bankruptcy.

The second book, *Bankruptcy Not Bailout: A Special Chapter 14,* published in 2012, built on those original ideas and crafted an explicit bankruptcy reform called Chapter 14 (because there was no such numbered chapter in the US bankruptcy code); it also considered the implications of the "orderly liquidation authority" in Title II of the Dodd-Frank Wall Street Reform and Consumer Protection Act, which was passed into law after the first book was written.

This third book, *Making Failure Feasible: How Bankruptcy Reform Can End "Too Big To Fail,"* centers around Chapter 14 2.0, an expansion of the 2012 Chapter 14 to include a simpler and quicker recapitalization-based bankruptcy reform, analogous to the single-point-of-entry approach that the Federal Deposit Insurance Corporation (FDIC) proposes to use under Title II of the Dodd-Frank Act. And while Chapter 14 2.0 is the centerpiece of the book, each of the chapters is a significant contribution in its own right. These chapters provide the context for reform, outline the fundamental principles of reform, show how reform would work in practice, and go beyond Chapter 14 2.0 with needed complementary reforms.

Recent bills to modify bankruptcy law in ways consistent with the overall mission of the Resolution Project have been introduced in the US Senate (S. 1861, December 2013) and House of Representatives (H. 5421, August 2014). We hope that this new book will be helpful as these bills and others work their way through Congress in the months ahead. Importantly, in this regard, a major finding of this book is that reform of the bankruptcy law is essential even after the passage of the Dodd-Frank Act. First, that act requires that bankruptcy be the standard against which the effectiveness of a resolution process is measured; and, second, that act requires that resolution plans must be found credible under the bankruptcy law, which is nearly impossible for existing firms without a reform of bankruptcy law.

Ken Scott's leadoff chapter, "The Context for Bankruptcy Resolutions," examines several key regulations that are still being proposed or adopted which would affect the resolution process, and it considers how Chapter 14 might deal with them. Scott recommends other measures that would facilitate successful resolutions and emphasizes that there may be cases in which a great many firms need to be resolved simultaneously and therefore may be "beyond the reach of Title II or Chapter 14." This speaks to the need for further reform efforts to reduce risk along the lines George Shultz emphasized in his original "Make Failure Tolerable" piece.

The detailed proposal for Chapter 14 2.0 and its rationale are carefully explained by Tom Jackson in the chapter "Building on Bankruptcy: A Revised Chapter 14 Proposal for the Recapitalization, Reorganization, or Liquidation of Large Financial Institutions." The chapter outlines the basic features of the initial Chapter 14 proposal and then focuses on the provisions for a direct recapitalization through a holding company.

David Skeel's chapter, "Financing Systemically Important Financial Institutions in Bankruptcy," considers the issue of providing special government financing arrangements for financial firms going through bankruptcy. Currently, Chapter 11 does not provide such arrangements, and some recently proposed legislation explicitly prohibits government funding. Critics of bankruptcy approaches (especially in contrast with Title II resolution, which provides for funding from the US Treasury) point to the absence of such funding as a serious problem. Skeel argues, however, that a large financial firm in bankruptcy would likely be able to borrow sufficient funds from non-government sources to quickly finance a resolution in bankruptcy. Nevertheless, he warns that potential lenders might refuse to fund, especially if a firm "falls into financial distress during a period of market-wide instability." He therefore considers prearranged private funding and governmental funding as supplements.

The chapter by Darrell Duffie, "Resolution of Failing Central Counterparties," explains the essential role of central counterparties (CCPs) in the post-crisis financial system and notes that they too entail substantial risks. However, as he points out, it "is not a completely settled matter" whether Dodd-Frank "assigns the administration of the failure resolution process" to the FDIC under Title II. Since Chapter 14 would exclude CCPs, this leaves an area of systemic risk that still needs to be addressed.

In "The Consequences of Chapter 14 for International Recognition of US Bank Resolution Action," Simon Gleeson examines an extremely difficult problem in the resolution of failing financial institutions: "the question of how resolution measures in one country should be given effect under the laws of another." He notes that "most courts find it easier to recognize foreign bankruptcy proceedings than unclassified administrative procedures which may bear little resemblance to anything in the home jurisdiction." Thus, after comparing Chapter 14 and Title 11, he concludes that "replacing Title II with Chapter 14 could well have a positive impact on the enforceability in other jurisdictions of US resolution measures."

In the chapter "A Resolvable Bank," Thomas Huertas gets down to basics and explains the essence of "making failure feasible." He considers the key properties of a bank that make it "resolvable" both in a single jurisdiction and in multiple jurisdictions. As he explains, "A resolvable bank is one that is 'safe to fail': it can fail and be resolved without cost to the taxpayer and without significant disruption to the financial markets or the economy at large." A separation of "investor obligations" such as the bank's capital instruments and "customer obligations" such as deposits is "the key to resolvability." If customer obligations are made senior to investor obligations, then a sufficiently large amount of investor obligations can create a solvent bank-in-resolution which can obtain liquidity and continue offering services to its customers.

In "The Next Lehman Bankruptcy," Emily Kapur examines how the September 15, 2008, Lehman Brothers bankruptcy would have played out were Chapter 14 available at the time, a question essential to understanding whether and how this reform would work in practice. The chapter finds that "under certain assumptions, applying Chapter 14 to Lehman in a timely manner would have returned it to solvency and thereby forestalled the run that occurred in 2008." Chapter 14 "could have reduced creditors' direct losses by hundreds of billions of dollars" and these more favorable expectations would have reduced the "risk of runs" and avoided some of the worst consequences of Lehman Brothers' bankruptcy.

William Kroener's chapter, "Revised Chapter 14 2.0 and Living Will Requirements under the Dodd-Frank Act," considers the important connection between bankruptcy reform and post-crisis reforms already passed in Dodd-Frank. As Kroener points out, Dodd-Frank now requires that resolution plans submitted by large financial firms show how these firms can be resolved in cases of distress or failure in a "rapid and orderly resolution" without systemic spillovers under the existing law, which of course includes existing bankruptcy law. However, thus far the plans submitted by the financial firms have been rejected. He shows how Chapter 14 would facilitate the ability of a resolution plan to meet the statutory requirements.

The chapter "The Cross-Border Challenge in Resolving Global Systemically Important Banks," by Jacopo Carmassi and Richard Herring, concludes the book with a warning that, even with the Chapter 14–style reforms proposed here, there is more work to do. They argue, "More effective bankruptcy procedures like the proposed Chapter 14 reform would certainly help provide a stronger anchor to market expectations about how the resolution of a G-SIB [Global Systemically Important Bank] may unfold," but they conclude, "Although too-big-to-fail is too-costly-to-continue, a solution to the problem remains elusive."

So one might look forward to yet another book in this series, or at the least to more policy-driven research by the members of the Resolution Project on the ongoing theme of ending the too-big-to-fail problem by making failure of financial institutions safe, tolerable, and feasible. In the meantime, the material in this book provides a detailed roadmap for needed reform.

CHAPTER 1

The Context for Bankruptcy Resolutions

Kenneth E. Scott

Introduction

Any process for resolving the affairs of failed financial institutions other than banks, whether under Title II of the Dodd-Frank Act of 2010 or the Resolution Project's proposed new version of a Chapter 14 of the Bankruptcy Code, takes as its starting point a firm whose organizational form and financial structure have been determined by a complex set of statutory and regulatory requirements. At this writing, many of those requirements are still being developed, important aspects are uncertain, and terminology is not set.

A note on terminology: the phrase "systemically important financial institution" or SIFI is nowhere defined (or even used) in the Dodd-Frank Act, though it has come into common parlance. I will use it here to refer to those financial companies whose distress or failure could qualify for seizure under Title II and Federal Deposit Insurance Corp. (FDIC) receivership, as threatening serious adverse effects on US financial stability. Presumably they come from bank holding companies with more than $50 billion in consolidated assets and nonbank financial companies that have been designated for supervision by the Federal Reserve Board.

Revised Chapter 14 2.0, at places, makes assumptions about pending requirements' final form, and may have to be modified in the light of what is settled on. It also contains recommended changes in the application of stays to QFCs (qualified financial contracts), which are also relevant to a separate chapter in this volume by Darrell Duffie on the resolution of central clearing counterparties.

The Resolution Project's original proposal (Chapter 14 1.0) contemplated resolving a troubled financial institution through reorganization of the firm in a manner similar to a familiar Chapter 11 proceeding, with a number of specialized adjustments. Subsequently, the FDIC has proposed that the failure of those large US financial institutions (mostly bank holding company groups) that are thought to be systemically important (SIFIs) and not satisfactorily resolvable under current bankruptcy law will be handled by (1) placing the parent holding company under the control of the FDIC as a Title II receiver and (2) transferring to a new "bridge" financial company most of its assets and secured liabilities (and some vendor claims)—but not most of its unsecured debt. Exactly what is to be left behind is not yet defined, but will be here referred to as bail-in debt (BID) or capital debt. (Any convertible debt instruments—CoCos—that the firm may have issued are required to have been already converted to equity.) The losses that created a fear of insolvency might have occurred anywhere in the debtor's corporate structure, but the takeover would be of the parent company—a tactic described as a "single point of entry" (SPOE).

The desired result would be a new financial company that was strongly capitalized (having shed a large amount of its prior debt), would have the capacity to recapitalize (where necessary) operating subsidiaries, and would have the confidence of other market participants, and therefore be able to immediately continue its critical operations in the financial system without any systemic spillover effects or problems. But all of that depends on a number of preconditions and assumptions about matters such as: the size and locus of the losses, the amount and terms of capital debt and where it is held, the availability of short-term (liquidity) debt to manage the daily flow of transactions, and agreement on priorities and dependable cooperation among regulators in different countries where the firm and its subsidiaries operate—to name some of the most salient.

If the failed financial institution is not deemed to present a threat to US financial stability, even though large, it is not covered by Title II but would come under the Bankruptcy Code. Chapter 14 2.0 is our proposal for a bankruptcy proceeding that is especially designed for financial institutions and includes provisions for the use of SPOE bridge transfers where desired, and it too will be affected by the regulatory regime in force—especially as it relates to BID.

Not all of these matters are, or can be, determined by Dodd-Frank or in the Bankruptcy Code. But they can be affected for better or worse by regulations still being proposed or adopted. This paper represents my attempt, for readers not unfamiliar with these topics, to highlight some of the problems and Chapter 14's responses, and to recommend some other measures that would facilitate successful resolutions.

Capital Debt

Definition

1) In FDIC's proposal, the debt that is not to be transferred (and thus fully paid) is not precisely specified. It is suggested that accounts payable to "essential" vendors would go over, and "likely" secured claims as well (at least as deemed necessary to avoid systemic risk), but not (all?) unsecured debt for borrowed funds. Unless ultimately much better specified, this would leave a high degree of uncertainty for creditors of financial institutions, with corresponding costs.

There are some specifics that have been suggested—for example, that capital debt be limited to unsecured debt for borrowed money with an original (or perhaps remaining) maturity of over a year. That would imply a regulatory requirement that a SIFI hold at all times a prescribed minimum amount of such debt—at a level yet to be determined but perhaps equal to its applicable regulatory capital requirements and buffers, giving a total loss absorbing capacity (TLAC) of as much as 20 percent to 25 percent of risk-weighted assets

Would that total amount be sufficient to cover all losses the firm might encounter, and enough more to leave it still well capitalized? That depends on the magnitude of the losses it has incurred. In effect, the debt requirement becomes a new ingredient of required total capital (beyond equity), and impaired total capital could trigger resolution (but not necessarily continuance of operations, unless a grace period of a year or more for restoration of the mandated TLAC were included). The operative constraint is the mandated total amount of regulatory capital plus BID; the exact split between the two is less significant, and could be a matter for management judgment. Until such requirements are actually specified and instituted, however, their effectiveness is hard to analyze.

The definition of bail-in debt continues to be controverted. Is it a species of unsecured bonds for borrowed money, with specified staggered maturities? Is it all unsecured liabilities, with an extensive list of exceptions? Whatever the category, does it apply retroactively to existing liabilities? Will investors realize their risk status? Should disclosure requirements be spelled out? (It is hard to see why it is not defined simply as newly issued subordinated debt, without any cumbersome apparatus for conversions or write-downs or loss of a priority rank.)

2) A capital debt requirement would function the same way in Chapter 14, but without discretionary uncertainty. Section 1405 provides for the transfer to a bridge company of all the debtor's assets (which should include NOL [net operating loss] carry-forwards) and liabilities (*except* for the capital debt and any subordinated debt); in exchange, the debtor estate receives all of the stock in the new entity. And the external capital debt is given a clear definition: it must be designated unsecured debt for borrowed money with an original maturity of one year or more. To be effective, minimum capital debt requirements (an issue outside of bankruptcy law) would again need to be specified.

It should be noted that Chapter 14 applies to all financial companies, not just SIFIs that pose systemic risk and not just to resolution through a bridge. The firm may go through a familiar Chapter 11 type of reorganization, following on a filing by either management or supervisor after losses have impaired compliance with whatever are the total capital plus BID (TLAC) requirements then in force. In that case, the BID is not "left behind" but should all automatically (under the provisions of its indenture) either be written down or converted to a new class of senior common stock, or to preferred stock or subordinated debt with similar terms. (If conversion were to a security on a parity with outstanding common stock, there would be immediate time-consuming and disputable issues about how to determine asset valuations and losses and the possible value of existing common shares. These are avoided by simply converting instead to a new class with a priority above outstanding common and below ordinary liabilities.)

3) What is the locus of the capital debt? The question is central to whether subsidiaries necessarily continue in operation. The FDIC proposal seems to contemplate that it is issued by a parent holding company (or, in the case of a foreign parent, its intermediate US holding company), and thus removed from the capital structure of the new bridge company, which is thereby rendered solvent.

But what if the large losses precipitating failure of the US parent were incurred at a foreign subsidiary? There have been suggestions that the new bridge parent would be so strongly capitalized that it *could* recapitalize the failed subsidiary—but who makes that decision, and on what basis? The supervisory authorities of foreign host countries have understandably shown a keen interest in the answer, and it is high on the agendas of various international talks.

A core attribute of separate legal entities is their separation of risk and liability. Under corporation law, the decision to pay off a subsidiary's creditors would be a business judgment for the parent board, taking into account financial cost, reputational cost, future prospects, and the like—and the decision could be negative. In a Title II proceeding, perhaps the FDIC, through its control of the board, would override (or dictate) that decision—and perhaps not.

The clearest legal ways to try to ensure payment of subsidiary creditors would be (1) to require parents to guarantee all subsidiary debt (which amounts to a de facto consolidation) or (2) to have separate and hopefully adequate "internal" capital debt (presumably to the parent) requirements for all material subsidiaries. Again, at time of writing it is an issue still to be resolved, and perhaps better left to the host regulators and the firm's business judgment in the specific circumstances.

Coverage

1) The FDIC's SPOE bridge proposal seemingly applies only to domestic financial companies posing systemic risk (currently, eight bank and three or four non-bank holding companies are so regarded, although more may be added, even at the last minute), not to the next hundred or so bank holding companies with more than $10 billion in consolidated assets, or to all the (potentially over one thousand)

"financial companies" covered by Dodd-Frank's Title I definition (at least 85 percent of assets or revenues from financial activities). Will the capital debt requirement be limited to those dozen SIFIs, or will it be extended to all bank holding companies with more than $250 billion or even $50 billion in consolidated assets (though posing no threat to US financial stability)? That will determine how failure resolutions may be conducted under the Bankruptcy Code, as they must be for all but that small number of SIFIs that Title II covers.

2) Resolution under Chapter 14 (in its original version) can take the form essentially of a familiar Chapter 11 reorganization of the debtor firm (often at an operating entity level). Where systemic risk or other considerations dictate no interruptions of business operations, it may (in its current version 2.0) take the form of transfers to a new bridge company (usually at the holding company level—thus leaving operating subsidiaries out of bankruptcy). Therefore, any capital debt requirement should apply explicitly to both situations, and Chapter 14 would accommodate both options.

3) What triggers the operation of the capital debt mechanism? A filing of a petition under Chapter 14, for which there are two possibilities. The management of a firm facing significant deterioration in its financial position can choose to make a voluntary filing, to preserve operations (and perhaps their jobs) and hopefully some shareholder value, as often occurs in ordinary Chapter 11 proceedings. Depending on circumstances, this could take the form of a single-firm reorganization or a transfer of assets and other liabilities to a new bridge company in exchange for its stock.

The second possibility is a filing by the institution's supervisor, which could be predicated on a determination (1) that it is necessary to avoid serious adverse effects on US financial stability (as our proposal now specifies) or (2), more broadly, that there has been a substantial impairment of required regulatory capital or TLAC. There can be differing views on how much regulatory discretion is advisable, so this too is to some extent an open issue. But the ability of the supervisor to force a recapitalization short of insolvency might alleviate concern that institutions that are "too big to fail" must be broken up or they will inevitably receive government bailouts.

Liquidity

Significance

Banks perform vital roles in intermediating transactions between investors and businesses, buying and selling risk, and operating the payments system. They have to manage fluctuating flows of cash in and out, by short-term borrowing and lending to each other and with financial firms. Bank failures often occur when creditors and counterparties have lost confidence and demand full (or more) and readily marketable collateral before supplying any funds. Even if over time a bank's assets could cover its liabilities, it has to have sufficient immediate cash or it cannot continue in business. For that reason, the Basel Committee and others have adopted, and are in the process of implementing, regulations governing "buffer" liquidity coverage ratios that global systemically important banks (G-SIBs) would be required to maintain.

FDIC's SPOE Proposal

The new bridge company is intended to be so well-capitalized, in the sense of book net worth, that it will have no difficulty in raising any needed funds from other institutions in the private market. But this is an institution that, despite all the Title I regulations, has just failed. There may be limited cash on hand and substantial uncertainty (or controversy) about the value of its loans and investments. So if liquidity is not forthcoming in the private market, Dodd-Frank creates an Orderly Liquidation Fund (OLF) in the Treasury, which the FDIC as receiver can tap for loans or guarantees (to be repaid later by the bridge company or industry assessments) to assure the necessary cash. Critics fear that this will open a door for selected creditor bailouts or ultimate taxpayer costs.

Chapter 14

As with the FDIC proposal, under favorable conditions there may be no problem. But what if cash is low or collateral value uncertain, and there is a problem? It depends on which type of resolution is being pursued.

In a standard Chapter 11 type of reorganization, the debtor firm can typically obtain new ("debtor in possession" or DIP) financing because the lenders are given top ("administrative expense") priority in payment; those provisions remain in effect under Chapter 14. In a bridge resolution, the new company is not in bankruptcy, so the existing Bankruptcy Code priority provision would not apply. Therefore, Chapter 14 2.0 provides that new lenders to the bridge would receive similar priority if it were to fail within a year after the transfer.

In addition, a new financial institution could be given the same access to the Fed's discount window as its competitors have. In a time of general financial crisis it could be eligible to participate in programs established by the Fed under its section 13(3) authority. If all that is not enough assurance of liquidity in case of need, skeptics might support allowing (as a last resort) the supervisor of the failed institution (as either the petitioner or a party in the bankruptcy proceeding) the same access to the OLF as under Title II.

Qualified Financial Contracts

Even with a prompt "resolution weekend" equity recapitalization and measures to bolster liquidity, the first instinct of derivatives counterparties could well be to take advantage of their current exemption from bankruptcy's automatic stay and exercise their contractual termination rights—which could have an abrupt and heavy impact on the firm's ability to continue to conduct business.

Therefore, to simplify a bit, the proposed Chapter 14 amends the Bankruptcy Code to treat a counterparty's derivatives as executory contracts and make them subject to a two-day stay, for the debtor to choose to accept or reject them as a group—provided the debtor continues to fulfill all its obligations. If they are accepted, they remain as part of the firm's book of continuing business.

This would enact into governing US law some of what the International Swaps and Derivatives Association (ISDA) has sought to achieve in its 2014 Resolution Stay Protocol, to stay or override certain cross-default and close-out rights, through amending the master agreements of adhering parties (initially the eighteen largest dealer banks).

Due Process

Title II of Dodd-Frank Act

Section 202 of the Act prescribes a procedure to take over a SIFI posing systemic risks that the Secretary of the Treasury has determined to be in danger of default, with FDIC as receiver instructed to immediately proceed to liquidate it. The secretary's determination, if not consented to, is filed in a petition in the District of Columbia federal district court to appoint the receiver. Unless in twenty-four hours the district court judge has held a hearing, received and considered any conflicting evidence on the financial condition of a huge firm, and either (1) made findings of fact and law, concluded that the determination was arbitrary and capricious, and written an opinion giving all the reasons for that conclusion, or (2) granted the petition, then (3) the petition is deemed granted by operation of law.

Obviously, the pre-seizure judicial hearing is an empty formality, and it is quite possible that most judges would prefer to simply let the twenty-four-hour clock run out. The company can appeal the outcome as arbitrary and capricious (although the record may be rather one-sided), but the court cannot stay the receiver's actions to dismantle the firm (or transfer operations to a bridge), pending appeal. So in the unlikely event that there is a successful appeal, an adequate remedy would be hard to design. The whole procedure invites constitutional due process challenge.

Chapter 14

Most debtors are likely to go through a straightforward, one-firm reorganization, which entails claimant participation, public hearings, and well-defined rules, all presided over by an Article III (life tenure) judge. Criteria of due process and fundamental fairness are observed in a procedure developed over many years.

In the case of a SIFI going through the bridge route in order to promote continuity of essential services, the transfer motion is subjected to a somewhat more substantial hearing, in terms of both time and content. If the Fed is filing the motion, it has to certify (and make a statement of the reasons) that it has found (1) that a default by the firm would have serious adverse effects on US financial stability and (2) that the new bridge company can meet the transferred obligations. If the Treasury Secretary decides to assert authority to put the proceeding into Title II, he would be required in addition to certify and make a statement of the reasons for having found that those adverse effects could not adequately be addressed under the Bankruptcy Code (as amended by Chapter 14).

Nonetheless, the court would not be in a position, given the time constraints, to conduct a genuine adversary hearing and make an independent judgment. To overcome the serious due process shortcomings attached to the Title II section, Chapter 14 provides for an ex-post remedy under section 106 of the Bankruptcy Code: an explicit damage cause of action against the United States. And rather than the very narrow judicial oversight possible under the "arbitrary and capricious" standard of review (as in Title II), there is the standard of whether the relevant certifications are supported by "substantial evidence on the record as a whole."

International Coordination

Most SIFIs are global firms (G-SIFIs), with branches and subsidiaries in many countries. To resolve them efficiently and equitably would require cooperation and similar approaches by regulators in both home and host nations. Optimally, that would mean a multilateral treaty among all the countries affected—a daunting undertaking that would take years at best. The Financial Stability Board, in its Key Attributes paper, has outlined a framework for procedures and cooperation agreements among resolution authorities, but they are in general not legally binding or enforceable in judicial proceedings.

The response of ISDA in its Resolution Stay Protocol was to seek a contractual solution in the master agreements, with the expectation that it would be enforced under the laws of six major jurisdictions. But since adherence is voluntary and coverage will be partial, there are gaps best filled by a statutory approach.

To make a modest legal beginning, a binding international agreement just between the United States and the United Kingdom would cover a large fraction of total transactions. The FDIC and Bank of

England in a 2010 Memorandum of Understanding agreed to consult, cooperate, and exchange information relevant to the condition and possible resolution of financial service firms with cross-border operations. The Memorandum specifically, however, does not create any legally binding obligations.

A treaty, or binding executive agreement, could go further to determine how a resolution would proceed between the United States and United Kingdom as home or host countries. To get that process under way, the Resolution Project would provide in Chapter 15 (added to the code in 2005 to deal with cross-border insolvencies) new substantive provisions dealing with US enforcement of foreign home country stay orders and barring domestic ring-fencing actions against local assets, provided that the home country has adopted similar provisions for US proceedings. Unilateral action by the United States, conditioned on such a basis of reciprocal treatment, would be desirable on its merits and might contribute to much broader multilateral efforts.

The Problem of Systemic Risk

The special concern with the failure of a systemically important financial institution is based on the fear that it may lead to a collapse of the financial system which transfers savings, loans, and payments throughout the economy and is essential to its functioning. There are several different ways in which this might occur.

Knock-On Chains

In this scenario, a giant, "interconnected" financial firm incurs very large losses (from poor investment decisions, fraud, or bad luck) and defaults on its obligations, inflicting immediate losses on its counterparties, causing some of them to fail in turn. As a wave of failures spreads, the whole financial system contracts and so does the real economy.

Some observers attribute the panic of 2008 to losses caused by the failure of Lehman Brothers. That belief powered much of the Dodd-Frank Act and in particular its Title II mechanism for taking over a SIFI and putting it into a government receivership. It is not clear how a government receivership per se of a failed firm (without any bailout) is supposed to prevent direct spillover losses, other than that the process will be more "orderly" than was the case for Lehman. The fact that Lehman had done absolutely zero planning for a bankruptcy reorganization makes that a low standard, and the Dodd-Frank section 165 "living wills" requirement for firms to have resolution plans can't help but be an improvement, however limited their "credibility" in an actual case may turn out to be. Their best practical use might be as rough preliminary drafts for "pre-packaged" bankruptcy petition filings.

In any event, Title II and FDIC's SPOE proposal are all focused on a new procedure for handling the impending failure of an individual SIFI, and accordingly so is the Chapter 14 proposal for bankruptcy reform.

Common Shocks

In this scenario, a very widely held class of assets or investments turns out to perform unexpectedly poorly and becomes increasingly hard to value and trade. The example in 2007 and 2008 was asset-backed securities, and in particular over $2 trillion in residential (and commercial) real estate mortgage-backed securities that had been promoted as a matter of government policy and were held by financial institutions and investors around the world.

Until December 2006, subprime mortgages had been sustained by the Fed's drastically low interest rates and ever-increasing house prices. But then that bubble burst. Delinquencies and foreclosures started rising, adversely affecting the tranches of complex securitizations. Rating agencies downgraded hundreds of subprime mortgage bonds. Financial firms became concerned about the solvency of counterparties with large but opaque holdings, and they responded by reducing or cutting off extensions of credit.

The situation came to a head in early September 2008. The giant mortgage insurers Fannie Mae and Freddie Mac were put into conservatorships, Merrill Lynch was forced into acquisition by Bank of America, Lehman filed for bankruptcy, and the Fed made an $85 billion loan to AIG—all in a ten-day period. With such unmistakable signals of the scope and severity of the problem, the flow of funds through the financial system dried up and business firms in general were forced to contract operations. A severe recession in the real economy was under way.

This kind of common asset problem affecting a great many firms cannot be prevented or cured by the early resolution of an individual SIFI. It should be understood to be beyond the reach of Title II or Chapter 14, though they remain relevant to the extent the two categories of systemic risk overlap and some SIFIs can be resolved.

CHAPTER 2

Building on Bankruptcy: A Revised Chapter 14 Proposal for the Recapitalization, Reorganization, or Liquidation of Large Financial Institutions

Thomas H. Jackson

Introduction

In 2012, building off of work first published in 2010, the Resolution Project proposed that a new Chapter 14 be added to the Bankruptcy Code, designed exclusively to deal with the reorganization or liquidation of the nation's larger financial institutions.[1] This proposal was, in turn, the Resolution Project's studied perspective on the most appropriate way to respond to the financial crisis of 2008 and the federal government's role in it, highlighted by the bankruptcy of Lehman Brothers. There quickly emerged a consensus—certainly among our working group, but more widespread—that the institutions, and the government, lacked important tools to deal effectively with financially distressed large financial institutions without the Hobson's choice of either potential systemic consequences affecting the nation's economy as a whole or a bailout—a financial "rescue" of the institution so that it would not fail. Chief among the perspectives that new tools were necessary was the widespread perception that bankruptcy, as it existed at that time, was simply not up to the task of resolving, according to

---

1. Kenneth E. Scott and John B. Taylor, eds., *Bankruptcy Not Bailout: A Special Chapter 14* (Stanford, CA: Hoover Institution Press, 2012); Kenneth E. Scott, George P. Shultz, and John B. Taylor, *Ending Government Bailouts as We Know Them* (Stanford, CA: Hoover Institution Press, 2010), particularly chapter 11, pp. 217–51.

the rule of law, such institutions in a fashion that would contain systemic effects.

This conclusion was the result of a number of subsidiary beliefs—some correct, some not. The bankruptcy process was too slow and cumbersome. The adversarial bankruptcy process was conducted before a judicial officer who might know the law, but didn't have the requisite economic or financial expertise or the power to consider systemic consequences. Bankruptcy had too many exclusions to deal effectively with a complex financial group (depository banks and insurance companies were wholly excluded; stockbrokers and commodity brokers were assigned to a specialized provision of Chapter 7).[2] And a series of amendments to the Bankruptcy Code, originally driven by the International Swaps and Derivatives Association (ISDA) and the Federal Reserve Board, had increasingly immunized counterparties on qualified financial contracts from the major consequences of bankruptcy, prominently including bankruptcy's automatic stay under section 362.[3]

While members of the Resolution Project believed that a number of those criticisms were justified, we also believed that thoughtful revisions to the Bankruptcy Code could ameliorate or eliminate many of them, improving the prospect that our largest financial institutions—particularly with pre-bankruptcy planning—could be reorganized or liquidated pursuant to the rule of law (especially respecting priorities to ensure that losses fell where they were anticipated). Out of that grew our proposal for a special chapter designed for such financial institutions: a Bankruptcy Code Chapter 14.[4] Key features in that proposal included: (a) allowing an entire covered financial institution, including its non-bank subsidiaries, to be resolved in bankruptcy without the existing Bankruptcy Code's potpourri of

---

2. These criticisms are outlined more fully in Scott et al., *Ending Government Bailouts*, 218.

3. Criticized both in Scott and Taylor, *Bankruptcy Not Bailout*, 45–46; and in David Skeel and Thomas Jackson, "Transaction Consistency and the New Finance in Bankruptcy," *Columbia Law Review* 112 (2012): 152.

4. See Scott and Taylor, *Bankruptcy Not Bailout*.

exemptions; (b) the ability of the institution's primary regulator, who may be aware of potential systemic consequences otherwise not before a bankruptcy court, to file an involuntary petition, including one based on "balance sheet" insolvency, as well as to have standing to be heard as a party or to raise motions relevant to its regulation, including filing a plan of reorganization notwithstanding a debtor's exclusive period and motions for the use, sale, and lease of property; (c) numerous changes to the protections afforded by existing bankruptcy law to holders of qualified financial contracts, especially derivatives and swaps, to ensure that they were treated according to their basic underlying attributes (that of secured liabilities, in the case of repos; that of executory contracts, in the case of derivatives and swaps); (d) provisions allowing, with designated protections against favoritism or bailout, funding for the pre-payment of certain distributions to identified creditors; and (e) the assignment of Chapter 14 cases and proceedings to designated Article III district judges, rather than to bankruptcy judges without the political independence provided by Article III.[5]

In proposing this, we wrote:

> We, the members of the Resolution Project group, believe it is possible through these changes to take advantage of a judicial proceeding—including explicit rules, designated in advance and honed through published judicial precedent, with appeals challenging the application of those rules, public proceedings, and transparency—in such a way as to minimize the felt necessity to use the alternative government agency resolution process recently enacted as a part of the Dodd-Frank Wall Street Reform and Consumer Protection Act. The new chapter could be adopted either in addition or as an alternative to the new resolution regime of Dodd-Frank.
>
> The crucial feature of this new Chapter 14 is to ensure that the covered financial institutions, creditors dealing with them, and other market participants know in advance, in a clear and predictable way, how losses will be allocated if the institution fails. If the creditors of a

---

5. For more detail, see ibid., 26–70.

failed financial institution are protected (bailed out), then the strongest and most rapidly responding constraint on risk taking by the financial institution's management is destroyed, and their losses are transferred to others.[6]

Even with the passage of the Dodd-Frank Wall Street Reform and Consumer Protection Act of 2010,[7] with its own Title II resolution process run by the Federal Deposit Insurance Corporation—the Orderly Liquidation Authority—we believe these changes to bankruptcy law remain vital to accomplish several of the announced goals of Dodd-Frank itself. First, Title I's resolution plans—which we believe are an important part of pre-bankruptcy planning—require a focus on using bankruptcy as the standard against which their effectiveness will be measured.[8] And, second, invocation of Title II itself can only occur if the government regulators find that bankruptcy is wanting.[9] Unless bankruptcy can be seen as a viable alternative for the resolution of a large and complex systemically important financial institution (SIFI) in economic distress, (a) the resolution plans could technically be found not credible or facilitating an orderly liquidation (since they are to be based on bankruptcy) and (b) breakup, or use of Title II of Dodd-Frank, will be the only perceived effective responses to the "too big to fail" problem.[10]

Those remain important reasons for the adoption of many of the proposals the Resolution Project put forth in its original 2012 Chapter 14 proposal. That proposal, however, consistent with most of

---

6. Ibid., 26.

7. Pub. L. No. 111-203, 124 Stat. 1376 (Dodd-Frank Act).

8. Dodd-Frank Act, section 165(d). The ways in which a proposal such as the one contained in this chapter would bring congruity to those provisions is explored in William Kroener, "Revised Chapter 14 2.0 and Living Will Requirements under the Dodd-Frank Act," chapter 8 in this volume.

9. Ibid., sections 203(a)(1)(F) and (a)(2)(F); sections 203(b)(2) and (3).

10. Reducing the size, and not just the complexity, of large financial institutions may be independently desirable, but that goal—if indeed it is one—should not be conflated with designing an appropriate mechanism for the effective resolution of a financial institution in distress.

the thinking and work being done at that time, was focused on the resolution of an operating institution—which, in the case of a large financial institution, is usually at the subsidiary level of a holding company. Yet, in addition to the concerns with existing bankruptcy law, Title II, as enacted, had its own set of difficulties with effective resolution of any such financial institutions. Title II is designated the "Orderly *Liquidation* Authority,"[11] and section 214(a) explicitly states: "All financial companies put into receivership under this subchapter shall be liquidated."[12] A first-day lesson in a corporate reorganization course is that "understanding that financial and economic distress are conceptually distinct from each other is fundamental to understanding Chapter 11 of the Bankruptcy Code."[13] Thus, what of a company whose going-concern value exceeds its liquidation value? But if bankruptcy is perceived not to be up to the task and Title II required an actual liquidation of the business, there may be many cases in which the condition precedent for the use of Title II—that it will be more effective than bankruptcy—will not be met, and current bankruptcy will (or, under the terms of Dodd-Frank, should) be the (rather inefficient) result.

Since then, however, a sea change in perspective has occurred.[14] Increasingly, the focus, in Europe as well as in the United States, has been on a reorganization or recapitalization that focuses, in the first instance, on the parent holding company (many or most of the assets of which are the equity ownership of its subsidiaries). Europe has focused on a

---

11. Dodd-Frank Act sections 206 and 208 (emphasis added).

12. Ibid., section 214(a). See also Thomas Jackson and David Skeel, "Dynamic Resolution of Large Financial Institutions," *Harvard Business Law Review* 2 (2012): 435, 440–41.

13. Barry Adler, Douglas Baird, and Thomas Jackson, *Bankruptcy: Cases, Problems, and Materials,* 4th ed. (St. Paul, MN: Foundation Press, 2007), 28.

14. A useful discussion of whether and how well Title II of Dodd-Frank would have responded to the 2008 crisis—prior to the development of the SPOE proposal—is contained in David Skeel, "Single Point of Entry and the Bankruptcy Alternative," in *Across the Great Divide: New Perspectives on the Financial Crisis* (Stanford, CA: Hoover Institution Press, 2014). Cf. Emily Kapur, "The Next Lehman Bankruptcy," chapter 7 in this volume.

"one-entity" recapitalization via bail-in[15] while the FDIC has focused in its single-point-of-entry (SPOE) proposal on a "two-entity" recapitalization.[16] Under the FDIC's approach, a SIFI holding company (the "single point of entry") is supposed to effectively achieve "recapitalization" of its business virtually overnight by the transfer of its assets and liabilities, except for certain long-term unsecured liabilities and any subordinated debt, to a new bridge institution. The bridge institution then is supposed to forgive intercompany liabilities or contribute assets to recapitalize its operating subsidiaries. Because of the splitting off of the long-term unsecured debt, the bridge institution, in the FDIC's model, looks very much like a SIFI holding company following a European-like bail-in. The major difference is that in the bail-in, the SIFI holding company before and after the recapitalization is the same legal entity (thus, the one-entity recapitalization), whereas in the FDIC's SPOE proposal, the recapitalized bridge institution is legally different than the pre-SPOE SIFI holding company (thus, the two-entity recapitalization).

There are preconditions for making this work. Important among them are legal rules, known in advance, setting forth a required amount of long-term debt to be held by the holding company that would be legally subordinate to other unsecured debt—in the sense of being known that it would be bailed-in (in a one-entity recapitalization) or left behind (in a two-entity recapitalization).[17] And its

---

15. Financial Stability Board, *Progress and Next Steps Towards Ending "Too-Big-to-Fail,"* Report of the Financial Stability Board to the G-20, September 2, 2013, www.financialstabilityboard.org/publications/r_130902.pdf; Thomas Huertas, "The Road to Better Resolution: From Bail-out to Bail-in," speech at The Euro and the Financial Crisis Conference, September 6, 2010, http://www.fsa.gov.uk /library/communication/speeches/2010/0906_th.shtml; Christopher Bates and Simon Gleeson, "Legal Aspects of Bank Bail-Ins," Clifford Chance client briefing, May 3, 2011.

16. FDIC SPOE, Federal Deposit Insurance Corporation, The Resolution of Systemically Important Financial Institutions: The Single Point of Entry Strategy, 78 Fed. Reg. 76614 (Dec. 18, 2013).

17. See Kenneth E. Scott, "The Context for Bankruptcy Resolutions," chapter 1 in this volume; see also John Bovenzi, Randall Guynn, and Thomas Jackson, "Too Big to Fail: The Path to a Solution," panel discussion, Bipartisan Policy Center, Failure Resolution Task Force, Washington, DC, May 2013.

effective use in Title II—as of this writing the FDIC has promulgated for comments a working document on its SPOE proposal[18]—needs to straddle the tension between Title II's liquidation mandate (literally met because, following the transfer to the bridge company, the original holding company will be liquidated) and the notion of limiting financial contagion and using Title II only when its results are better than would occur in bankruptcy. That said, many recognize that the FDIC's SPOE proposal for Title II of Dodd-Frank, consistent with parallel work in Europe, is a significant advance in terms of undermining the presumption that some firms are "too big to fail."[19]

But it also comes with the defects that have always made us uncomfortable with a resolution proceeding run and dominated by a government agency. The FDIC retains discretion to prefer some creditors over others of equal rank, without limiting it to occasions where there is background legal authority (which will rarely occur at the holding company level), and at important points the FDIC, rather than the market, is making critical determinations regarding the bridge financial company and its equity.[20] Thus, the FDIC proposes that the bridge financial institution created in the SPOE process (treated as a government entity for tax purposes[21]) is effectively run, for a while at least, by the FDIC.[22] In addition, the FDIC's SPOE proposal relies on expert (and FDIC) valuations of the new securities that will form the basis of the distribution to the long-term creditors and old equity interests "left behind,"[23] and the FDIC retains the authority to distribute them other than according to the absolute priority rule so well known in bankruptcy law.[24]

---

18. See FDIC SPOE.

19. See Bovenzi et al., "Too Big to Fail," and Skeel, "Single Point of Entry."

20. See FDIC SPOE, 76616–18.

21. Dodd-Frank Act, section 210(h)(10) ("a bridge financial company . . . shall be exempt from all taxation now or hereafter imposed by the United States, by any territory, dependency, or possession thereof, or by any State, country, municipality, or local taxing authority").

22. FDIC SPOE, 76617.

23. Ibid., 76618.

24. Ibid., 76619.

Moreover, the SPOE proposal for Title II has the potential to create an even greater disconnect with both Title I of Dodd-Frank and the presumptive preference for use of bankruptcy in Title II. The first occurs because Title I's resolution plans are to be focused on what would happen to the financial institution *in bankruptcy*.[25] Without the ability to do a comparable recapitalization at the holding company level in bankruptcy, any resolution plan would not be focused on how to most effectively do such a recapitalization. And that would be particularly unfortunate because, without the kind of changes in bankruptcy law we propose, Title II—and its SPOE process—would become the default, not the extraordinary, process, which runs contrary to the express preference in Dodd-Frank for bankruptcy as a resolution process for financial institutions.[26]

Accordingly, the Resolution Project focused on what further changes might be appropriate in its Chapter 14 proposal to both (a) meet the original goals of an effective reorganization or liquidation of an operating company and (b) provide an effective mechanism that would accomplish the goals inherent in the one- or two-entity recapitalizations of the holding company suggested by bail-in and SPOE proposals. Again, the bones of a response to this are already inherent in the Bankruptcy Code. While it is probably the case that the original intent of section 363 of the Bankruptcy Code—a provision providing for the use, sale, and lease of property of the estate—was to permit piecemeal sales of unwanted property, following the enactment of the Bankruptcy Code of 1978, Chapter 11 practice began, over time, to move in the direction of both (a) pre-packaged plans and (b) plans whose essential device was a going-concern sale of some or all of the business, leaving the original equity and much of the debt behind— with the proceeds of the sale forming the basis of their distribution according to the absolute priority rule.[27] It doesn't fit perfectly, but it

---

25. Dodd-Frank Act, section 165(d); and Kroener, "Revised Chapter 14 2.0."

26. Dodd-Frank Act, sections 203(a)(1)(F) and (a)(2)(F); sections 203(b)(2) and (3).

27. David Skeel, *Debt's Dominion: A History of Bankruptcy Law in America* (Princeton, NJ: Princeton University Press, 2001), 227; and Adler et al.,

has been used, repeatedly, as a way of creating a viable business outside of bankruptcy while the claimants, left behind, wind up as the owners of the estate of the former business entity.

Thus, the Resolution Project Working Group decided to expand its 2012 Chapter 14 proposal (which, for the purpose of clarity, we will designate Chapter 14 1.0) to include a direct recapitalization-based bankruptcy alternative—a Chapter 14 2.0. Chapter 14 2.0 accommodates *both* a conventional reorganization of an operating company *and* a two-entity recapitalization of a holding company (as well as, in appropriate circumstances, an operating company).[28] While there is a great deal of merit in considering ways of successfully implementing one-entity recapitalization, especially for the many financial companies that are not systemically important (and we have considered those possibilities extensively among ourselves), in the United States, at least, it is simpler for SIFIs to build upon the two-entity recapitalization model. This is both because (a) Chapter 14 may operate in parallel to the FDIC's SPOE proposal under Title II of Dodd-Frank and because Dodd-Frank itself looks to bankruptcy as the primary "competitor" to Title II[29] and (b) because it is, for a variety of reasons, easier to use the existing bankruptcy framework for a two-entity recapitalization than it is for a one-entity recapitalization.

While there are certainly overlaps with the way Chapter 14 1.0 works—and would continue to work for conventional reorganizations of operating companies—the features that facilitate a two-entity recapitalization through bankruptcy are structurally somewhat distinct. They—together with the basic features of Chapter 14 1.0—are incorporated in the Chapter 14 2.0 proposal.[30] In this paper, we will,

---

Bankruptcy: Cases, Problems and Materials, 466–67 ("Between [1983 and 2003] a sea change occurred through which an auction of the debtor's assets has become a commonplace alternative to a traditional corporate reorganization").

28. A section-by-section outline of this Chapter 14 2.0 proposal is contained in the Appendix, and will be referred to throughout.

29. Dodd-Frank Act, sections 203(a)(2)(F) and (b)(2).

30. A Senate bill, S. 1861, 113th Congress, 1st Sess. ("The Taxpayer Protection and Responsible Resolution Act") (December 2013) focuses on amending the Bankruptcy Code so as to incorporate provisions for a two-entity recapitalization,

first, outline the basic features of Chapter 14 1.0 vis-à-vis the reorganization or liquidation of an operating company and point to where they (sometimes with modifications) are located in Chapter 14 2.0. We will then focus on the additional provisions that form the basis for the two-entity recapitalization of a holding company that is at the center of the differences between the two versions.

But, first, a brief description of the differences between the two processes. The reorganization or liquidation of an operating company that was the focus of Chapter 14 1.0, and the "quick sale" recapitalization that is the major driver of the changes in Chapter 14 2.0, trigger off of whether there is a motion for, and approval of, a "section 1405 transfer"[31] (as defined in our section-by-section proposal that forms an appendix to this chapter) within the first forty-eight hours of a bankruptcy case. If the court approves such a section 1405 transfer, then the covered financial corporation's operations (and ownership of subsidiaries) shift to a new bridge company *that is not in bankruptcy,* in exchange for all its stock.

Through the transfer, this new bridge company will be (effectively) recapitalized, as compared to the original covered financial corporation, by leaving behind in the bankruptcy proceeding certain pre-identified (by regulators such as the Federal Reserve Board or by the parties themselves through subordination or bail-in provisions) long-term unsecured debt (called in the proposal "capital structure debt") of the original covered financial corporation. *After* the transfer, the covered financial corporation (the debtor) remains *in bankruptcy* but is effectively a shell, whose assets usually will consist only of beneficial

---

without ancillary provisions for a more traditional reorganization or liquidation as contemplated by Chapter 14 1.0. The House Judiciary Committee has introduced a similar bill, "The Financial Institution Bankruptcy Act," H. 5421 (August 2014) on a unanimous voice vote. That bill, with minor changes, was subsequently approved by the full House, also via a voice vote, on December 1, 2014—although, without action by the Senate, the process is restarted with the new session of Congress in 2015. We believe this is a positive step, though a complete bankruptcy solution should incorporate not just two-entity recapitalization provisions, but also provisions teed off of Chapter 14 1.0.

31. Appendix, section 2(6).

ownership of the equity interests in the bridge company (held on its behalf by a special trustee) and whose claimants consist of the holders of the long-term debt, any subordinated debt, and the old equity interests of the covered financial corporation. It has no real business to conduct, and essentially waits for an event (such as an IPO for public trading in equity securities of the bridge company) that will value its assets (all equity interests in the new, recapitalized entity) and permit a sale or distribution of those assets, pursuant to bankruptcy's normal distribution rules, to the holders of the long-term and subordinated debt and original equity interests of the debtor (the original covered financial corporation).

Essentially, Chapter 14 2.0 includes four types of rules. One set, centered around the section 1405 transfer, is specific to the mechanics of the two-entity recapitalization's transfer to the bridge company—keeping the other assets, debts, executory contracts, qualified financial contracts, and the like, "in place" and "intact" so they can be transferred to the bridge company. Another set of Chapter 14 rules, as noted above, is specific to the mechanisms of the reorganization of an operating company by keeping the covered financial corporation a "going concern" during its reorganization. A third set of rules deals with the conceivable possibility that the section 1405 transfer won't be approved, and thus provides for the transition from rules appropriate to the two-entity recapitalization to those appropriate to the reorganization (or liquidation) of the covered financial corporation in bankruptcy. Finally, a fourth set of rules is common for all cases in Chapter 14, and thus applies to both a one-entity reorganization and a two-entity recapitalization. Many of these rules are those provided by Chapters 1, 3, 5, and 11 of the current Bankruptcy Code, which Chapter 14 expressly makes relevant (unless overridden by a provision of Chapter 14 itself) to all Chapter 14 cases, as augmented by the proposals suggested in our 2012 Chapter 14 1.0 proposal.

Chapter 14 1.0

The 2012 Chapter 14 1.0 proposal centered around five basic areas where new provisions were added and existing bankruptcy provisions were modified. They were: (A) provisions applying to the creation of a new Chapter 14;[32] (B) provisions relevant to the commencement of a Chapter 14 case;[33] (C) provisions involving the role of the primary regulator in the bankruptcy proceeding;[34] (D) provisions involving debtor-in-possession financing;[35] and (E) provisions applicable to qualified financial contracts in Chapter 14.[36] The essence of these proposals is summarized next, although fuller treatment, of course, is contained in the 2012 Chapter 14 1.0 proposal itself.

Provisions Applying to the Creation of a New Chapter 14

Recognizing that the provisions for a reorganization proceeding in Chapter 11 and a liquidation proceeding in Chapter 7 provided a solid starting point—together with the general provisions in Chapters 1, 3, and 5—Chapter 14 was built around the premise that a large financial institution (and its subsidiaries) would generally use those rules *except* where Chapter 14 was designed to explicitly change them. It accordingly called for a large financial institution[37] to concurrently file for both Chapter 14 and either Chapter 7 or Chapter 11.[38] Because of concerns about political independence, as well as judicial expertise, a Chapter 14 case would be funneled to pre-designated district judges in the Second and District of Columbia circuits, who were expected to hear the cases themselves rather than referring them to bankruptcy judges.[39] The district judges were given the express right to appoint a special master from a predesignated panel to hear Chapter 14 cases and proceedings connected with a Chapter 14 case, as well as the designation of bankruptcy judges and experts to provide advice and input.[40]

---

32. Scott and Taylor, *Bankruptcy Not Bailout*, 27–33.
33. Ibid., 34–38.
34. Ibid., 39–40 and 44–45.
35. Ibid., 40–44.
36. Ibid., 45–66.
37. See Scott and Taylor, *Bankruptcy Not Bailout*, 28; Appendix, section 1(1).
38. Ibid., 29–30; Appendix, section 1(2).
39. Ibid., 33; Appendix, section 3(1).
40. Ibid., 33; Appendix, section 3(1).

Provisions Relevant to the Commencement of a Chapter 14 Case

To ensure that the entire financial institution could be dealt with in the Chapter 14 case, Chapter 14 1.0 proposed to eliminate the exclusion in existing bankruptcy law for domestic and foreign insurance companies, as well as stockbrokers and commodity brokers, from Chapter 11 when a Chapter 14 case applied, although existing rules for the treatment of customer accounts would be made applicable to the bankruptcy proceedings of stockbrokers and commodity brokers. The Securities Investor Protection Corporation (for stockbrokers) or the Commodity Futures Trading Commission (for commodity brokers) would be given a right to be heard and file motions.[41] Chapter 14 1.0, however, did not change the current resolution practice of the FDIC over depository banks.[42]

Provisions Involving the Role of the Primary Regulator in the Bankruptcy Proceeding

In addition, a financial institution's primary regulator would be given the right to file an involuntary case against that financial institution and the right to do so, if contested, not just in the case of the institution generally not paying its debts as they become due, but also on the ground that either the financial institution's assets were less than its liabilities, at fair valuation, or the financial institution had an unreasonably small capital.[43]

Beyond the filing of an involuntary petition by a financial institution's primary regulator, the regulators of the business of a financial institution or any subsidiary thereof would have standing, with respect to the financial institution or the particular subsidiary, to be heard as parties and to raise motions relevant to their regulation.[44] The primary regulator would additionally be given the power, in parallel with the trustee or debtor-in-possession, to file motions for the use, sale, or lease of property of the estate pursuant to the procedures of section

---

41. Ibid., 35–36; Appendix, section 1(1).
42. Ibid., 36; Appendix, section 1(1).
43. Ibid., 37–38; Appendix, sections 2(3) and (4).
44. Ibid., 39; Appendix, sections 2(2) and (5).

363 of the Bankruptcy Code.[45] Either the primary regulator or a creditors' committee would be permitted to file a plan of reorganization at any time.[46]

Provisions Involving Debtor-in-Possession Financing

The Chapter 14 1.0 proposal would make it clear that debtor-in-possession (DIP) financing is available in Chapter 14, pursuant to section 364's procedures and limitations, for financing that will permit partial or complete payouts to some or all creditors where liquidity or solvency of those creditors is a systemic concern, with those payments intended as "advances" for the likely payouts such creditors would receive in a liquidation or a reorganization at the end of the bankruptcy process. To ensure that this was not a backdoor way of providing financial favoritism, these distributions would be subject to several burden-of-proof requirements, to be passed on by the district judge, as well as subordination of the claim of the entity providing such funding to the extent that the creditors receiving such distributions received more than they would have in the bankruptcy proceeding absent such funding. Moreover, if the government was the entity providing such funding, it would additionally be required to show that no private funding on reasonably comparable terms was available within the time frame required.[47]

---

45. Ibid., 40; Appendix, section 2(2).

46. Ibid., 45; Appendix, section 2(5).

47. Ibid., 43–44; Appendix, section 2(14). That provision, which adds a section 1413, picks up the provisions regarding debtor-in-possession financing from Chapter 14 1.0. This provision is essentially for use in Chapter 14 1.0's reorganization of an operating entity model that is carrying on an active business and that needs liquidity in the bankruptcy proceeding, and perhaps may need, for financial stability purposes, prepayments to some claimants. It builds on the debtor-in-possession financing provisions of section 364 of the Bankruptcy Code. In the case of a section 1405 transfer (see Appendix, section 2(6)), the judge will retain jurisdiction over the bridge company, on its application, sufficient to allow the Chapter 14 court to authorize for a limited period comparable funding, subject to conditions, available to a debtor-in-possession under section 1403.

Provisions Applicable to Qualified
Financial Contracts in Chapter 14

Rules written into the Bankruptcy Code over the past several decades have increasingly exempted counterparties on qualified financial contracts from many of bankruptcy law's special rules, including the automatic stay and preference law. Occasionally, these exemptions make underlying sense, but often they do not. In Chapter 14 1.0, our Working Group proposed revisiting all these Code provisions, and treating the counterparties according to the underlying attributes of the contracts they possessed. In the case of counterparties on repo (repurchase) contracts, which are comparable to secured loans, the automatic stay would not apply in terms of netting, setoff, or collateral sales by the counterparty of cash-like collateral that is in its possession—each being an instance of rights that the counterparty could exercise without detriment to the debtor or its estate.[48] In the case of counterparties on derivatives, however, more significant short-term changes in existing law were proposed, again consistent with the idea that most derivatives were comparable to executory contracts, and should be treated as such. Thus, for three days, the counterparty would be subject to bankruptcy's automatic stay, so as to enable the debtor to exercise its choice between assumption and rejection of the derivative (although the debtor would need to accept or reject all of the counterparty's derivatives without cherry-picking). After three days, and unless the debtor had previously assumed the derivative, the counterparty would be free to exercise any rights it may have to terminate the derivative and, upon termination (either by action of the counterparty or by rejection by the debtor), the counterparty will have the netting, setoff, and collateral sale rights of a repo counterparty in bankruptcy.[49]

Finally, counterparties on qualified financial contracts would be given no blanket exemption from the trustee's avoiding powers, including preference law, although preference law would be amended

---

48. Ibid., 50–52; Appendix, section 2(8).
49. Ibid., 56–60; Appendix, section 2(8).

to provide a "two-point net improvement test" safe harbor for certain payments and collateral transfers.[50]

Incorporating a "Quick Sale" Recapitalization into Chapter 14

While most of these provisions continue to make sense, and apply as well to the reorganization or liquidation of an operating company, they—by themselves—are not focused sufficiently on a rapid recapitalization of a financial institution at the holding company level (or, indeed, the rapid recapitalization of an operating covered financial corporation), in which—in the course of a very short period of time—it is intended that the financial institution, through the recapitalization, would (a) likely be solvent, (b) appear solvent to market participants, and (c) be subject to market discipline, rather than be under the "protection" of a bankruptcy proceeding (or subject to the interference with market-based decisions by a judge overseeing the bankruptcy proceeding of the holding company).

Doing this requires several new provisions and counsels for some modifications in the proposals contained in Chapter 14 1.0. The most significant change in the Chapter 14 2.0 proposal is its focus on provisions implementing a quick recapitalization of a covered financial corporation (usually a holding company), via a sale of its assets and liabilities (other than certain pre-identified long-term unsecured debt and subordinated debt) to a bridge company immediately following the commencement of a bankruptcy case.[51] In essence, this quickly removes the assets from the bankruptcy process, in the form of a new,

---

50. Ibid., 62–66; Appendix, section 2(12).

51. Appendix, section 2(6) (describing a section 1405 "Special Transfer"). If the entity does not have regulatory-required capital structure debt, and does not have contractually subordinated debt, it will be unlikely to be able to use section 1405's "quick transfer," as there will be little, if anything, left behind in the transfer (other than equity). This will almost certainly mean the financially distressed covered financial institution will be unable to demonstrate, as section 1405 requires, that the bridge company can provide adequate assurance of future performance of the debts and contracts being transferred to it. Thus, while not limited to holding companies, the use of section 1405 will require that the covered financial

and hopefully clearly solvent, company, while leaving full beneficial ownership rights of that company (as between the holders of the long-term and subordinated debt that is not transferred and the old equity holders who are also left behind) to be realized over time in the bankruptcy estate. In addition to requiring pre-identified long-term debt in sufficient quantity—a non-bankruptcy issue but critical to the ability of *either* Chapter 14's quick sale *or* the FDIC's SPOE process to succeed[52]—it requires a series of rules permitting assets, liabilities, contracts, and permits to be transferred to the bridge company notwithstanding restrictions on transfer, or change-of-control provisions, or the like. In essence, a number of rules need to be in place to ensure that, but for the recapitalization, the bridge company has all of the rights and liabilities that the holding company had the moment before the commencement of the bankruptcy case. Virtually all of the new rules in the Chapter 14 2.0 proposal are designed to deal with this, although there are also some transitional rules, some changes in the Chapter 14 1.0 proposal based on making the "quick sale" effective, and some (modest) changes in the Chapter 14 1.0 proposal based on our current thinking.

The Section 1405 Transfer

The heart of the change is what we have denominated the section 1405 transfer.[53] This transfer is, in many ways, the key concept implementing the two-entity recapitalization idea in Chapter 14. It permits the debtor or either the Board (in cases where the Board has supervisory authority over the debtor—usually the largest financial institutions) or its primary regulator (in other cases)[54] that commences a bankruptcy case to immediately make a motion for a transfer of the property of the estate, contracts, and liabilities (except for "capital

---

corporation have debt that can be left behind, thus accomplishing the financial reorganization contemplated by the section 1405 transfer.

52. See Scott, "The Context for Bankruptcy Resolutions."

53. Appendix, section 2(6).

54. Defined in Appendix, section 2(3) (and slightly modified from the Chapter 14 1.0 proposal).

structure debt"—our term for the debt that is left behind—and, of course, equity)[55] of the debtor to a newly created bridge company.[56] If the transfer is approved, every asset, liability, and executory contract of the debtor will be included in the transfer to the bridge company *except* for capital structure debt (and equity). If the debtor owns collateral that secures a loan (other than via a qualified financial contract) with an original maturity of at least one year, upon its transfer pursuant to section 1405 to the bridge company, the secured lender's claim against the bridge company will be non-recourse if its deficiency claim would otherwise be considered capital structure debt.[57] However, through that definition of capital structure debt, such a lender will, if the collateral is insufficient, continue to have an unsecured claim for any deficiency in the Chapter 14 case.[58]

The section 1405 transfer motion shall be heard by the court no sooner than twenty-four hours after the filing (so as to permit twenty-four-hour notification to the debtor, the twenty largest holders of the capital structure debt, the Board and the FDIC [in the case of a debtor over whom the Board has supervisory authority], and also the primary financial regulatory authority—whether US or foreign—with respect to the debtor as well as any subsidiary whose ownership is proposed to be transferred to the bridge company in the section 1405 transfer).[59] Based on limited stays in other provisions in Chapter 14, the transfer decision essentially must be made within forty-eight hours after the filing.[60] The court can order the transfer only if it finds, or the Board or primary regulator (as the case may be) certifies that it

---

55. Defined in Appendix, section 2(3). A part of this definition of capital structure debt begins the idea, finished in Appendix, section 2(6), that under-collateralized long-term secured debt will be treated as follows: (a) the secured portion of the debt will be transferred (along with the collateral) to the bridge company on a non-recourse basis and (b) the debt holder will retain an unsecured claim in the debtor's bankruptcy for the remainder.

56. Ibid., section 2(3).

57. Ibid., sections 2(3) and (6).

58. Ibid., section 2(3).

59. Ibid., section 2(6).

60. See ibid., sections 2(7) and (8).

has found, that the bridge company adequately provides assurance of future performance of any executory contract, unexpired lease, or debt agreement being transferred to the bridge company.[61] The court must also confirm that the bridge company's bylaws allow its board to be replaced, pursuant to a decision of the Chapter 14 judge after a notice and hearing for the equity owners of the bridge company (collectively, the debtor; individually, the holders of the capital structure debt and equity interests of the debtor), and other parties in interest (such as the Board and/or primary regulator), during the first thirty days following the section 1405 transfer to that bridge company.[62] Moreover, while the bridge company is not otherwise subject to the jurisdiction of the Chapter 14 judge following the transfer, that judge shall retain jurisdiction for one year, upon application of the bridge company, to award financing on the terms and conditions applicable to DIP financing pursuant to section 1413. This is done in order to provide access to liquidity in the (hopefully rare) occasions where market-based liquidity to the presumptively solvent bridge company is unavailable. It is limited to six months on the view that any market-based liquidity restrictions (whether local or global) will have dissipated or otherwise been dealt with by that time and the bridge company is thereafter on its own.[63]

Commencing the Chapter 14 Case

While many of the commencement provisions in the Chapter 14 1.0 proposal have been carried forward, there have also been some modest changes, based largely on the necessity for a decision on a section 1405 transfer within forty-eight hours of the filing. While Chapter 14 itself is new, there will be provisions noting that, except where otherwise expressly provided by Chapter 14, the "non-substantive" chapters of the Bankruptcy Code (Chapters 1, 3, and 5) apply in Chapter 14, and

---

61. Ibid., section 2(6). If the certifications are challenged, the Chapter 14 judge, after appropriate proceedings, may award damages, ibid., section 2(4), and sovereign immunity is to that extent abrogated, ibid., section 1(3).

62. Ibid.

63. The more general subject of financing such institutions is explored in David Skeel, "Financing Systemically Important Financial Institutions in Bankruptcy," chapter 3 in this volume.

that, again except where otherwise expressly provided by Chapter 14, the provisions of Chapter 11 apply in a case under Chapter 14.[64] While there is no provision for the direct use of Chapter 7, liquidations are permitted under Chapter 11 and a conversion to Chapter 7 under section 1112 of the Bankruptcy Code is expressly allowed.[65] Because Chapter 14 generally incorporates the provisions of Chapter 11, there is no need for a concurrent filing under Chapters 14 and 11, as proposed in Chapter 14 1.0, although the substance is the same. (The current Chapter 14 2.0 proposal is, in substance, similar to making the provisions of Chapter 14 a new subchapter of Chapter 11.)

Chapter 14 can only be used by a "covered financial corporation,"[66] whose definition picks up institutions that are "substantially engaged in providing financial services or financial products," including subsidiaries that are neither banks (that currently are, and would remain, subject to FDIC resolution procedures), nor a stockbroker or commodity broker (which goes into special Chapter 7 provisions).[67] (While subsidiaries of a covered financial corporation—that are themselves excluded banks, stockbrokers, or commodity brokers—cannot file in Chapter 14, a parent institution owning such subsidiaries can nevertheless use Chapter 14.) In common with Chapter 14 1.0, there is no exclusion of insurance companies.[68] The minimum size requirement of Chapter 14 1.0 has been dropped on the view that Chapter 14 provides a superior reorganization mechanism for all financial institutions. The definition of "covered financial corporation," however, specifically excludes financial market infrastructure corporations (such as central counterparty clearinghouses) as unsuited for Chapter 14, even if they otherwise meet the definition of a covered financial corporation.[69]

As for the commencement of a Chapter 14 case, Chapter 14 2.0 picks up on, but modifies, the provisions for the commencement of

---

64. Appendix, section 1(2).

65. Ibid., section 1(3).

66. Ibid.

67. Ibid., section 1(1).

68. Ibid.

69. Ibid. See Darrell Duffie, "Resolution of Failing Central Counterparties," chapter 4 in this volume.

a Chapter 14 case in Chapter 14 1.0. It continues with the ability of the covered financial corporation itself (the debtor) to file a voluntary petition under section 301 of the Bankruptcy Code.[70] It does not, however, permit three or more creditors of a covered financial corporation to file an involuntary petition under section 303 of the Bankruptcy Code, as this was thought to be both potentially disruptive and unnecessary, particularly when a section 1405 transfer might be the preferred solution, as the time-table for that determination simply doesn't accommodate time for a distinct hearing and resolution on the merits of the involuntary petition itself.[71] It does allow the Federal Reserve Board to file what is tantamount to a voluntary petition for covered financial corporations over which it has supervisory authority, in legal effect (e.g., the filing commences the case and constitutes an order for relief), if the Board certifies (and makes a statement of the reasons) that it has determined (after consultation with the secretary of the treasury and the FDIC) that either the commencement of a Chapter 14 case is necessary to avoid serious adverse effects on the financial stability of the United States[72] or the covered financial corporation has substantial impairment of regulatory capital. In other cases, the primary regulator may file a comparable petition in which the commencement of the case and the order for relief are simultaneous, upon a certification that the primary regulator has determined that the covered financial corporation's assets are less than its liabilities, at fair valuation, or the covered financial corporation has unreasonably small capital. This substitutes the Board, in instances where it is has supervisory authority, for Chapter 14 1.0's proposal regarding the primary regulator, makes several other changes in the standard, and makes the petition function equivalent to a voluntary petition (i.e., immediate order for relief) rather than an involuntary petition (that can be challenged before an order for relief). This was done with the thought that because of the very tight time constraint to approve a section 1405 transfer (after notice and hearing), in cases

---

70. Appendix, section 2(4).

71. Ibid.

72. Ibid.

where it is otherwise appropriate, there simply wasn't time to have a meaningful insolvency hearing; in addition, once the filing was made, it was likely to be a self-fulfilling prophecy. In its place is a Board certification regarding impairment of regulatory capital or financial stability or a primary regulator's certification concerning balance sheet insolvency (e.g., assets less than liabilities) or unreasonably small capital. However, the court would retain jurisdiction to subsequently hear and determine damages proximately caused by such filing, if it finds that the Board's or primary regulator's certification was not supported by substantial evidence on the record as a whole (analogous in some respects to the damages provision of section 303(i)(2)(A)), so that there is an understanding that aggrieved parties (mostly the original equity holders of the debtor) could have ex post damage remedies.[73]

In terms of who oversees the Chapter 14 case, the Chapter 14 1.0 proposal essentially displaced non–Article III bankruptcy judges with Article III district judges to handle Chapter 14 cases, and funneled all such cases to the Second and District of Columbia circuits. We propose the same basic idea of using district judges, but have made some modifications in the original proposal. First, rather than funneling cases to the Second Circuit or the DC Circuit, it has at least one designated district court judge (selected by the chief justice of the United States) in each circuit who will be involved in Chapter 14 cases.[74] Ordinary venue rules (in 28 USC section 1408) determine where the covered financial corporation files (or the Board commences a case involving a covered financial corporation). Because a designated judge, while within the judicial circuit, may not be within the judicial district where the Chapter 14 case is commenced, the provision deems the judge to be temporally assigned to the district in which the bankruptcy case is commenced.[75] (This decision to involve a judge

---

73. Ibid., section 2(4). Sovereign immunity is thereby abrogated. Section 1(3). Cf. Scott, "The Context for Bankruptcy Resolutions."

74. Appendix, section 3. No need to exclude the Federal Circuit Court of Appeals, as that circuit has no district judges.

75. Ibid.

from every judicial circuit, rather than funneling cases to the Second or DC Circuit, is responsive to likely political reactions by senators and representatives who focus on their own respective jurisdictions.) Moreover, the designated judge "goes with the case," so if venue is changed, the district judge will be deemed temporarily assigned to the new district.[76] Second, it requires two-entity recapitalization cases—those involving a section 1405 transfer—to be handled up to the point of the transfer by the designated district judge, but not necessarily thereafter (again, since most of the debtor's business has been transferred to the bridge company).[77] In other cases—conventional reorganization cases of the type contemplated by the original Chapter 14 1.0 proposal—the designated district judge, as with the *Bankruptcy Not Bailout* proposal, must keep the case and proceedings without referral to a bankruptcy judge.[78] Referral to a bankruptcy judge, however, can occur if there is a decision to convert the case to Chapter 7 pursuant to section 1112.[79] Third, the designated district judge can appoint a bankruptcy judge to assist the district judge as a special master.[80] Finally, because some circuits require that appeals from bankruptcy judges go to the Bankruptcy Appellate Panel (consisting of non–Article III bankruptcy judges), and the remaining circuits may otherwise send appeals to other district judges, this provision will require 28 USC section158(a) appeals from bankruptcy judges to go to the designated district judge.[81] (As usual, appeals from the designated district judge in cases and proceedings that haven't been referred to a bankruptcy judge will go to the relevant court of appeals.)

Role of Regulators

In addition to the Board's ability to file what is tantamount to a voluntary petition, as discussed above, Chapter 14 2.0 provides several

---

76. Ibid.
77. Ibid.
78. Ibid.
79. Ibid.
80. Ibid.
81. Ibid.

other roles for regulators.[82] First, it gives the Board standing to be heard on any issue relevant either to the regulation of the debtor by the Board or to the financial stability of the United States.[83] It gives the FDIC more limited standing—to be heard in connection with a section 1405 transfer.[84] And it gives the primary financial regulator of any subsidiary (domestic or foreign) or its parent standing to be heard on any issue relevant to its regulation of that entity (including transfer of its ownership interests in a section 1405 transfer as well as its ownership by the debtor in a reorganization rather than a two-entity recapitalization).[85] If there is a section 1405 transfer, where the bridge company effectively continues as the recapitalized debtor (in a two-entity recapitalization), the Board's regulatory interest should shift to the bridge company, so Chapter 14 provides that, after such a section 1405 transfer, the Board's remaining standing vis-à-vis the debtor is with respect to its equity ownership of the bridge institution.[86] If there is not a section 1405 transfer, the Board, analogous to the primary regulator in the original Chapter 14 proposal, can file a plan of reorganization at any time. (In the typical section 1405 transfer, we propose the appointment of a trustee immediately after the section 1405 transfer, and thus all parties in interest, including the Board, are authorized to file a plan of reorganization without delay under section 1121(c) of the Bankruptcy Code.)[87]

---

82. References to the United States trustee as having a role are removed (Appendix, section 2(2)), and our proposal essentially substitutes the (Federal Reserve) Board (a defined term from Appendix, Section 2(3)), thus, for example, giving the Board the power to move for the appointment of a trustee under section 1104. While Chapter 14 1.0 had provisions to give the primary regulator a role in the Chapter 14 proceeding, nothing exactly parallel to this exists in the Chapter 14 2.0 proposal. Appendix, section 2(5), follows, and modifies, the "regulator standing" proposal from Chapter 14 1.0.

83. Appendix, section 2(5).

84. Ibid.

85. Ibid.

86. Ibid.

87. Ibid.

Provisions Related to Making the Section 1405 Transfer Effective

As noted, at the heart of the two-entity recapitalization are two principles: first, that there is sufficient long-term unsecured debt—capital structure debt—to be "left behind" in the transfer to a bridge company so as to effectuate the recapitalization; and, second, that the bridge company otherwise have the assets, rights, and liabilities of the former holding company. A number of provisions in Chapter 14 2.0 are designed to effectuate this latter principle.

First, there are provisions applicable to debts, executory contracts, and unexpired leases, including qualified financial contracts.[88] Conceptually, the goal of these provisions is to keep assets and liabilities in place so that they can be transferred to the bridge company (within a forty-eight-hour window) and, thereafter, remain in place so that business as usual can be picked up by the bridge company once it assumes the assets and liabilities. This requires overriding "ipso facto" clauses (of the type that would otherwise permit termination or modification based on the commencement of a Chapter 14 case or similar circumstance, including credit-rating agency ratings), and it requires overriding similar provisions allowing for termination or modification based on a change of control, since the ownership of the bridge company will be different than the ownership of the debtor prior to the bankruptcy filing.[89] It needs to be broader than section 365 of the Bankruptcy Code, for at least two reasons. First, bankruptcy doesn't have a provision expressly allowing for the transfer of debt (although many debts are in fact transferred as a matter of existing practice under Chapter 11 "going concern sales"). Unlike executory contracts, which might be viewed as net assets (and thus something to "assume") or as net liabilities (and thus something to "reject"), debt is generally considered breached and accelerated (think "rejected") upon the filing of a petition in bankruptcy. But, if there is going to be a two-entity recapitalization, the bridge company needs to take the debt "as if nothing has happened." Thus, Chapter 14 2.0 has provisions (sections 1406

---

88. See generally Appendix, sections 2(7) and (8).
89. Ibid.

and 1407) that are designed to accomplish that.[90] Second, section 365 doesn't deal with change-of-control provisions; these provisions add that and extend it to debt agreements as well.[91]

A complexity is that the brief stay to allow the section 1405 transfer needs itself to be terminated with respect to the termination or modification of any debt agreement if there is no section 1405 transfer but, rather, a regular bankruptcy of the type contemplated by the original Chapter 14 proposal.[92] (Debts—liabilities that normally are deemed breached upon the filing of bankruptcy—are in this respect treated differently than executory contracts and unexpired leases, since the provisions of sections 362 and 365 of the Bankruptcy Code are expected to continue, as they do in other reorganization cases.)

With respect to qualified financial contracts, similar rules apply. If there is a filing with a motion for a section 1405 transfer, there is a stay of efforts to liquidate, terminate, or accelerate a qualified financial contract of the debtor or subsidiary or to offset or net out, other than rights that exist upon the normal maturation of a qualified financial contract.[93] (Unlike the detailed provisions in the qualified financial contracts proposal in Chapter 14 2.0, these provisions are distinct in that they apply rules that didn't apply—and continue not to apply—in the Chapter 14 1.0 reorganization proposal, particularly with respect to repo counterparties and their ability to sell cash-like collateral.)

The stay applies for the period essentially until the section 1405 transfer occurs, it is clear it won't occur, or forty-eight hours have passed.[94] Because of this interregnum, when there is a likelihood that the section 1405 transfer will be approved, and all of these qualified financial contracts go over in their original form to the bridge company, there is a requirement that the debtor and its subsidiaries shall continue to perform payment and delivery obligations.[95] And,

---

90. Ibid.
91. Ibid.
92. Ibid., section 2(7).
93. Ibid., section 2(8).
94. Ibid.
95. Ibid.

as long as the debtor and/or its subsidiaries are performing payment and delivery obligations, a counterparty is expected to comply with its contractual obligations as well; the failure to do so shall constitute a breach in accordance with the terms of the qualified financial contract.[96] Finally, if the filing of the bankruptcy case does not involve a motion for a section 1405 transfer, or if the motion is denied, or if forty-eight hours pass, then the case will be considered to be a conventional reorganization case (rather than a two-entity recapitalization case), and thus the original proposed rules for qualified financial contracts in Chapter 14 1.0 shall come into play.[97]

Just as the principle of having the bridge company have the same rights, assets, and liabilities drives the provisions regarding debts, executory contracts, and unexpired leases just discussed (including qualified financial contracts), a similar provision is necessary to keep licenses, permits, and registrations in place, and does not allow a government to terminate or modify them based on an ipso facto clause or a section 1405 transfer.[98]

---

96. Ibid.

97. Ibid. These provisions are somewhat complex. To summarize them, without every nuance, under our provisions, from Chapter 14 1.0, we treat repos as debts, and consider them automatically breached by the commencement of the case. (Although there may be a stay up to forty-eight hours, if there is a motion for a section 1405 transfer, as described above.) However, we allow a counterparty to dispose of highly liquid collateral in its possession and exercise set-off rights without court permission, and allow it to sell other, non-firm-specific collateral in its possession upon motion to the court and the court's determination of the collateral's value. We also give the counterparty the right to reach comparable collateral in the hands of the debtor on motion of the court. We treat most swaps/derivatives as executory contracts, and give the debtor seventy-two hours to decide to accept or reject them (without permitting cherry-picking within a counterparty's portfolio). If they are accepted, then the swap/derivative continues as an enforceable contract, notwithstanding ipso facto clauses and the like. If they are breached, then the swap/derivative counterparty has essentially the rights of a repo counterparty (i.e., to sell highly liquid collateral, etc.).

98. Ibid., section 2(10). We assume that the "name" of the bridge company will be close enough to that of the debtor that filed financing statements will remain effective under Article 9, Section 9-508, of the Uniform Commercial Code.

Many avoiding power provisions use as a baseline what a creditor would receive in a Chapter 7 liquidation. That potentially brings into play various avoiding powers, such as preference law, against holders of short-term debt (such as commercial paper) who, in a Chapter 7 liquidation, might not be paid in full, but in a two-entity recapitalization under a section 1405 transfer, will be paid in full. Thus, section 1411 is designed to call off avoiding powers (other than section 548 (a)(1) (A) of the Bankruptcy Code dealing with intentional fraud) in the case of a section 1405 transfer, except with respect to transfers to, or for the benefit of, holders of long-term unsecured debt or subordinated debt (which is not transferred and is likely not to be paid in full) and transfers to the debtor's equity holders (such as dividends made pre-bankruptcy while the SIFI was insolvent).[99]

Finally, while all of these provisions deal with those in a relationship with the holding company, similar provisions need to be implemented with respect to contracts and permits held by a subsidiary whose ownership interests are transferred to the bridge company. Thus, we provide that a counterparty to such contracts with the subsidiary cannot terminate, accelerate, or modify any executory contract, unexpired lease, or debt agreement based on either an anti-assignment provision or a change-of-control provision.[100] Nor may a party to an agreement

---

99. Appendix, section 2(12). In an ordinary recapitalization case (not involving a section 1405 transfer), there are special avoiding power rules specified in Chapter 14 1.0 for holders of qualified financial contracts. Those provisions have been incorporated in Appendix, section 2(12) as well.

100. Ibid., Section 2(9). While these provisions affect the contracts of entities not themselves in bankruptcy, we believe they are fully authorized, if not by Congress's Article I bankruptcy power, then by application of the "necessary and proper" clause of Article I, as interpreted since McCulloch v. Maryland, 4 Wheat. 316 (1819). See also United States v. Comstock, 560 U.S. 126 (2010). The issue of reaching foreign subsidiaries cannot be directly resolved by US bankruptcy law and, in general, cross-border issues of international institutions remain nettlesome. See Jacopo Carmassi and Richard Herring, "The Cross-Border Challenge in Resolving Global Systemically Important Banks," chapter 9 in this volume. That said, domestic and foreign regulators and banks, in conjunction with the International Swaps and Derivatives Association (ISDA), have promulgated a Resolution Stay Protocol that will (with sufficient regulatory support) impose similar rules

with a subsidiary enforce a cross-default provision involving the debtor for the period during which a section 1405 transfer motion is under consideration.[101] Again, these provisions, like sections 1406 and 1407, are designed to allow the two-entity recapitalization effected by a section 1405 transfer to occur seamlessly with respect to the bridge company's ownership of the debtor's subsidiaries. Similarly, in the case of a subsidiary whose ownership is transferred to the bridge company in a section 1405 transfer, those licenses, permits, and registrations cannot be terminated based on a "change-of-control" provision.[102]

Transitional Provisions Designed to Make the Section 1405 Transfer Effective

Upon consummation of a section 1405 transfer, the newly created bridge company will have little to no long-term unsecured debt (as capital structure debt has been left behind with the debtor). It will, however, presumably have residual (equity) value—which is, indeed,

---

on qualified financial contract counterparties in major foreign jurisdictions (as well as the United States). See ISDA, "Resolution Stay Protocol—Background," October 11, 2014; see also Tom Braithwaite and Tracy Alloway, "Banks Rewrite Derivative Rules to Cope with Future Crisis," *Financial Times*, October 7, 2014. There are two points to note about the ISDA Resolution Stay Protocol. First, it does not supplant the need for the provisions in proposed sections 1407 and 1408. They originally apply (as of January 1, 2015) to eighteen major financial institutions and certain of their affiliates, although this is described as "[t]he first wave of banks." Second, they are, in principle, voluntary, although the eighteen financial institutions have committed themselves to the Protocol, and there are expectations that governmental regulators, who pushed for the ISDA Protocol, will make compliance effectively necessary. The provisions of sections 1407 and 1408 apply irrespective of whether a particular financial institution is bound to the ISDA Resolution Stay Protocol. See Scott, "The Context for Bankruptcy Resolutions." Second, to the extent that an institution *is* subject to the ISDA Resolution Stay Protocol, and foreign regulators recognize a Chapter 14 resolution proceeding, the Protocol will go a long way to resolving the inability of US bankruptcy law to impose, at least vis-à-vis derivatives, the provisions of section 1408 directly on foreign subsidiaries (and their counterparties) of a covered financial corporation that is in Chapter 14.

101. Appendix, section 2(9).

102. Ibid, section 2(10).

the basis ultimately for payment to the debtor's claimants that were not transferred to the bridge company. Whether the bridge will be able to meet legal and regulatory capital requirements with that equity value alone will depend both on ex post valuation and on whether the regulatory scheme requires (as we believe it must in order to effectuate a two-entity recapitalization in the first place) a certain amount of debt (and not just equity) for loss absorbency purposes. The bridge will initially have substantial capital (equity) on a book basis, but its initial book value may not be validated by market performance. Moreover, initially the bridge company will have little to no long-term unsecured debt—since capital structure debt was left behind—and such debt may be crucial in terms of regulatory requirements.[103] The equity value in market terms will need to be sufficient for the bridge company, over time, to issue new long-term unsecured debt, but until that occurs, the bridge company is likely to be non-compliant with the debt side of minimum capital requirements. Thus, Chapter 14 2.0 proposes giving the bridge company a window in which it does not have to be in compliance with those capital requirements. That period of effective exemption from those capital requirements ends at the earlier of (a) the confirmation of the debtor's plan of reorganization involving (as will usually be the case) the distribution of securities (or proceeds from their sale) of the bridge company or (b) the passage of one year from the section 1405 transfer.[104] By the end of that window of exemption, the bridge company must be in compliance with relevant regulatory capital requirements, including those involving minimum long-term unsecured debt.

Section 1145 of the Bankruptcy Code allows a reorganized debtor to issue securities pursuant to a plan of reorganization without complying with most securities laws, the idea being that the required disclosure in a plan of reorganization, under section 1125, confirmed by a court, should substitute. Given that an envisioned end of a bankruptcy case of a debtor where there has been a section 1405 transfer will be the sale or distribution of securities of the bridge company

---

103. Ibid, section 2(11).
104. Ibid.

pursuant to a plan of reorganization, section 1412 treats this situation as equivalent to the typical reorganization case involving securities of the debtor, and thus provides that a security of the bridge company shall be treated as a security of a successor to the debtor under a plan of reorganization, in cases where the court has approved the plan's disclosure statement as providing adequate information about the bridge company and the security—thus fitting it within the provisions of section 1145.[105] Additionally, the exemption from any law imposing a stamp tax or similar tax, in section 1146(a), applicable to securities issued pursuant to a conventional plan of reorganization, is provided to securities of the bridge company in connection with a confirmed plan of reorganization following a section 1405 transfer.[106] (Importantly, unlike the ill-advised provision in Title II of Dodd-Frank that treats a bridge financial institution as equivalent for a government entity not subject to federal, state, or local tax,[107] there is no comparable provision for the bridge company created in a section 1405 transfer. It is, and should be thought of as, a private company subject to no favorable tax considerations not applicable to its competitors. This is distinct from the issue of a holding company's tax loss carry-forwards that should be treated as an asset that can be transferred to the bridge company in the Section 1405 transfer.)

If there is a section 1405 transfer, the management, at least originally, of the bridge company is very likely to be the management of the entity that filed for bankruptcy. Given that, it would be a conflict of interest to have that same management having the status of the "debtor in possession" of the debtor, which is now the equity owner of the bridge company. As a consequence, and given (as noted in the prior numbered paragraph) that the debtor after the section 1405 transfer isn't likely to be operating an ongoing business, there really is no need for prior management to be the "debtor in possession."

Thus, section 1414 requires the replacement of the debtor in possession with a trustee, appointed by the court after a notice and

---

105. Ibid, section 2(13).
106. Ibid.
107. Dodd-Frank Act, section 210(h)(10).

hearing, who shall be chosen from a preapproved list of trustees.[108] This trustee will represent the estate before the judge, together with a creditors' committee (consisting of representatives of the holders of capital structure debt), an equity holders committee (consisting of representatives of the former equity owners of the debtor), and other parties in interest.[109] The appointment of the trustee will also, importantly, permit "a party in interest" to file a plan of reorganization without needing to wait out (or call off) the exclusivity period for the debtor in possession in section 1121(c) of the Bankruptcy Code. In cases not involving a section 1405 transfer—that is to say, cases involving a conventional reorganization as contemplated by the Chapter 14 1.0 proposal—this will permit, but not require, the appointment of a trustee, but if a trustee is appointed, it will be from the same preapproved list.[110]

In addition, because of the concern that the Chapter 14 trustee will be subject to conflicting pressures from his constituents (debt and equity left behind) concerning using the equity ownership of the bridge company to direct the bridge company's actions, which would be resolved by the judge overseeing the bankruptcy case, Chapter 14 2.0 places the actual equity interests of the bridge in the hands of a special trustee, appointed by the court at the time of the section 1405 transfer. The special trustee will hold the equity interests for the sole benefit of the Chapter 14 estate. This additional step, albeit a complicating feature, is designed to give third parties additional assurance that the bridge company is, indeed, not being run by an entity in bankruptcy or by the judge overseeing the Chapter 14 case. The special trustee will have ongoing reporting requirements to the Chapter 14 trustee; major corporate decisions that require equity input or approval can be taken by the special trustee only after consultation with the Chapter 14 trustee. The bridge company shall be responsible for paying the reasonable expenses of the special trustee.

---

108. Appendix, section 2(15).
109. Ibid.
110. Ibid.

In the situation of a Chapter 14 case where there is a two-entity recapitalization pursuant to a section 1405 transfer, resolution of the Chapter 14 case will involve the debtor essentially awaiting a sale or distribution of equity securities of the bridge company that will be valued by the market. This distribution of stock or proceeds from it will form the basis of a plan of reorganization, including disclosure, solicitation of acceptances, a court hearing, and court confirmation of the plan (sections 1123–1129 of the Bankruptcy Code). While the Bankruptcy Code does not expressly provide a timetable for these events, it seems appropriate, given the hoped-for market-based determination of the value of the bridge company's equity securities that will be distributed in a plan, together with the desire to conclude the bankruptcy case (and wind down the debtor), to authorize explicitly a rapid time frame for solicitation, voting, and the court's hearing (and decision) on confirmation of the plan.[111]

Interface with Title II of Dodd-Frank

Currently, in order to commence an orderly liquidation proceeding under Title II of Dodd-Frank against a "covered financial company," where the board of that company does not acquiesce or consent to the proceeding, the secretary of the treasury must petition the District Court for the District of Columbia.[112] The court is given twenty-four hours to determine that the secretary's findings (a) that the "covered financial company is in default or in danger of default" or (b) that the company "satisfies the definition of a financial company under section 2019a)(11)" are arbitrary and capricious; if the court does not make a determination within that time frame, Dodd Frank provides that the petition is granted by operation of law.[113]

Given this very tight timetable, and given that if a Chapter 14 case was previously commenced there is already an involved district judge, the revised Chapter 14 proposal would amend Dodd-Frank by substituting the Chapter 14 district court (and judge) for the District

---

111. Ibid., section 2(16).
112. Dodd-Frank Act, section 202(a)(1)(A)(i).
113. Ibid., section 202(a)(1)(A)(v).

Court for the District of Columbia.[114] It would, in addition, subject the finding required of the government agencies under Dodd-Frank section 203(a)(2) that bankruptcy is not a viable alternative for the resolution of the financial institution to the same determination and issuance procedures currently outlined under section 202(a)(1)(A) (iii) and (iv) for the section 202(a)(1)(A)(iii) determination "that the covered financial company is in default or in danger of default and satisfies the definition of a financial company under section 201(a)(11)."[115]

APPENDIX
Proposed Bankruptcy Code Chapter 14 2.0

*Section 1: General Provisions Relating
to Covered Financial Corporations*

1) Amend **Section 101** of the Bankruptcy Code by adding a new subsection defining a "covered financial corporation" as any corporation that is substantially engaged in providing financial services or financial products (other than financial market infrastructure corporations such as central counterparty clearinghouses), and any subsidiary of that corporation that both (i) is substantially engaged in providing financial services or financial products and (ii) is neither (a) an entity, other than a domestic insurance company, that is included on the lists in Section 109(b)(2) and (b)(3)(B) nor (b) a stockbroker (Section 741) nor (c) a commodity broker (Section 761).

2) Amend **Section 103** of the Bankruptcy Code to provide that (a) except as provided in Chapter 14, Chapters 1, 3, and 5 of the Bankruptcy Code apply in a case under Chapter 14 and (b) the provisions of Chapter 14 apply only in a case where the debtor is a covered financial corporation. Also, amend Section 103 to provide that, except as

---

114. Appendix, section 4 (amending Dodd-Frank Act, section 202(a)(1)(A)(i)).
115. Dodd-Frank, section 203(a)(2) (the FDIC and the Board must both "contain . . . (F) an evaluation of why a case under the Bankruptcy Code is not appropriate for the financial company. . . .").

provided in Chapter 14, the provisions of Chapter 11 apply in a case under Chapter 14.

3) Amend **Section 106** of the Bankruptcy Code by adding Section 1403 to the list of sections where sovereign immunity is abrogated.

4) Amend **Section 109** of the Bankruptcy Code to provide that only a covered financial corporation may be a debtor under Chapter 14. Also, exclude the ability of a covered financial corporation to be a debtor under Chapter 11 or under Chapter 7 (unless, in the case of Chapter 7, it is pursuant to the application of Section 1112 in the Chapter 14 case).

5) Amend **Section 1506** of the Bankruptcy Code to provide that the court has the discretion not to enforce foreign home country stay orders, or not to issue orders barring domestic ring-fencing actions against US-based assets, if the foreign home country has not adopted comparable provisions respecting ancillary proceedings in that foreign home country for U.S.-based home proceedings.

Section 2: Liquidation, Reorganization, or Recapitalization of a Covered Financial Corporation

1) Amend the Bankruptcy Code by adding a new **Chapter 14** ("Liquidation, Reorganization, or Recapitalization of a Covered Financial Corporation").

2) Add a **Section 1401**, "Inapplicability of other sections," that provides that Sections 321(c) (allowing the U.S. trustee for the district to serve as a trustee) and 322(b) (essentially the same) do not apply to a case under Chapter 14. References to "the United States trustee" in Chapter 11 shall be deemed replaced by references to "the Board" (defined below).

3) Add a **Section 1402**, "Definitions for this chapter," that defines (a) the "Board" as referring to the Board of Governors of the Federal Reserve System, (b) "bridge company" as the recipient of the transfer under Section 1405, whose equity interests are received by the Chapter 14 debtor in that transfer, (c) "capital structure debt" as unsecured debt (including the under-secured portion of secured debt that would otherwise constitute capital structure debt), other than a qualified financial contract, of the debtor for borrowed money with an original

maturity of at least one year that is either (i) of a kind required by the Board or other applicable government agency, (ii) contractually subordinated to other unsecured debt, or (iii) convertible upon specified financial events or conditions to a security that would have a lower priority in bankruptcy than unsecured debt; (c) "qualified financial contract" as contracts as defined in Section 101(25), (38A), (47), or (53B), Section 741(7), or Section 761(4), (5), (11), or (13); (d) "special trustee" as the trustee of a trust created under Section 1405.

4) Add a **Section 1403**, dealing with the "Commencement of a case concerning a covered financial corporation," that permits a case to be commenced (a) by the filing of a voluntary petition by the debtor under Section 301, (b) in the case of a covered financial corporation as to which the Board has supervisory authority, by the Board if the Board certifies that it has determined, following consultation with the Secretary of the Treasury and the FDIC, that the immediate commencement of a Chapter 14 case is necessary to avoid serious adverse effects on the financial stability of the United States or that the covered financial corporation has substantial impairment of regulatory capital, or (c) in the case of other covered financial corporations, by the filing of a petition by the primary regulator of that corporation if the primary regulator certifies that it has determined that the covered financial corporation's assets are less than its liabilities, at fair valuation, or the covered financial corporation has unreasonably small capital. A filing by the Board under (b) or by the primary regulator under (c) with the requisite certification will be treated as equivalent to a Section 301 voluntary filing (that is, the commencement of the case will itself constitute an order for relief), except that, analogous to Section 303(i)(2)(A), the court, before or after a Section 1405 transfer, would retain jurisdiction so as, on motion and hearing, to determine any damages proximately caused by such a filing or transfer pursuant to Section 1405, if the court further makes the determination that the certifications required by either Section 1403 or Section 1405 were not supported by substantial evidence on the record as a whole.

5) Add a **Section 1404**, "Regulators," permitting (a) the Board to be heard on any issue relevant to the regulation of the debtor by the

Board or to financial stability in the United States, (b) the FDIC to be heard in connection with a transfer under Section 1405, (c) the primary financial regulatory agency (as defined in section 2(12) of Dodd-Frank) of the covered financial corporation, any subsidiary of the covered financial corporation, or the primary financial regulator of any foreign subsidiary of the covered financial corporation or its parent, to be heard on any issue relevant to its regulation of that entity. If there is a transfer under Section 1405, following that transfer, the Board can be heard only in connection with the debtor's ownership of the bridge company. If there is not a transfer under Section 1405, then the Board is deemed a party in interest who can file a plan of reorganization at any time after the later of (a) the order for relief and (b) the failure to timely approve of a transfer under Section 1405, in a case where such transfer is sought.

6) Add a **Section 1405**, "Special Transfer of Property of the Estate, Contracts, and Debts." On motion by the debtor, the Board, or the primary regulator (in the latter two cases, only if the Board or the primary regulator was eligible to file a petition under Section 1403) at the time of the commencement of the case, and after a hearing, the court may order a transfer of the property of the estate, executory contracts, unexpired leases, and debt agreements, with the exception noted next, from the debtor to a bridge company. Neither capital structure debt nor equity interests may be transferred. All other assets and liabilities of the debtor shall be transferred to the bridge company if the court orders a transfer under this section. The transfer under this section shall specify that any debt for borrowed money that (a) is secured by collateral included in the transfer, (b) is not associated with a qualified financial contract, and (c) has an original maturity of at least one year, shall be non-recourse upon the transfer if the deficiency claim would otherwise constitute capital structure debt. Prior to the hearing, 24-hour electronic or telephonic notice shall be given to (a) the debtor, (b) the 20 largest holders of capital structure debt, (c) the Board and the FDIC (if the Board has supervisory authority over the debtor), and (d) each primary financial regulatory authority, whether US or foreign, of the covered financial corporation and any subsidiary whose ownership is proposed to be transferred, each of

whom have standing, with respect to its particular regulatory juris-diction, concerning the motion for a Section 1405 transfer. After the hearing, the court may not order the transfer unless it finds (or the Board or the primary regulator, as the case may be, certifies to the court that it has found) that the bridge company provides adequate assurance of future performance of any executory contract, unexpired lease, or debt agreement being transferred to the bridge company. In addition, the court may not authorize the transfer to the bridge company unless it determines that the by-laws of the bridge company will allow a thirty-day period in which the debtor, with the approval of the Chapter 14 judge after notice and a hearing, can determine the composition of the board of the bridge company, notwithstand-ing the charter or by-laws of the bridge company or applicable non-bankruptcy law. A transfer under this section shall provide for the transfer to a special trustee, appointed by the court, of all of the equity securities of the bridge company to be held in trust for the sole benefit of the Chapter 14 estate, as well as the responsibility of the bridge company to pay the reasonable expenses of the special trustee. The court shall approve the trust agreement and shall require the special trustee to inform and consult with the Chapter 14 trustee about mate-rial corporate actions of the bridge company. The special trustee shall distribute the assets held in trust, and shall thereafter terminate the trust, upon either (a) the effective date of a confirmed plan of reor-ganization of the covered financial corporation or (b) the conversion of the case to Chapter 7. Finally, while the court otherwise does not retain jurisdiction over the bridge company following the transfer, it does retain jurisdiction for one year, on application by the bridge company, for liquidity financing at the priority levels of, and on the conditions specified in, Section 1413.

7) Add a **Section 1406**, dealing with "Automatic Stay; Assumed Debt." (I) Provide in this section that the filing of a petition operates as a stay, applicable to all entities, of the termination, acceleration, or modification of any debt agreement (other than a capital structure debt agreement or a qualified financial contract), executory contract (other than a qualified financial contract), or unexpired lease with the

debtor, or of any right or obligation under any such debt, contract, lease, or agreement, solely because of a provision that is conditioned on (a) the insolvency or financial condition of the debtor at any time before the closing of the case; (b) the commencement of a Chapter 14 case; (c) a cross-default, or (d) a change in a credit-rating agency rating (i) of the debtor at any time after the commencement of the case or (ii) of a subsidiary during the 48 hours after the commencement of the case, or (iii) of the bridge company or a subsidiary of the bridge company prior to the earlier of 90 days or the confirmation of a plan involving the debtor under Section 1129. The stay under this Section 1406 terminates, as to the debtor and with respect to any debt agreements with the debtor, upon the earliest of (a) a commencement of a Chapter 14 case without a motion for a Section 1405 transfer, (b) 48 hours after the commencement of the case, (c) the transfer of the debt agreement under an order authorizing a Section 1405 transfer, or (d) a determination by the court not to order a Section 1405 transfer. In addition, in the case of a subsidiary, the stay terminates not only upon the foregoing conditions but by a determination by the court not to order the transfer of the interests of the debtor in the subsidiary to the bridge company.

(II) Provide, as well, in this section, that such a debt agreement, executory contract, or unexpired lease of the debtor, may be transferred (and thus assumed) by the bridge company under Section 1405 notwithstanding any provision in an agreement or applicable non-bankruptcy law that (a) prohibits, restricts, or conditions the assignment of such debt agreement, executory contract, or unexpired lease, or (b) terminates, accelerates, or modifies any such debt agreement, executory contract, or unexpired lease, based on a change in control in any party.

8) Add a **Section 1407**, "Treatment of Qualified Financial Contracts," that provides that the filing of a petition to commence a Chapter 14 case that is accompanied by a motion for a Section 1405 transfer operates as a stay, notwithstanding Sections 362(b)(6), (b)(7), (b)(17), (b)(27), 555, 556, 559, 560, and 561, for the period specified in the stay duration in Section 1406, above, of the exercise of any contractual

right (i) to liquidate, terminate, or accelerate a qualified financial contract of the debtor or a subsidiary or (ii) to offset or net out any termination value, payment amount, or the like except the exercise of contractual rights that arise upon the non-accelerated maturity of a qualified financial contract shall not be subject to the stay. During the period in which this Section 1407 stay is applicable, the debtor and its subsidiaries shall perform all payment and delivery obligations under a qualified financial contract that become due after the commencement of the case; if the debtor or a subsidiary, as the case may be, fails to perform any such obligation, the stay provided by this Section 1407 terminates. As long as the debtor and/or its subsidiaries are performing all payment and delivery obligations under a qualified financial contract that become due after the commencement of the case, the failure of a counterparty to perform its obligations under that qualified financial contract shall constitute a breach of such contact according to its terms. A Section 1405 transfer of a qualified financial contract to the bridge company may not occur unless (i) all qualified financial contracts between the counterparty and the debtor are transferred to the bridge company and (ii) all property acting as security to the qualified financial contract is likewise transferred to the bridge company. Upon the transfer of a qualified financial contract to the bridge company under Section 1405, notwithstanding any provision in the qualified financial contract or in applicable law, that qualified financial contract may not be terminated, accelerated, or modified, for a breach of a provision of the type identified in Section 1406 (I) between the time of the Section 1405 transfer until the conclusion of the Chapter 14 case involving the debtor. If there is not a request for a transfer under Section 1405, or if such transfer is not approved, or 48 hours from the filing of the petition have expired, then the provisions for qualified financial contracts originally outlined in "Chapter 14 version 1.0" in BANKRUPTCY *NOT* BAILOUT apply.

9) Add a **Section 1408**, "Subsidiary Contracts," that provides that, notwithstanding any provision in an agreement or applicable non-bankruptcy law, an agreement of a subsidiary (including an executory contract, unexpired lease, or agreement under which the subsidiary issued or is obligated for debt) where the subsidiary's ownership

interests that are property of the estate are transferred to the bridge company in a Section 1405 transfer, such agreement may not be terminated, accelerated, or modified, at any time after the commencement of the case, because of a provision prohibiting, restricting, or conditioning the assignment of the agreement or because of the change-of-control of a party to the agreement. Nor may a cross-default provision respecting the debtor in an agreement of the subsidiary be enforced in any case of the debtor involving a Section 1405 transfer motion during the earliest of 48 hours from the commencement of a case under this Chapter involving the debtor or the denial of a Section 1405 transfer motion.

10) Add a **Section 1409**, dealing with "Licenses, Permits, and Registrations," that provides, notwithstanding any other provision of nonbankruptcy law, a Section 1405 transfer motion stays, for the period of time specified in Section 1406, any termination or modification of any Federal, State, or local license, permit or registration that the debtor or a subsidiary had immediately before the commencement of the case that is proposed to be transferred, based upon (i) the insolvency or financial condition of the debtor at any time before the closing of the case, (ii) the commencement of a case under this title, or (iii) a transfer under Section 1405. Following a Section 1405 transfer, all such licenses, permits, and registrations shall vest in the bridge company. In addition, where a subsidiary's ownership interests that are property of the estate are proposed to be transferred to the bridge company in a Section 1405 transfer, a Section 1405 transfer motion stays, for the period of time specified in Section 1406 and thereafter if the subsidiary's ownership interests that are property of the estate are transferred to the bridge company in a Section 1405 transfer, any termination or modification of any Federal, State, or local license, permit or registration that the subsidiary had immediately before the commencement of the case, based on a change-of-control of the subsidiary.

11) Add a **Section 1410**, "Bridge Company Capital Requirements," giving the bridge company an exemption from applicable debt or capital requirements (such as might be required by the Board or Basel III) until such time as (a) the confirmation of a plan of reorganization for the debtor that involves the distribution or sale of securities of

the bridge company or (b) one year from the Section 1405 transfer, whichever is earlier.

12) Add a **Section 1411**, "Avoiding Powers," providing that in a case where there is a request for a Section 1405 transfer, and such transfer occurs, the avoiding powers in Sections 544, 547, 548(a)(1)(B), or 549, do not apply, except for transfers of (i) an interest of the debtor in property to or for the benefit of a holder of capital structure debt under Section 547 or (ii) an interest of the debtor in property to or for the benefit of a holder of equity of the debtor under Section 548(a)(1)(B). Additionally, if there is not a motion for a Section 1405 transfer or if such transfer is not approved, the provisions for the application of avoiding powers with respect to qualified financial contracts contained in BANKRUPTCY NOT BAILOUT apply.

13) Add a **Section 1412**, "Exemption from Securities Laws and Special Tax Provisions," providing that, for purposes of Section 1145, a security of the bridge company shall be deemed to be a security of a successor to the debtor under a plan of reorganization if the court approves the disclosure statement for the plan as providing adequate information (as defined in Section 1125(a)) about the bridge company and the security. In addition, securities issued by the bridge company in connection with a confirmed plan of reorganization shall have the protection from any law imposing a stamp tax or similar tax under Section 1146(a).

14) Add a **Section 1413**, "Debtor-in-Possession Financing," that picks up the provisions regarding Section 364 in the original Chapter 14 version 1.0.[116]

15) Add a **Section 1414**, "Trustee in a Chapter 14 Case" that provides, if there is an approved Section 1405 transfer, then there shall be a trustee appointed by the court, after notice and a hearing, in lieu of the debtor in possession, for all purposes of the debtor after the Section 1405 transfer. The trustee shall be appointed by the court from a pre-approved list of trustees that has been determined by the Chief Judge of the Circuit. In other cases, a trustee, chosen from the

---

116. Pursuant to section 1405, these provisions will also be applicable to the bridge company. See section 2(6).

pre-approved list of trustees, can be appointed pursuant to the provisions of Section 1104.

16) Add a **Section 1415**, "Solicitation, Acceptance, and Confirmation of a Plan," providing that, in the case of a plan of reorganization proposed at or following the approval of a Section 1405 transfer, that a court may hold a confirmation hearing under Section 1128, within ten days of the circulation of the plan if voting for purposes of Section 1126 is sufficient, at the time of the hearing, to allow the court to make the determinations required by Section 1129.

Section 3: Amendments to Title 28

1) Provide, in **Section 298**, that, notwithstanding Section 295, the Chief Justice of the United States shall designate at least one district judge from each circuit to be available to hear a case under Chapter 14. And that district judge, again notwithstanding Section 295, shall hear a Chapter 14 case filed in that circuit, and shall be considered, for purposes of the case, to be temporally assigned to the district in which the bankruptcy case is commenced or any district to which the case is removed pursuant to 28 USC §1412. The district judge may not refer a motion for a Section 1405 transfer to a bankruptcy judge, notwithstanding Section 157. In a case in which there is not a motion for a Section 1405 transfer, or the motion is denied, the district court may not assign the case or proceedings under the case to a bankruptcy judge, unless there has been approved a motion to convert the case to Chapter 7 pursuant to Section 1112. In all cases where the district judge may not refer a case or proceeding to a bankruptcy judge, the district judge may appoint a bankruptcy judge as a special master. Appeals under Section 158(a) in a Chapter 14 case shall be heard by the assigned district judge.

Section 4: Amendment to Dodd-Frank Wall Street Reform and Consumer Protection Act

1) Amend **Section 202** by adding at the end of (a)(1)(A)(i) that, notwithstanding the provisions of this subsection, if a case has been commenced under Chapter 14 of Title 11, the relevant district court shall be the district court where the Chapter 14 case is pending, and

the judge overseeing the Chapter 14 case shall be assigned to hear and decide the order under (a)(1)(A) of this section. In addition, amend (a)(1)(A)(iii) and (iv) so as to subject the finding required of the government agencies under section 203(a)(2)(F) to the same determination and issuance procedures currently outlined under (a)(1)(A)(iii) and (iv) of this section for the (a)(1)(A)(iii) determination.

CHAPTER 3

Financing Systemically Important Financial Institutions in Bankruptcy

David A. Skeel Jr.

Introduction

When railroads failed in the second half of the nineteenth century, as many did in the rush to link America's markets to its frontiers, their creditors and the Wall Street professionals who represented them faced a vexing problem. Although the creditors held mortgages on railroad assets and thus were nominally secured, a mortgage on a stretch of railroad track was worth very little unless the railroad continued to operate. Many railroads had been cobbled together through mergers, so the creditors often had mortgages on parts of the business rather than the business as a whole. As a result, the railroads' secured creditors were as anxious to see the railroads restructured as were the shareholders, suppliers and—because of the national interest in improved transportation—the general public. It was against this backdrop that the Wall Street banks and lawyers who represented the secured creditors devised America's first reorganization framework for large-scale corporations—the equity or railroad receivership.[1]

Among the many problems that the architects of the equity receiverships encountered was the question of how to finance the receivership process. The equity receiverships were crafted from foreclosure law,

---

I am grateful to Kenneth Ayotte, Daniel Bussel, Darrell Duffie, Bruce Grohsgal, Ken Scott, and John Van Etten for helpful comments on previous drafts.

1. For a much more complete history of the emergence of railroad receiverships in the United States, see David A. Skeel Jr., *Debt's Dominion: A History of Bankruptcy Law in America* (Princeton, NJ: Princeton University Press, 2001), 52–69.

which provided for the foreclosure and sale of collateral after a default; and from receivership law, which authorized a court to vest authority over a debtor's assets in a receiver. Because equity receiverships were much more complex and often took significantly longer than a traditional foreclosure or receivership, and because railroads were usually starved for cash when the receivership began, they often needed to borrow money to finance the receivership process. But few lenders were anxious to lend money to an insolvent railroad that already had multiple layers of secured debt unless they could be assured priority over the existing debt. Here, too, the architects of the early receiverships devised an ingenious solution: the receiver's certificate. If the railroad needed financing during the receivership process, the receiver would ask the court to authorize a receiver's certificate in the amount of the desired financing. The holder of a receiver's certificate would be promised a first priority charge against the railroad's current income; only the net income, after the debtor's obligations under the receiver's certificates were paid, would be made available to the debtor's other creditors. Receiver's certificates are the direct ancestors of the debtor-in-possession financing provision in current Chapter 11.[2]

A year or so after the enactment of the Dodd-Frank Act in 2010, the Federal Deposit Insurance Corporation devised a mechanism for restructuring troubled, systemically important financial institutions — "single-point-of-entry" resolution — that bears an unmistakable resemblance to the nineteenth-century receiverships.[3] In a

---

2. See David A. Skeel Jr., "The Past, Present and Future of Debtor-in-Possession Financing," *Cardozo Law Review* 25 (2004): 1905, 1908–13.

3. For early descriptions of this strategy, before it was dubbed single-point-of-entry, see Randall D. Guynn, "Are Bailouts Inevitable?" *Yale Journal on Regulation* 29, no. 121 (2012): 147–50; and comment letter from the Securities Industry and Financial Markets Association and The Clearing House Association to FDIC on its second notice of proposed rulemaking under Title II of the Dodd-Frank Act, May 23, 2011, http://www.fdic.gov/regulatios/laws/federal/2011/11c16Ad73 .PDF. Douglas Baird and Ed Morrison also pointed out early on that Title II could be used to recapitalize a systemically important financial institution. See Douglas G. Baird & Edward R. Morrison, "Dodd-Frank for Bankruptcy Lawyers," *American Bankruptcy Institute Law Review* 19 (2011). The FDIC formally endorsed and

single-point-of-entry resolution, regulators would put the holding company of a SIFI into Title II resolution, then transfer the holding company's assets, secured debt, and short-term debt, if any,[4] to a newly created bridge institution, leaving the holding company's long-term debt and stock behind.[5] As with the equity receivership, the FDIC's single-point-of-entry strategy is in form a sale of the debtor's assets but in reality a recapitalization. And both required a creative reinterpretation of laws that were intended for liquidation rather than recapitalization—foreclosure law in the nineteenth century in the first case and the "thou shalt liquidate" commandment in Title II of the Dodd-Frank Act in the second.[6]

---

outlined single-point-of-entry in Federal Deposit Insurance Corporation, "The Resolution of Systemically Important Financial Institutions: The Single Point of Entry Strategy," 78 Fed. Reg. 76614 (Dec. 18, 2013).

4. US bank holding companies generally have very little secured debt or short-term unsecured debt, virtually all of which is issued at the operating subsidiary level. In addition, the Financial Stability Board (FSB) has issued a proposal for imposing new total loss-absorbing capacity (TLAC) on global systemically important banking groups (G-SIBs) that would supplement Basel III regulatory capital requirements. Financial Stability Board, "Consultative Document: Adequacy of Loss-Absorbing Capacity of Global Systemically Important Banks in Resolution" (Nov. 10, 2014). TLAC-eligible instruments would include common equity, other regulatory capital instruments and long-term unsecured debt with a remaining maturity of one year or more. They would exclude short-term unsecured debt. The FSB's proposal would also require TLAC-eligible instruments to be contractually, legally, or structurally subordinate to short term unsecured debt. This would effectively require the bank holding company parents of US G-SIBs either to push any short-term unsecured debt from the parent to the operating subsidiary level or to make such short-term debt contractually senior to the parent's TLAC-eligible instruments. The Federal Reserve has indicated that it intends to issue a regulation imposing TLAC requirements on US G-SIBs similar to the FSB proposal.

5. For additional details, see FDIC, "Resolution of Systemically Important Financial Institutions," note 4.

6. See Dodd-Frank Act section 214 (liquidation requirement). For a skeptical assessment of the single-point-of-entry strategy, see Paul H. Kupiec and Peter J. Wallison, "Can the 'Single Point of Entry' Strategy be Used to Recapitalize a Failing Bank?" AEI Economic Working Paper 2014-08 (December 3, 2014).

The same lawyers who persuaded the FDIC to pursue the single-point-of-entry strategy subsequently realized that a very similar approach might work in Chapter 11 if lawmakers made a handful of amendments to current bankruptcy law. If a SIFI's holding company filed for Chapter 11, it could transfer its assets, secured debt, and any short-term liabilities to a newly created corporation, leaving its stock and long-term debt behind.[7] The bankruptcy alternative to the single-point-of-entry approach does not yet have a generally agreed-upon moniker. As this volume reflects, the Hoover working group on financial institution insolvency incorporated a version of the bankruptcy alternative into a proposal for a new Chapter 14. Those of us in the group generally refer to our proposal as a "quick sale" or "quick section 363 sale," and the proposed statutory framework for implementing it as Chapter 14 2.0. As this book goes to press, lawmakers have included the central features of Chapter 14 2.0 in two bills, one introduced in the Senate and the other both introduced in and passed by the House.[8]

My objective in this chapter is to explore the options for financing SIFIs in bankruptcy, especially in connection with the quick sale process.[9] Financing is the issue on which the proposal to effect a quick sale in Chapter 11 differs most starkly with the single-point-of-entry

---

7. See Randall D. Guynn, "Framing the TBTF Problem: The Path to a Solution," in *Across the Great Divide: New Perspectives on the Financial Crisis,* ed. John B. Taylor and Martin Neal Baily (Stanford, CA: Hoover Institution Press, 2014); John Bovenzi, Randall Guynn, and Thomas Jackson, "Too Big to Fail: The Path to a Solution," panel discussion for Bipartisan Policy Center, May 14, 2013; and Donald S. Bernstein, Testimony on "The Financial Institution Bankruptcy Act of 2014" Before the Subcommittee on Regulatory Reform, Commercial and Antitrust Law, US House of Representatives (July 15, 2014).

8. The Senate Bill is the Taxpayer Protection and Responsible Resolution Act, S. 1861, 113th Cong. (2013); the House Bill is the Financial Institution Bankruptcy Act of 2014, H.R. 5421, 113th Cong. (2014).

9. Throughout this chapter, I use the term SIFI broadly, to refer to bank holding companies that meet the $50 billion threshold for inclusion in Title I of the Dodd-Frank Act, as well as systemically important nonbank financial institutions. Most or all of the bank holding companies with less than $250 billion in assets actually are not systemically important. Where the distinction between institutions that

approach to Title II of the Dodd-Frank Act. Although the financing arrangements in Title II are controversial, there is little doubt that the receiver of a troubled SIFI would have access to sufficient financing to meet even the most pressing liquidity needs. Title II authorizes the receiver to borrow up to 10 percent of a SIFI's pre-resolution value or 90 percent of its post-resolution value from the United States Treasury.[10] Chapter 11, by contrast, does not currently provide any special financial arrangements for SIFIs, and neither of the pending bills would introduce additional funding for a SIFI bankruptcy. (Indeed, the Senate bill prohibits the government from providing funding in connection with a quick sale.) Advocates of Title II often single out the absence of SIFI-specific financing as an insuperable obstacle to successful resolution of a SIFI in Chapter 11.[11]

I argue in this chapter that the widespread pessimism about a SIFI's ability to borrow sufficient funds—sufficiently quickly—to finance resolution in Chapter 11 is substantially overstated. The criticism appears to be based on the assumption that the largest banks have essentially the same structure as they had prior to the 2008 panic, thus ignoring the effects of the regulatory changes that have taken place as a result of the Dodd-Frank Act. Critics also do not seem to have fully considered the likelihood that the quick sale resolution of a SIFI—like

---

are and are not systemically important is significant, I will signal which institutions I have in mind in the text.

10. See Dodd-Frank Wall Street Reform and Consumer Protection Act, Pub. L. No. 111-203, § 210(n)(2010).

11. Stephen Lubben is among those who have voiced this concern. Stephen J. Lubben, "Resolution, Orderly and Otherwise: B of A in OLA," *University of Cincinnati Law Review* 81 (2012): 485, 517 (arguing that the "key difficulty" with Chapter 14 "rests on funding," and concluding that "something like" the Title II funding mechanism "is a prerequisite to a viable resolution authority"). Also see Stephen J. Lubben, "What's Wrong with the Chapter 14 Proposal," *New York Times*, April 10, 2013 (questioning "the dubious assumption in Chapter 14 that private debtor-in-possession financing will be available in times of financial distress, especially in the size a large financial institution would need"), http://dealbook .nytimes.com/2013/04/10/whats-wrong-with-the-chapter-14-proposal/?_r=0. See also Guynn, "Are Bailouts Inevitable?" (identifying funding limitations as a shortcoming of bankruptcy).

prepackaged bankruptcies of other firms—should require less new liquidity than the traditional bankruptcy process.

Although bankruptcy is better able to handle the financing needs of a troubled SIFI than is generally acknowledged, the doubts of Chapter 14 2.0's critics are not altogether unfounded. The old debtor and new corporation would need to put any financing in place very quickly, which might cause potential lenders to balk, especially if a SIFI fell into financial distress during a period of market-wide instability. I therefore consider two other potential sources of funding: prearranged private funding and governmental funding.

I begin, in the first section, by exploring the financing options that would be available to a SIFI that filed for bankruptcy today, as well as several factors that would determine the extent of the SIFI's financing needs. I conclude both that bankruptcy provides greater access to liquidity than is often appreciated—through its debtor-in-possession financing provision and through several other key rules—and that post-2008 regulation and the quick sale strategy have reduced the amount of liquidity that a SIFI debtor would need at the outset of its restructuring. Although critics may be right about the need for additional liquidity, the limitations of existing bankruptcy law seem much less severe than the conventional wisdom suggests.

In the second section, I explore the possibility that a SIFI could boost its access to liquidity by putting private financing in place prior to a bankruptcy filing—a strategy I refer to as prearranged financing. Prearranged financing could remove much of the uncertainty over a troubled SIFI's ability to obtain enough liquidity for an effective bankruptcy resolution. But the strategy would also face a series of significant obstacles. The most important obstacles are (1) a bankruptcy rule that automatically terminates any pre-bankruptcy loan commitment made to the debtor itself[12] and (2) the likely cost of arranging financing for a hypothetical crisis that may not occur in the foreseeable future. I consider a variety of responses to these obstacles, and also point out that SIFIs are not likely to implement a prearranged financing strategy voluntarily. The Federal Reserve could counteract SIFIs' reluctance

---

12. 11 USC § 365(c)(2).

to incur the costs of prearranged financing by incorporating prearranged financing into the living-will process. Given the obstacles and the likely availability of funding at the time a SIFI falls into financial distress, I question whether a prearranged funding requirement would make sense.

In the final section, I consider whether an additional source of governmental financing may be necessary. In my view, lawmakers could plausibly conclude that they do not need to authorize either of the most likely sources of government funding: a designated fund analogous to Title II's orderly liquidation fund (OLF) or access to Federal Reserve funding. Given the residuum of uncertainty about a SIFI's ability to obtain adequate liquidity, I conclude that lawmakers should give SIFIs limited, explicit access to Fed funding, preferably by expanding the Fed's emergency lending authority under section 13(3) of the Federal Reserve Act.

Funding Options in Current Chapter 11

In their assessment of a SIFI's funding capacity in a Chapter 11 reorganization, skeptics of the existing bankruptcy rules have emphasized the magnitude and immediacy of a SIFI's likely financing needs.[13] Skeptics question whether a SIFI could arrange adequate financing from private sources quickly enough to fund an effective Chapter 11 sale and resolution. To assess this objection, I begin by describing bankruptcy's debtor-in-possession (DIP) financing provision, which critics fear is too slow and limited in scope to meet a SIFI's immediate financing needs. Although critics are right to worry about the adequacy of traditional DIP financing, a more complete analysis of the liquidity available after the bankruptcy filing and the likely scope of a SIFI's liquidity needs will invite a somewhat more optimistic conclusion.

Bankruptcy's Debtor-in-Possession Financing Provision

Bankruptcy's debtor-in-possession financing provision, which is set forth in section 364 of the Bankruptcy Code, provides a variety of financing options. Section 364 first authorizes a debtor to borrow on

---

13. See, e.g., Lubben, "What's Wrong with the Chapter 14 Proposal."

an unsecured basis, with the promise of administrative expense treatment for the lender, without first seeking court approval.[14] If unsecured financing is unlikely to be available, the court can give the DIP financer priority over all other administrative expenses or authorize a lien on either unencumbered or already encumbered property.[15] The court's most dramatic power is the right to authorize a new "priming" lien that has priority over an existing lien on the same property.[16] The broad borrowing powers afforded by the financing provision are one of the most striking features of Chapter 11.

In the general run of cases, Chapter 11's DIP financing provision provides extensive access to funding for the bankruptcy process; indeed, it is one of Chapter 11's most noteworthy features. Although DIP financing requires court approval, a debtor often can put the financing in place quite quickly. Bankruptcy courts regularly grant interim approval for proposed financing at the outset of the case. When Eastman Kodak filed for bankruptcy, for instance, it put nearly $1 billion of funding in place within twenty-four hours of its bankruptcy filing.[17]

Whether this would be sufficient for the liquidity needs of a bank holding company or other SIFI is less clear, however. Bankruptcy skeptics argue a SIFI could not borrow nearly enough under a standard DIP financing facility to assure creditors and other market actors that the SIFI is stable and capable of meeting its obligations. On this view, the Chapter 11 quick sale strategy cannot work effectively unless lawmakers provide an additional source of lender-of-last-resort funding.

In our original Chapter 14 proposal—now known as Chapter 14 1.0—we proposed an amendment to bankruptcy's DIP financing provision that would authorize the debtor to make immediate partial payments of its obligations to derivatives counterparties and other creditors that might be destabilized by the debtor's default on

---

14. 11 USC § 364(a).

15. 11 USC § 364(b) and (c).

16. 11 USC § 364(d).

17. See, e.g., Joseph Checkler, "Judge Says Kodak Can Tap $950M Bankruptcy Loan from Citi," *Daily Bankruptcy Review,* January 20, 2012.

its obligations. "There may be situations," our principal drafter wrote, "where liquidity or other systematic concerns suggest that the appropriate action—without involving a government bailout of any sort— would be for certain liquidity-sensitive creditors to be 'advanced' a portion of their likely bankruptcy distribution."[18] Because existing bankruptcy law does not seem to contemplate partial payments, Chapter 14 1.0 proposed amending section 364 to "permit partial or complete payments to some or all creditors where liquidity of those creditors is a concern."[19] Although our proposal would alleviate the liquidity problems of a SIFI debtor's counterparties, it would not alter the current process for obtaining DIP financing, and it would not address the debtor's own liquidity needs. Indeed, by directing funds to the debtor's counterparties, it actually could reduce the *debtor's* liquidity.

In my view, the question whether bankruptcy would provide sufficient liquidity, sufficiently quickly, is a weighty one. Indeed, I have raised it in my own work,[20] and I will argue below that limited Federal Reserve financing should be extended to the new holding company created by a quick sale in bankruptcy. Yet the concerns seem much less serious in the context of a quick sale of a SIFI than for the ordinary bankruptcy process. In my view, the standard critiques underappreciate the liquidity that would be available to a SIFI in connection with a quick sale, and overestimate the amount of liquidity that would be necessary.

Additional Sources of Liquidity under Current Bankruptcy Law

To appreciate the full extent of the liquidity available in bankruptcy, we need to look beyond the DIP financing provision alone. In addition to the expansive DIP financing rules, bankruptcy provides several

---

18. Thomas H. Jackson, "Bankruptcy Code Chapter 14: A Proposal," in *Bankruptcy Not Bailout: A Special Chapter 14*, ed. Kenneth E. Scott and John B. Taylor (Stanford, CA: Hoover Institution Press, 2012), 25, 41.

19. Ibid., 43.

20. See, e.g., Thomas H. Jackson and David A. Skeel Jr., "Dynamic Resolution of Large Financial Institutions," *Harvard Business Law Review* 2 (2012): 435, 449–50.

other liquidity-generating mechanisms that would expand the liquidity available to a SIFI that filed for bankruptcy.[21] First, bankruptcy imposes an automatic stay on creditor collection activities as of the moment a debtor files for bankruptcy.[22] A bank holding company or other SIFI could therefore halt payments on its bond debt and other obligations, freeing up those funds for its bankruptcy financing needs. The benefit of suspending current payments to long-term creditors could prove significant, given that systemically important financial institutions will be required to continue to hold a large swath of bond debt.[23]

The second source of liquidity is more subtle and far more important. The bankruptcy provision that permits a debtor to sell most or all of its assets can enhance a debtor's financing capacity, because the sale is free and clear of debt obligations that might otherwise interfere with a debtor's capacity to borrow money.[24] Once they are sold, the assets can be used as collateral for new loans, shorn of the debt overhang that might otherwise prevent the debtor from borrowing.

A version of this financing technique has already been used in Chapter 11 cases involving smaller financial institutions. When AmericanWest Bancorporation, the holding company of American-West Bank, fell into financial distress in 2011, it could not restructure its debt outside of bankruptcy because it had issued a substantial amount of trust-preferred securities that precluded alteration unless

---

21. In addition to the two rules discussed in the text that follows, bankruptcy provides a variety of other liquidity-generating mechanisms. If any of the debtor's creditors are secured, for instance, the secured creditor's lien extends only to its current collateral and any proceeds of the collateral. See 11 USC § 552(a). For a more complete analysis, see Kenneth Ayotte & David A. Skeel Jr., "Bankruptcy Law as a Liquidity Provider," *University of Chicago Law Review* 80 (2013): 1557.

22. 11 USC § 362(a).

23. The Financial Stability Board has outlined its expectations for what has become known as the total loss-absorbing capacity, or TLAC. See Financial Stability Board, "Adequacy of loss-absorbing capacity of global systemically important banks in resolution," press release, November 10, 2014. The Federal Reserve has not yet released its TLAC rules for American SIFIs, but is expected to do so in early 2015.

24. 11 USC § 363.

two-thirds of the generally passive investors agreed.[25] The holding company raised $200 million in new funding from a private equity group by arranging to file for bankruptcy and then sell the stock of AmericanWest Bank to the private equity group pursuant to a section 363 sale.[26] The bankruptcy was completed in forty-two days, and achieved a recapitalization similar to the recapitalization envisioned by the Chapter 11 quick sale strategy.

Chapter 14 2.0 contemplates that the holding company SIFI would transfer any secured and short-term debt to the newly formed corporate buyer, while leaving its long-term debt and stock behind. The reduction in overall debt could facilitate borrowing by the new corporation, much as the section 363 sale of AmericanWest Bank's stock did for its holding company. Because the new corporation formed to acquire the SIFI holding company's assets and some of its debt would not be in bankruptcy itself, it would not need court approval for any new loan it obtained.[27] The buyer could arrange financing before proposing a sale transaction, and have it in place the moment the transaction was approved (and possibly even before).

The recapitalized SIFI's borrowing options may not be quite as simple as I have suggested thus far. The holding company's principal asset is likely to be the stock of its subsidiaries. Although lenders

---

25. For a description of the AmericanWest Bankcorporation bankruptcy, see Henry M. Fields, Kenneth E. Kohler, Barbara R. Mendelson, and Alexandra Steinberg Barrage, "AmericanWest Bancorporation: How a Section 363 Sale in Bankruptcy Provides a Viable Recapitalization Option for Troubled Banks," Morrison and Foerster, February 2011.

26. Ibid., 4. The private equity group, whose investors reportedly included Goldman Sachs and Oaktree Management, bid $6.5 million for the stock and agreed to lend up to $200 million. A total of $185 million was ultimately committed. See *In re re American Bancorporation*, 2010 WL 6415766, (Bankr. E.D. Wash), cited in Lev Breydo, "Banking on Bankruptcy: Bank Recapitalization through Chapter 11" (unpublished manuscript, December 2014).

27. Chapter 14 2.0 currently proposes to extend the judge's power to authorize financing to the newly created corporation. See, e.g., Thomas E. Jackson, chapter 2 in this volume. But the new corporation would not be required to ask for court involvement. Judicial involvement would only be necessary if the new corporation wished to take advantage of the additional powers provided by 11 USC § 364.

might be willing to take the stock as collateral, this would leave them structurally subordinated to subsidiary creditors with respect to the subsidiaries' assets. Lenders may therefore require that their loans be secured by one or more subsidiaries' assets. In theory, a creditor of the subsidiary that pledged its assets could challenge the security interest as a fraudulent conveyance, arguing that the subsidiary did not receive reasonably equivalent value for the security interest, since the proceeds of the loan went to the holding company. But a subsequent fraudulent conveyance challenge is only a danger if the subsidiary is insolvent or nearly insolvent at the time of the loan.[28] Moreover, even if the insolvency requirement were met, courts have generally rejected fraudulent conveyance challenges if the subsidiary receives at least an indirect benefit from a loan or other arrangement.[29] A loan that would facilitate the recapitalization of a troubled SIFI, and which is intended to help restore the holding company's stability, would provide obvious benefits for the subsidiaries that pledged their assets to support the loan, even if the funds did not go directly to the subsidiaries.

In practice, a significant portion of the funds almost certainly would in fact go to the subsidiaries, since the liquidity strain is likely to be most pressing at the subsidiary level. The subsidiaries are the locus of most operations, and the holding company itself would have little debt after the quick sale. This suggests that the loans could be made directly to the subsidiaries, with a guarantee by the new holding company.

There are downsides to being outside of the bankruptcy process, such as the absence of court authority to approve extraordinary loan

---

28. Under Uniform Fraudulent Transfer Act § 4(a)(2), for instance, a creditor would need to demonstrate both that the subsidiary did not receive "reasonably equivalent value" and that it either had "unreasonably small" assets or intended to incur debts beyond the subsidiary's ability to pay.

29. See, e.g., Mellon Bank v. Metro Communications Inc., 945 F.2d 635 (3d Cir. 1991) (indirect benefit sufficient to justify guaranty by subsidiary); and *In re Fairchild Aircraft Corp.*, 6 F.3d 1119 (5th Cir. 1993) (indirect benefit justifies subsidiary agreement to make payments).

provisions. (As noted earlier, Chapter 14 2.0 would address this concern by temporarily extending the bankruptcy court's DIP lending authority to the new corporation if the debtor seeks authorization for a loan.[30]) These complications do not seem likely to prevent a SIFI debtor from arranging for liquidity, however, and by forgoing bankruptcy court authorization a debtor could put financing in place almost immediately.

Liquidity Needs in the New Regulatory Environment

Although the Dodd-Frank Act avoided making any adjustments to current bankruptcy law, it and subsequent regulatory reforms may have altered the liquidity needs of a bank holding company that files for bankruptcy. The most obvious change is a significant increase in the capital requirements for systemically important financial institutions. Under the Basel III standard, which the Federal Reserve has begun to implement, SIFIs will now be required to maintain as much as 10.5 percent capital, due to a 1 percent to 2.5 percent capital surcharge that is being added in the wake of the 2008 crisis. SIFIs also must maintain substantially higher leverage ratios—which are calculated without risk-weighting the SIFI's assets.

At least as important are new liquidity requirements the Federal Reserve now imposes on the largest financial institutions. In keeping with Basel III, the Fed rolled out a new liquidity rule in September 2014. As described in the Fed's press release, the liquidity coverage ratio, which applies to institutions with $250 billion in total assets or $10 billion in foreign exposure,

> will for the first time create a standardized minimum liquidity requirement for large and internationally active banking organizations. Each institution will be required to hold high quality, liquid assets (HQLA) such as central bank reserves and government and corporate debt that can be converted easily and quickly into cash in an amount equal to or greater than its projected cash outflows minus its projected cash inflows

---

30. See Jackson, chapter 2 in this volume, Appendix section 2(6)(describing § 1413).

during a 30-day stress period. The ratio of the firm's liquid assets to its projected net cash outflow is its "liquidity coverage ratio," or LCR.[31]

Both liquidity and capital also figure in a series of stress tests the Federal Reserve applies to large bank holding companies. Best known is the Comprehensive Capital Analysis and Review (CCAR) stress test that the Fed administers to the thirty-one bank holding companies that have $50 billion or more in assets.[32] The aim of the stress tests, which were first introduced in 2009, is "to ensure that large financial institutions have robust, forward-looking capital planning processes that account for their unique risks, and to help ensure that they have sufficient capital to continue operations throughout times of economic and financial stress."[33] The Fed tests the banks' ability to withstand adverse economic conditions, modeled in terms of twenty-eight variables ranging from increased unemployment to changes in interest or exchange rates. Bank holding companies that fail the stress test are not permitted to make dividends or other distributions to their shareholders.

Recent history warns us not to put too much confidence even in significantly stiffened capital and liquidity requirements.[34] And a SIFI that winds up in bankruptcy will inevitably have run short on capital, liquidity, or both. But the stringent new rules should reduce the magnitude of a SIFI's liquidity needs at the time of a potential bankruptcy as compared to the rules in place before the recent crisis.

If the SIFI seeks to resolve its financial distress through a quick sale, rather than a traditional bankruptcy process, its liquidity needs should be further reduced. The quick sale is somewhat analogous to

---

31. Federal Reserve System and FDIC, "Federal Banking Regulators Finalize Liquidity Coverage Ratio," press release, September 3, 2014, http://www.federal reserve.gov/newsevents/press/bcreg/20140903a.htm.

32. The Dodd-Frank Act calls for additional stress tests.

33. Federal Reserve System, press release, October 23, 2014, http://www .federalreserve.gov/newsevents/press/bcreg/20141023a.htm.

34. Bear Stearns had considerable liquidity only a week before its collapse. And Citigroup appeared to be adequately capitalized in early 2008, yet it was almost certainly insolvent a month or two later.

the prepackaged bankruptcy of a traditional corporation, in which a corporation that wishes to restructure some of its unsecured debt (usually bonds) files its Chapter 11 petition and its proposed reorganization plan at the same time. Because prepackaged bankruptcies quickly recapitalize the troubled company, they require much less DIP financing than other Chapter 11 cases: debtors often do not seek any DIP financing for their prepackaged bankruptcy case. SIFIs are quite different from the companies that generally file prepackaged bankruptcy cases, of course; their liquidity can disappear much more quickly, and liquidity is central to their business model.[35] But the general pattern should hold true. Just as prepackaged bankruptcies do not require as much liquidity as traditional Chapter 11 cases, the quick sale resolution of a SIFI in Chapter 11 should be less liquidity-intensive than a more traditional SIFI bankruptcy.

Just how much financing would be necessary? It is of course hard to predict in advance, but we can perhaps arrive at a ballpark number by comparison to the rescue financing that was secured during the 2007–2009 recession. When Bear Stearns threatened to default, the Federal Reserve provided $29 billion in loan guarantees to facilitate its sale to J. P. Morgan Chase. The bankruptcy of a large SIFI might require more funding—perhaps $30–50 billion, and possibly more for the very largest—but if resolution is achieved through a quick sale, it is unlikely to require the huge amounts skeptics seem to envision. And smaller SIFIs could probably achieve a quick sale with significantly less financing. Although even $10–20 billion is substantially more than debtors have obtained from private lenders in previous Chapter 11 cases,[36] it seems plausible that a smaller SIFI could obtain private funding of this magnitude for its newly created holding company and its subsidiaries, especially if it planned for its bankruptcy in advance.

---

35. Interestingly, banks do sometimes recapitalize through a prepackaged bankruptcy. Anchor Bancorp Wisconsin Inc. recently did precisely this, recapitalizing its secured debt and its TARP obligations through a prepackaged bankruptcy that took only eighteen days. See, e.g., Brian D. Christiansen, Van C. Durrer II, and Sven G. Mickisch, "The Use of Pre-Packs in Bank Restructuring and M&A," *Financier Worldwide,* January 2014.

36. I discuss some of the largest recent DIP facilities in the next subsection.

If I am right about the effect of bankruptcy's liquidity enhancing rules and about the reduced need for funding in the Chapter 14 2.0 context, it seems plausible that a bank would be capable of raising adequate funding for its bankruptcy case from private lenders, or at the least much more plausible than before the Dodd-Frank reforms.

Do Private Markets Work in a Crisis?

It is of course possible that private lending would dry up altogether in a crisis as widespread as the 2008 crisis. Auto czar Steven Rattner and other commentators have argued that the government needed to bail out General Motors and Chrysler because the DIP financing market had completely collapsed in 2008 and 2009. This logic suggests that financing might not be available when it is most needed, even if it would be available under ordinary circumstances.

Although the DIP financing market clearly was stressed in 2008 and 2009, the rumors of its demise have been significantly exaggerated. In 2009, for instance, during the crisis, the CIT Group obtained $5.5 billion in funding for its reorganization. Also in 2009, Lyondell Chemical Co. obtained $8 billion in DIP financing. A significant portion of the Lyondell loan was "rolled up" pre-petition debt, but roughly $3 billion was new financing. Prior to Lehman Brothers' bankruptcy filing in September 2008, a group of lenders had tentatively agreed to a multibillion-dollar loan package to facilitate the sale of Lehman's brokerage operations to Barclays. (The arrangement faltered when UK regulators declined to waive the regulatory requirements that impeded an immediate sale.) A large troubled SIFI would need to secure considerably more funding, but the private lending market did not shut down altogether, even during the crisis. This suggests that private financing may be available in all but the most severe, market-wide crises.

Could the Government Serve as Financer?

If private financing really did dry up due to a market-wide crisis, the Federal Reserve could fill in the gap.[37] The Dodd-Frank Act restricted

---

37. At least, this is the case under existing law or under the subchapter V proposal that was recently approved by the House. The Toomey-Cornyn legislation

the Fed's authority to provide extraordinary financing like its rescue loans to Bear Stearns, Lehman, and AIG in 2008. Dodd-Frank amended the Fed's so-called 13(3) powers—its emergency lending authority under section 13(3) of the Federal Reserve Act—to prohibit the Fed from making emergency loans to individual institutions.[38] But the Dodd-Frank Act does authorize the Fed to provide industry-wide lending programs. In the event of a market-wide crisis, the Fed could presumably set up an industry-wide mechanism for borrowing that would be available to the new holding company created for the purposes of a SIFI restructuring or to the SIFI's subsidiaries. I will consider below the question of whether lawmakers should provide explicit authorization for Fed funding in a financial institution bankruptcy. Even without additional authorization, however, the Fed could step in under an industry-wide program.

I do not mean to suggest that concerns about the adequacy of bankruptcy funding are unfounded. But once we consider the full range of bankruptcy's liquidity-enhancing mechanisms, together with the likelihood that the new capital and liquidity rules have reduced the magnitude of the loan that would be necessary, it seems plausible that private funding sources would suffice for the purposes of a quick sale in bankruptcy.

Prearranged Bankruptcy Funding Alternatives

The funding strategies I have considered thus far would not require any advance coordination or legislative change. A second strategy would be to establish a prearranged private funding mechanism that could be quickly deployed if a SIFI fell into financial distress. The chief benefit of prearranged funding is that it would significantly reduce concerns about a troubled SIFI's ability to put together a big enough financing package at the outset of its bankruptcy case. The chief limitations are a legal impediment under current bankruptcy

---

introduced in the Senate in late 2013 would preclude the federal government from providing financing in connection with a SIFI restructuring.

38. Dodd-Frank Act § 1101(a) (extraordinary loans must be part of a "program or facility with broad-based eligibility").

law and the costs of putting in place a funding package that may never be used.

Prearranged funding would formalize an approach that was used in more ad hoc (and ex post) fashion to handle several major financial collapses in the late 1990s. When South Korea threatened to default on its sovereign debt in 1997, the International Monetary Fund put together a substantial rescue package—totaling $55 billion—but the financing failed to reassure the markets.[39] As lenders exited Korean debt, the US Treasury and Fed convened a meeting of major lenders at the New York Fed on December 22, 1997, and pressured the bank lenders to roll over their loans.[40] In effect, the roll-over amounted to a new $22 billion loan package provided by a group of the world's largest banks.

When the high-profile hedge fund Long-Term Capital Management faced collapse in 1998 due to the Russian crisis, regulators responded in similar fashion. Convened in New York by the New York Fed, sixteen major banks agreed to provide $3.625 billion to LTCM.[41] The rescue financing was used to close out LTCM's positions and unwind its portfolio. Similarly, as noted earlier, shortly before Lehman Brothers filed for bankruptcy, a group of banks had tentatively agreed to provide a multibillion-dollar loan to Lehman to facilitate its sale to Barclays.

In theory, regulators and leading banks could use the same ad hoc strategy in connection with the quick sale of a troubled SIFI in bankruptcy. The Fed could convene a group of the largest banks and prod them to provide funding to their troubled peer. But the ad hoc approach has several important limitations. First, if the funding is not prearranged, there may be considerable uncertainty as to whether the SIFI would successfully obtain the funding. This uncertainty would make it more difficult to assure markets that the troubled SIFI is stable.

---

39. See Paul Blustein, *The Chastening: Inside the Crisis That Rocked the Global Financial System and Humbled the IMF* (New York: Public Affairs, 2001), 148.

40. Ibid., 177–205.

41. Goldman Sachs, AIG, and Berkshire Hathaway had previously offered LTCM's partners $250 million for their partnership interests and $3.75 billion in funding, but the one-hour deadline for the offer elapsed before a deal was reached. See Roger Lowenstein, *When Genius Failed: The Rise and Fall of Long-Term Capital Management* (New York: Random House, 2000), 203–4.

Second, the ad hoc approach depends heavily on moral suasion; lenders are not under any obligation to contribute. Particularly in a period of industry-wide stress, lenders might decline to participate. (Ironically, the one major Wall Street bank that resisted the moral suasion, and declined to contribute to the LTCM bailout, was Bear Stearns.) Finally, the ad hoc approach significantly constrains the range of potential lenders. If regulators need to quickly convene a group of potential lenders, they inevitably will limit their gaze to a small group of the largest financial institutions.

A more coordinated approach theoretically could address these shortcomings (although at a stiff cost, as we shall see). If the financing were already in place and the markets were informed of its general scope, the threat of destabilizing uncertainty would be substantially reduced. Prearranged funding also would greatly reduce the risk that lenders would decline to provide funding. And the funding would not necessarily need to come entirely from a small group of the largest banks if a SIFI arranged for financing in advance, before the urgency of an actual crisis. If SIFIs were required to have prearranged funding in place, additional lenders such as smaller banks, hedge funds, or savvy investors like Warren Buffett might commit to provide some of the funding. Some or all of these other lenders might be less likely than other SIFIs to have fallen into financial distress themselves at the same time as the troubled SIFI.

Although prearranged financing has considerable attractions, it also would face several important obstacles. The first is a surprising and somewhat dubious bankruptcy provision. Under current law, any pre-bankruptcy loan commitment made by a lender to the debtor itself is terminated the moment the debtor files for bankruptcy.[42] Congress would do well to remove this automatic termination provision, which lacks any compelling policy basis, and to give debtors the same right to enforce loan commitments that they have with other contracts.[43] Fortunately, so long as the old SIFI holding company would not need new

---

42. 11 USC § 365(c)(2).

43. For a more detailed argument for amending § 365(c)(2), see Ayotte and Skeel, 1608–9.

funding after filing for bankruptcy, the new holding company or the SIFI's operating subsidiaries could arrange for the loan commitment. So long as none of the borrowers were in bankruptcy themselves, the termination provision would not apply. An alternative strategy would be to create a bail-in fund, either for a single institution or for a group of institutions. If funds were escrowed under such an arrangement, and released if the debtor defaulted, the arrangement could provide bankruptcy liquidity to a debtor as well as the new holding company and the debtor operating subsidiaries without running afoul of the bankruptcy termination provision.[44]

The second, more intractable obstacle is cost. A financial institution would be required to take a capital charge in connection with the loan arrangement. In addition, the prearranged financing could be quite costly, given that it would commit lenders for a potentially lengthy period of time to make loans to another financial institution based on pure speculation about the likely condition of the debtor at the time the loan would be needed and other factors that might affect the terms of the loan or escrow arrangement. As noted earlier, under the quick sale approach, the loan would not need to be as large as commentators often assume. A $20 billion loan commitment would probably be sufficient even for a fairly large financial institution. But given the uncertainties of the funding, the costs of even a manageable ex ante loan commitment could be steep.

A key design question would be whether to set the prearranged funds aside in advance, or whether the lenders should simply commit to provide the funds in the event the financial institution in question filed for bankruptcy. The tradeoffs between the two approaches are well known. Setting aside the funds assures that they will be available if needed, but it also can create moral hazard—the temptation to use the

---

44. This arrangement echoes the proposal J. P. Morgan has made for resolution of a troubled clearinghouse. See J. P. Morgan Chase & Co., Office of Regulatory Affairs, *What is the Resolution Plan for CCPs?* September 2014, discussed in Darrell Duffie's, "Resolution of Failing Central Counterparties," this volume. The multi-debtor version of this approach is similar in some respects to bank guaranty arrangements used in some states in the nineteenth century.

funds. The funds would be tied up for the duration of the loan commitment, which could interfere with the lenders' own liquidity needs. In my view, the moral hazard of a pre-committed fund is a relatively small concern in this context; it is the rare bank manager who would file for bankruptcy to get her hand in the honeypot. But the need to set the funds aside and manage them for potentially long periods is more problematic. If lenders committed to supply the funds if needed, by contrast, without actually providing the funding up front, the costs of setting the funds aside disappear. But there is a risk that lenders would default on their funding commitment if the debtor does indeed file for bankruptcy—especially if the debtor falls into distress during a period of general crisis.

One way to balance these effects would be to set a portion of the funds aside, rather than the full amount of a SIFI's potential liquidity needs, and to rely on lenders' lending commitments for the remainder. This approach is somewhat analogous to the obligations imposed on members of a clearinghouse, who make initial contributions to capital and also are liable for additional contributions if necessary in the event the clearinghouse defaults.[45]

From a SIFI's perspective, any of the prearranged funding mechanisms I have described imposes serious costs. In theory, the cost could be offset by the benefits to creditors of preserving the SIFI's value in the event of a subsequent bankruptcy. But there are good reasons to suspect that the benefits would not be fully priced. The risk of failure is quite small, for instance, which could dampen the price effects. Perhaps more importantly, if the most plausible alternative to an orderly bankruptcy is a governmental bailout, even an effective liquidity mechanism could diminish the value of the SIFI's debt by reducing the bailout subsidy traditionally enjoyed by creditors—especially bondholders—of systemically important financial institutions.

If prearranged funding were in fact desirable, industry coordination would be one way to overcome the disincentive each individual SIFI has to put such a liquidity mechanism in place. Since the number

---

45. Darrell Duffie analyzes these clearinghouse arrangements in detail in his chapter for this volume.

of financial institutions in question is small, industry coordination is a plausible response; the banking industry has used precisely this approach to address key resolution issues. The most important recent illustration is the adoption of a new industry protocol imposing a contractual stay on cross-default provisions.[46] But governmental pressure appears to have played a central role in the banks' newfound willingness to coordinate on a limited stay. The initiative seems to have originated with the head of the Bank of England, and it does not seem coincidental that it quickly gathered steam after the FDIC rejected as "not credible" the 2012 living wills prepared by eleven of the largest bank holding companies and the Fed indicated that they all contained various shortcomings that needed to be addressed.[47]

The Fed could, if it wished, use the living will process to insist that each of the largest bank holding companies put a liquidity mechanism in place. Under Title I of the Dodd-Frank Act, systemically important financial institutions must submit "rapid resolution plans," or living wills, explaining how the SIFI would restructure or liquidate in bankruptcy in an orderly fashion, without causing systemic harm.[48] As just noted, the Fed has already used its living will authority as a stick, requiring eleven banks to address various shortcomings identified in their 2012 living wills; it could require, as a condition for approval, that banks show that they have arranged for funding in the event they fall into financial distress. By refusing to approve a living will that does not include provision for liquidity in the event of a bankruptcy, the Fed could ensure that SIFIs provide adequately for the possibility of failure.[49] The liquidity mechanism would need to include a commit-

---

46. The new protocol, which has been endorsed by eighteen of the leading global banks, can be found at http://www2.isda.org/functional-areas/protocol-management/protocol/20.

47. Bill Kroener discusses the FDIC's rejection of the eleven SIFIs' 2012 living wills as "not credible" and the Fed's conclusion that those living wills had various shortcomings in his chapter for this volume, "Revised Chapter 14 2.0 and Living Will Requirements Under the Dodd-Frank Act."

48. The living will requirement comes from Dodd-Frank Act § 165(d).

49. For an analogous argument that the International Monetary Fund could play a credentialing role in connection with private lenders' rescue funding

ment to provide financing not just to the SIFI itself, but also to any new corporation created for the purposes of a quick sale, so that liquidity will be available for whatever bankruptcy option the SIFI chooses.

The principal question is whether the game would be worth the candle. Given the likely costs of prearranged funding and the need to sidestep bankruptcy's automatic termination of pre-bankruptcy loan commitments, prearranged funding would be expensive and potentially complex. It also is not clear it is necessary, given the liquidity options that are available at the time a financial institution files for bankruptcy. Perhaps the best argument for incorporating at least a limited expectation of prearranged funding into the living-will process is that it would encourage financial institutions to look to a broader range of potential lenders than they would if they were arranging funding after having fallen into financial distress. But the cost of even a limited facility would be steep.

My conclusion thus far is a cautiously optimistic one: the absence of massive, orderly liquidation fund-style funding in bankruptcy may not be as crippling a limitation as the conventional wisdom suggests. Bankruptcy has more tools for generating liquidity than is often recognized; a SIFI could put a financing package in place as soon as a quick sale was completed, since the newly created corporation would not be in bankruptcy itself. To further reduce the likelihood of liquidity shortfalls, the Fed could require that the largest SIFIs arrange for funding in advance as part of the living will process, although this seems ill-advised on balance given the likely costs.

Should Congress Provide Designated Governmental Funding?

One final question remains: what about government funding? Do the sources of liquidity that I have described make governmental funding unnecessary, or is governmental funding essential? And if governmental funding is needed, what form should it take?

---

arrangements with sovereign debtors, see Patrick Bolton and David A. Skeel Jr., "Redesigning the International Lender of Last Resort," *Chicago Journal of International Law* 6 (2005): 177, 196–201.

In my view, additional governmental funding is not absolutely essential for the bankruptcy process, given the potential availability of private funding and the last-resort backstop of a Federal Reserve lending program. The case for adding a more explicit governmental funding option is nevertheless strong. The first reason that governmental funding is desirable is the behavior of bank regulators themselves. Particularly if a SIFI falls into financial distress during a period of general market turmoil, as in 2008, bank regulators may be reluctant to leave a SIFI's fate to the bankruptcy process, no matter how promising the bankruptcy resolution strategy appears to be. Providing an explicit source of government funding might diminish the temptation for regulators to bail out the SIFI (as part of an "industry-wide" program, of course) rather than permit it to file for bankruptcy.[50] Second, if the SIFI did not have prearranged funding in place, there would likely be a short gap between the time the SIFI filed for bankruptcy and the moment when financing was fully available, since a lender might condition its financing on bankruptcy approval of the quick sale. By putting prearranged funding in place, the SIFI could eliminate even this small gap, but a residuum of market uncertainty might nevertheless remain until it was clear that the funding would indeed be made available. The presence of a governmental backstop would further reduce the uncertainty, and would strengthen the credibility of the bankruptcy option.

Although some form of governmental funding still seems desirable, the presence of substantial non-governmental liquidity options has significant implications for the issue of what form the governmental funding should take. The two principal options on offer are guaranteed funding comparable to the orderly liquidation fund and Federal Reserve funding under its discount window or emergency lending powers.

---

50. As noted earlier, the Fed theoretically could permit a SIFI to file for bankruptcy, while also providing DIP financing under an industry-wide funding arrangement. But the Fed might well conclude that it would rather provide the funding outside of bankruptcy, where the Fed has more control.

Guaranteed Funding (the OLF Approach)

The OLF's guaranteed funding approach has the great virtue of removing any serious doubts about the adequacy of the funding available to a troubled SIFI. In this sense, the use of the OLF in a SPOE recapitalization honors the memory of Walter Bagehot, whose classic lender-of-last-resort strategy called for unlimited funding to solvent institutions secured by good collateral in response to a liquidity crisis.[51] Although OLF funding is not unlimited, it is nearly so. And it would be available under all circumstances, even if the SIFI were not recapitalized, did not have sufficient unencumbered assets to support a secured loan, or could not demonstrate that it was solvent. The OLF approach removes any serious concerns about the availability of funding.

Yet the availability of very good alternative sources of funding suggests that it should not be necessary to put massive amounts of government funding in place. The conclusion is reinforced by the obvious downsides of the guaranteed funding approach. Because it does not distinguish between SIFIs that are insolvent and those that are simply illiquid, OLF-style funding could function very much like a bailout. The FDIC could flood funding into an insolvent SIFI and effectively bail out many of its creditors.[52] In Title II itself, neither the SIFI nor the bridge institution formed for the purposes of a single-point-of-entry resolution would be subject to taxes during the resolution, which adds to the bailout-like features of the process.[53]

---

51. Although he advocated unlimited rescue funding to solvent institutions secured by good collateral, Bagehot proposed that it come with a penalty rate of interest, to discourage reliance on the funding after the liquidity crisis had passed. Title II does not follow Bagehot quite so closely in this regard. It calls for an interest rate based on a basket of corporate bonds.

52. Given the potential abuses of OLF funding, I strongly endorse Randy Guynn's argument that the FDIC should commit to using the funds only on a fully secured basis.

53. Dodd-Frank Act § 210(h)(10) states that: "Notwithstanding any other provision of Federal or State law, a bridge financial company, its franchise, property, and income shall be exempt from all taxation now or hereafter imposed by the

In theory, at least, American taxpayers would not bear the costs of OLF funding that functioned like a bailout. If the SIFI is unable to repay its loans from the OLF fund, Title II provides for an assessment on other SIFIs.[54] The banking industry, rather than taxpayers, would make up the shortfall. In reality, however, taxpayers would at least indirectly bear the costs, since the other SIFIs would probably pass the costs onto their customers.[55] More importantly, if a SIFI failed during a period of market-wide crisis, the prospect of assessments could exacerbate the strain on the banking industry.

Extending the Fed's Emergency Liquidity Powers to a SIFI in Bankruptcy

The other principal option is Federal Reserve lending, either through the Fed's discount window, which enables banks to borrow money on a secured basis from the Federal Reserve,[56] or through its emergency lending powers under section 13(3) of the Federal Reserve Act. As compared to OLF-style liquidity, either of these options would be considerably more targeted and less likely to invite open-ended borrowing. Fed lending is limited to financial institutions that are solvent and are capable of providing adequate collateral. The new financial institution that acquired a troubled SIFI's assets should be able to meet both requirements, but a troubled financial institution that used the ordinary bankruptcy process could not, since it would almost certainly be insolvent. As a result, access to the funds would be tightly constrained. The risk of a disguised bailout would be significantly lower than with

---

United States, by any territory, dependency, or possession thereof, or by any State, county, municipality, or local taxing authority."

54. Dodd-Frank Act § 210(o).

55. See, e.g., John Taylor, "Who is Too Big to Fail: Does Title II of the Dodd-Frank Act Enshrine Taxpayer-Funded Bailouts?" Testimony before the Subcommittee on Oversight and Investigations, Committee on Financial Services, US House of Representatives, May 15, 2013.

56. The Fed's discount window authority comes from section 10B of the Federal Reserve Act. For an overview of discount window operations, see Board of Governors of the Federal Reserve System, "Discount Window Lending," http://www.federalreserve.gov/newsevents/reform_discount_window.htm.

OLF-style liquidity, and there would be no need either to set aside the funds in advance or to impose a tax on other SIFIs after the fact. Given that the new capital and liquidity standards should reduce the need for liquidity, as well as the other private sources of liquidity that are available, Federal Reserve lending is a more attractive source of government funding than an OLF-style approach.

Of the two options, the Federal Reserve's emergency lending powers are somewhat more restricted, and seem especially attractive for this reason. Not only is the Fed constrained under section 13(3) by the requirement that it lend on a fully secured basis; but the Fed must also determine that the loan is needed to prevent systemic or other harm. With the discount window, by contrast, the Fed provides access even in the absence of a crisis or risk of market-wide harm.

The systemic harm prerequisite to funding under section 13(3) would effectively limit governmental funding to bankruptcy recapitalizations of the largest SIFIs, but this is appropriate. The ordinary liquidity options should be adequate for effective resolution of financial institutions that are not systemically important.

The Federal Reserve backstop isn't foolproof. The presence or absence of adequate security is to some extent in the eye of the beholder, especially with a complicated financial institution whose assets are not easily valued. The Fed could manipulate access, much as it is thought by many to have manipulated its emergency lending powers in 2008. But it is subject to significantly more constraints than OLF-style funding.

Conclusion

The most surprising finding in this analysis of liquidity in a SIFI bankruptcy is the amount of liquidity that should be available even in the absence of additional government-supplied liquidity. A SIFI's ability to suspend payments on its long-term debt will free up a small amount of liquidity, and the borrowing capacity of the newly formed quick sale corporation should generate much more liquidity. Moreover, the liquidity needs of a troubled SIFI in 2015 or 2020 should be significantly less than they were in 2008, due to the much more stringent capital and liquidity requirements imposed in the wake of the crisis.

One interesting implication is that subchapter V of the Financial Institution Bankruptcy Act of 2014, the quick sale reforms approved by the House on December 1, 2014, may not be as incomplete as is sometimes supposed. Primarily due to concerns that adding a provision for governmental liquidity would provoke political opposition, subchapter V omits any reference to liquidity. My analysis of existing liquidity options suggests that additional liquidity may not be as necessary as I and others previously imagined.

In my view, Congress would do well to extend the Fed's emergency lending powers to the SIFI quick sale context even in the absence of an industry-wide program. The requirements that any loan be fully collateralized and be available only under emergency conditions would limit the risk of bailouts and provide a backstop for extraordinary cases. Explicitly authorizing the Fed to step in under these conditions also might reduce the Fed's temptation to manipulate the existing rules—by establishing an "industry-wide" program, for instance, that clearly is designed for a single financial institution.

Whether or not lawmakers extend the Fed's lending authority to SIFI bankruptcies, a SIFI's liquidity needs for a quick sale in bankruptcy appear to be manageable. This is further evidence, it seems to me, that the quick sale contemplated by Chapter 14 2.0 could work.

CHAPTER 4

Resolution of Failing Central Counterparties

Darrell Duffie

A central counterparty (CCP) is a financial market utility that lowers counterparty default risk on specified financial contracts by acting as a buyer to every seller, and as a seller to every buyer. Thus, if either of the original counterparties fails to perform, the CCP effectively guarantees payment to the other. When at risk of failure, a CCP could be forced into a normal insolvency process, such as bankruptcy, or an administrative failure resolution process. This chapter reviews some alternative approaches to the design of insolvency and failure resolution regimes for CCPs. I focus on the allocation of losses and the question of whether and how to provide for continuity of clearing services. I discuss how one might adapt to CCPs some of the failure resolution approaches currently being designed for other forms of systemically important financial institutions. A key policy question is when to interrupt a contractually based CCP default management process with an overriding failure resolution process, for example a bankruptcy or a government administered process.

I am grateful for discussions with the members of the Resolution Project Group and with participants in a Financial Stability Board workshop on resolution of systemically important financial market infrastructure held at the Federal Reserve Bank of New York on April 29, 2014. I am also grateful for conversations with and comments from Wilson Ervin, Tom Huertas, Antoine Martin, Dennis McLaughlin, Joanne Medero, Albert Menkveld, David Murphy, Ed Nosal, Sandie O'Connor, Marnie Rosenberg, Martin Scheicher, Ken Scott, Manmohan Singh, David Skeel, Penfield Starke, Robert Steigerwald, Guillaume Vuillemey, David Wall, David Weisbrod, and Haoxiang Zhu. For potential conflicts of interest, see www.stanford.edu/~duffie.

The balance sheet of a CCP is quite different from those of other major types of systemically important financial institutions such as banks, broker-dealers, and insurance companies. Special failure management procedures are suggested. The bulk of the financial risk of a CCP is not represented by conventional assets and liabilities. Rather, a CCP is essentially a nexus of contracts by which its clearing members net and mutualize their counterparty default risk. In the normal course of business, the daily payment obligations of a CCP automatically sum to zero. Because of this, a CCP tends to have tiny amounts of equity and conventional debt relative to its largest potential clearing obligations. Most of the tail risk of a CCP is allocated to its clearing members.

When the market value of a centrally cleared derivatives contract increases on a given day, any clearing member who is a buyer of that contract type collects a variation margin payment from its CCP on the next day, equal to the assessed change in market value of the position. Any seller is likewise required to make a variation margin payment to the CCP. Because the total amounts of cleared bought and sold contracts are identical, the CCP's positions are exactly balanced, long against short, leaving the CCP with zero net payment obligations. If, however, one or more clearing members fail to meet their payment obligations, the CCP has unbalanced exposures and must find the resources necessary to liquidate the failed positions and rebalance itself. If it cannot, its failure must be resolved.

Because there is now general international regulatory agreement that standard derivatives are to be centrally cleared, the failure of a major CCP could be a catastrophic event if its resolution procedures are not carefully designed and implemented. The greatest risks are (a) contagion, by which the failure of a clearing member could cause the CCP to fail to meet its obligations to other systemically clearing members; (b) fire sales of collateral or derivatives contracts, exacerbating broad market volatility; and (c) loss of continuity of critical clearing services on which the financial system has come to depend.

As an example of the significant counterparty risk managed by a single CCP, SwapClear, a cross-border central counterparty operated by LCH.Clearnet currently has a total notional amount of cleared interest-rate swaps of approximately $400 trillion.[1] Large CCPs are systemically important, and are becoming even more important as the implementation of new regulations forces more and more positions into CCPs. In the United States, the CCPs of the Chicago Mercantile Exchange and ICE Trust have been designated as systemically important by the Financial Stability Oversight Council.

The failure of a major CCP would probably come at an extremely stressful moment because it is most likely to be precipitated by the failure of one or more systemically important clearing members, who would probably have also failed to meet their payment obligations to many other major financial firms, including other CCPs. Ironically, the better the quality and depth of the risk-management resources of a CCP, the more likely it is that its failure could only have been caused by the collapse of extremely large clearing members, and probably by more than one of them. Under the principles of the CPMI (formerly known as the Committee on Payment and Settlement Systems-International Organization of Securities Commissions), a global systemically important CCP must have the resources necessary to cover the failures of its two largest clearing members.[2]

Beyond derivatives, central counterparties may also manage the counterparty risk associated with securities trade settlement and repurchase agreements. Failure resolution procedures for CCPs should vary according to the application. Here, I am focusing mainly on the case of derivatives clearing, although most of the principles apply to the failure resolution of other forms of CCPs.

---

1. See http://www.lchclearnet.com/swaps/swapclear_for_clearing_members/. Notional positions do not translate directly to risk. More commensurate to risk is the total amount of initial margin held, which for LCH Clearnet Group was 443 billion euros as of its most recent financial statements, for year-end 2013, http://www.lchclearnet.com/documents/731485/762550/LCH.Clearnet+ Group+Limited+Consolidated+Financial+Statements_2013/5c92c5c1-a69b -45f0-99fd-16debc19f9a2.

2. See Principle 4 of CPSS-IOSCO "Principles of Financial Market Infrastructure," CPSS-IOSCO, April 2012. The CPMI is the Committee on Payments and Market Infrastructure.

Recovery versus Resolution

Tensions can arise over the decision of whether to attempt the recovery of a CCP that has been weakened by the failure of some clearing members, given the alternative of placing the CCP into a failure-resolution procedure that aims for liquidation or recapitalization. Recovery and resolution processes share some features. Distinctions between them are based to a large extent on whether loss allocation is achieved contractually or via a more ad-hoc and externally administered insolvency process that overrides contracts.

Each clearing member gives its CCP access to initial margin funds in an amount that is intended to cover the shortfall that arises when the member fails to make payments due on its cleared positions. Clearing members also contribute to the default guarantee fund of the CCP. At the failure of one or more clearing members, whenever the cost of liquidating the failed members' positions exceeds the margin and default guarantee funds provided by the failed members, the surviving members and the CCP operator absorb the remaining cost of liquidating the failed positions, if that is actually possible with the available resources.

The surviving clearing members may absorb some of these losses through their contributions to the default guarantee fund. Some of these guarantee-fund contributions are paid in advance. If this paid-in fund is depleted, clearing members are obliged to make additional contributions to replenish the default guarantee fund, at least to some extent.

Some of the capital of the CCP operator is also designated to absorb losses. While the contribution of CCP capital to the default management resources is important as a loss absorber, it is typically most significant as a means of giving the CCP operator some skin-in-the-game incentive to design and manage the CCP safely. The incentive of the CCP operator to impose sufficient initial margin requirements and to monitor membership creditworthiness is improved by having a layer of CCP operator capital that is subject to loss immediately after the failed member's initial margin and guarantee fund contribution are exhausted, as illustrated in figure 1.

In a recovery process, a CCP might assign losses to its surviving members (and perhaps their clients) in a manner that causes significant

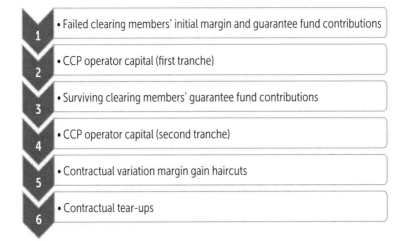

1 • Failed clearing members' initial margin and guarantee fund contributions

2 • CCP operator capital (first tranche)

3 • Surviving clearing members' guarantee fund contributions

4 • CCP operator capital (second tranche)

5 • Contractual variation margin gain haircuts

6 • Contractual tear-ups

Figure 4.1. Example of CCP Default-Management Waterfall of Recovery Resources

distress costs. The existence of a contractual recovery approach that avoids the insolvency of a CCP does not imply that the contractual recovery approach should be followed to its end regardless of the situation. The "creditors' bargain" suggested by Jackson (1982) recognizes that contracts cannot be written perfectly. There may be unforeseen circumstances in which total distress costs can be lowered by winding down or restructuring a CCP with a procedure that overrides contracts, such as bankruptcy or a government-administered resolution process.

Contractual agreements by clearing members to make guarantee-fund replenishment contributions should be robust but limited. The obligation to make uncapped guarantee-fund replenishment payments during a crisis could destabilize some clearing members. At some CCPs, these replenishment payments are already contractually capped. At some other CCPs, guarantee fund replenishment payment obligations have been uncapped, at least until recently.[3] Uncapped obligations to CCPs are increasingly rare because they now

---

3. For examples, see Annex Table 1A of Elliott (2013) and comments by The Clearinghouse (2012).

imply extremely onerous regulatory capital requirements for financial institutions.[4]

In any case, guarantee-fund replenishment payments may not arrive quickly enough to be a useful source of liquidity or capital, if they are paid at all. For example, in mid-December 2013, HanMag Investment Securities failed to meet its option margin payment obligations to the clearinghouse of Korea Exchange (KRX). After KRX was forced to use some of the clearinghouse guarantee fund to cover the losses, clearing members were contractually obliged to make replenishment payments within about one month. Some clearing members, however, failed to do so, and the replenishment payments were postponed until the end of March 2014.

The "waterfall" of recovery resources of some CCPs extends beyond the guarantee fund by permitting the CCP to contractually restructure its clearing payment obligations to clearing members. One such procedure is "variation margin gains haircutting" (VMGH). By this approach, the CCP can conserve or accumulate cash by cancelling or reducing the variation margin payments that it would otherwise have been required to make to clearing members. At the same time, the CCP collects 100 percent of the variation margin payments that it is due to receive from clearing members.[5] Beyond its role as a short-term liquidity backstop, VMGH could in some cases continue until the CCP has enough resources to pay for the liquidation of failed positions. There is no assurance that VMGH would be sufficient to entirely rebalance the CCP, although experts believe that VMGH would suffice in most scenarios.[6] Those clearing members suffering losses from VMGH could in principle be given compensating claims, for example equity or debt issued by the CCP.

---

4. Under Basel III, uncapped exposures to a CCP would rule out the lower risk-weighting of CCP exposures to the 2 percent level associated with "qualified" CCPs.

5. A version of this approach has been adopted by the Japanese Securities Clearing Association. See Japanese Securities Clearing Association, http://www.jscc .co.jp/en/cash/irs/loss.html.

6. See, for example, ISDA (2013) and Singh (2014).

Another potential contractual restructuring approach is a "tear-up," by which the CCP could cancel some or all of its outstanding notional derivatives positions with selected clearing members. For example, suppose the failure of a clearing member has left the CCP with a net short position in some specific class of derivatives that is 90 percent of the total of its outstanding long positions. In this case, the CCP could, assuming that it has the necessary contractual right, rebalance its exposure by stipulating that all long positions shall henceforth be 90 percent of their former notional size. An alternative is to simply tear up 100 percent of all outstanding positions of the affected type.

Variation margin gain haircuts and tear-ups have the beneficial incentive effect of encouraging clearing members to reduce the sizes of their positions with weak CCPs. They have the disadvantage of sharing losses unpredictably, given that it would be difficult to predict much more than a day in advance whether it would be long or short position holders that would be allocated the losses. This is unlike the situation facing normal creditors, who know they are in line for losses at the borrower's default, and know the priority order in which they will take losses. In terms of sharing distress costs, one would prefer to have losses borne by all CCP members, perhaps pro rata with some measure of the expected amount of potential loss that a clearing member would impose on the CCP, conditional on both the failure of the clearing member and the failure of the CCP.[7]

On a risk-corrected basis, this might suggest end-of-waterfall loss sharing that is proportional to total paid-in initial margins. Like VMGH and tear-ups, loss-sharing in proportion to total initial margins would also encourage clearing members to reduce their positions with weak CCPs. Unfortunately, there is no obvious method for collecting payments of this sort from clearing members. Initial margin funds are the property of clearing members. These funds are not legally accessible to CCPs, absent voluntary contracting to make

---

7. Both conditioning events are relevant, as explained by Dembo, Deuschel, and Duffie (2004).

them available at the end of the default-management waterfall.[8] It is not clear why many CCPs and clearing members prefer to use VMGH or tear-ups rather than to adjust their clearing agreements so as to allow legal end-of-waterfall access to initial margin funds.

In any case, more predictable loss-sharing is normally more efficient. There are no clear incentive benefits associated with disproportionate and unpredictable loss-sharing by clearing members who happen to be buyers, or who happen to be sellers. Moreover, economic principles suggest that it is better for a clearing member to suffer a moderate loss with certainty when a CCP fails to meet its clearing obligations than to "flip a coin" to determine whether the size of the loss is zero or not. The marginal cost to a clearing member of bearing an incremental unit of unexpected loss is normally increasing in the total amount of loss, a "convexity effect" that suggests sharing losses across all clearing members, pro rata to the loss exposures they impose on the CCP. This is one of the reasons that CCPs are supposed to ensure adequately sized paid-in guarantee funds, which do share losses predictably and broadly. When the default guarantee fund is revealed to be inadequate, and when it is deemed appropriate to attempt recovery through further contractual loss-sharing rather than resolution, there seems to be no persuasive reason to switch to a preference for unequal and unpredictable loss sharing.

Variants of these restructuring procedures are described by Elliott (2013) and by various commenters to a 2012 CPSS-IOSCO consultative report.[9] In principle, a CCP might also have the contractual right to assign derivatives positions to surviving clearing members at prices that are not equal to their fair market values, but are feasible for the CCP to cover with its available default-management resources.

---

8. See European Parliament (2012), which states that "A CCP shall have a right of use relating to the margins or default fund contributions collected via a security financial collateral arrangement, within the meaning of Article 2(1)(c) of Directive 2002/47/EC of the European Parliament and of the Council of 6 June 2002 on financial collateral arrangements provided that the use of such arrangements is provided for in its operating rules."

9. CPSS-IOSCO (2012b).

Not surprisingly, market participants are not fully aligned with each other on the net benefits of end-of-waterfall recovery approaches. For example, BlackRock,[10] a large asset-management firm, expressed the view in April 2014 that in the event that a CCP has exhausted its guarantee fund, end-user market participants would rather be "money good" than "position good." The assertion here is that investors would prefer to have the CCP immediately wound down than to be exposed to a CCP with a heavily impaired guarantee fund. BlackRock stated that recovery and continuity of CCP operations are not paramount in this situation. BlackRock's policy note recognizes the potential usefulness of VMGH in the context of a resolution process.[11]

On the other hand, in August 2013 the International Swaps and Derivatives Association (ISDA) stated[12] that "the primary goal in a default situation should be recovery and continuity of the CCP." (ISDA went on to say that "the need for resolution cannot be excluded and resolution mechanisms must also be in place.") ISDA advocated that variation margin gain haircuts should be applied in order to achieve recovery and continuity of the CCP. The exception suggested by ISDA is the "remote circumstance" that VMGH does not generate enough funds to liquidate the failed member positions, in which case ISDA believes there should be a 100 percent tear-up of all derivatives in the class of derivatives that had failed to be rebalanced.

For CCPs that have the contractual right to haircut variation margin or to tear-up positions in order to attempt recovery and continuity, government failure-resolution administrators may someday be faced with a decision of whether and when to halt the contractual recovery process, forcing the CCP into resolution. The right to do so

---

10. See "Central Clearing Counterparties and Too Big to Fail," BlackRock, April 2014.

11. A possibly analogous situation is the inability of insolvent US broker-dealers to reorganize, whether under the Securities Investor Protection Act (SIPA) or the Bankruptcy Code. Under both SIPA and subchapter III of Chapter 7 of the US Bankruptcy Code, a failed broker-dealer must be liquidated. This preference for liquidation may arise from the view that protection of client claims takes priority over general unsecured creditors.

12. See "CCP Loss Allocation at the End of the Waterfall," ISDA, August 2013.

presumably exists in the United States and United Kingdom, and will likely soon exist throughout the European Union whenever financial stability is threatened, even if the CCP is currently meeting its contractual obligations.

J. P. Morgan (2014) recently expressed the opinion[13] that "maintaining critical operations of the CCP should be the driving principle in default" and that "CCPs should be recapitalized rather than liquidated upon failure, to continue systemically important activities." J. P. Morgan suggested that VMGH could be a step toward resolution and continuity through recapitalization.

CCP Failure Resolution

Failure resolution procedures should be designed so as to minimize the total expected distress costs of all market participants, including clearing members and CCP operators, as well as unrelated market participants and taxpayers who could suffer from failure spillover costs.

Resolution procedures should be transparent and predictable, to the extent that this could be reasonably expected, so that the attendant risks can be better managed and priced into contracts, improving ex-ante incentives for lowering expected distress costs. Predictability may lessen costly failure-time defensive reactions, such as sudden runs or fire sales. "Slow runs," however, may be socially desirable. When clearing members are able to correctly foresee increasing expected future losses associated with their exposures to a weakening CCP, they have an incentive to lower their exposures to the CCP by entering offsetting positions cleared at that CCP. If there is enough predictability, this process can exploit market forces to reduce the amount of systemic damage that would occur if and when the CCP actually fails. It is critical, however, that a rush for the exits does not exacerbate a liquidity crisis for the CCP.

While the government bailout of a systemically important CCP should not be legally impossible, reliance on government capital should not be part of the failure resolution design, given the attendant

---

13. See "What Is the Resolution Plan for CCPs?" J. P. Morgan Chase & Co., Office of Regulatory Affairs, September 2014.

moral hazard. In order to align incentives in a socially efficient manner, the CCP operator and its clearing members should expect that they are on the hook for all of the losses, one way or another. The key questions are (a) how to efficiently allocate the CCP's losses, (b) how to mitigate fire sales, and (c) how to arrange for the prompt continuation of clearing services.

In the United States, it seems likely that Title II of the Dodd-Frank Act assigns the administration of the failure resolution process of systemically important CCPs to the Federal Deposit Insurance Corporation (FDIC). Whether this is in fact the case, however, is not a completely settled matter, as explained by Steigerwald and DeCarlo (2014). If Title II does apply, then the FDIC can become the receiver of a CCP in the event that the secretary of the treasury, the Federal Reserve Board, and the FDIC find that there would otherwise be a risk of financial instability. In that case, the FDIC could liquidate the CCP, or alternatively could assign its assets and obligations to another CCP or to a "bridge," which in principle could become a successor CCP.

CCPs can be legally structured in many ways, for example as bankruptcy-remote special-purpose entities operated by a firm that manages various such CCPs on a "silo by silo" basis. For example, LCH.Clearnet currently operates seven legally distinct CCPs, based in part on capital provided at the parent level. The capital of a CCP operator that is not contractually designated for loss-sharing in one silo remains available to back commitments to other silos operated by the same parent firm. It is important to design a multi-silo CCP so that obligations to and from clearing members that are common across CCPs can obtain legally enforceable close-out netting in the event that the CCP fails. Further discussion of this is found in section VI.A of ISDA (2013). Likewise, the resolution process for a CCP should be designed so as to avoid the breakup of netting sets. This raises particular concerns with the resolution of a CCP silo by transferring its assets to a bridge CCP, which could potentially block cross-silo netting. This concern is greater to the extent that CCP capital is held at the parent level relative to the CCP silo level. If the CCP must be resolved via a bridge at the parent level in order to take advantage of netting, then its other silos can be affected, adding to contagion risk. A potential disadvantage of resolution under the authority of Title II of the Dodd-Frank Act is the apparent preference for a bridge approach as opposed to reorganization of the existing entity. Chapter 11 of the US Bankruptcy Code could in principle provide for reorganization of a failed CCP, but is not currently well adapted to that purpose. For example, clearing agreements are exempted from bankruptcy.

At the point of resolution of a CCP, most or all of its waterfall of contractually available resources has likely been exhausted. As the resolution procedure begins, the CCP may therefore have very limited remaining resources with which to restructure its obligations to clearing members.

In principle, a resolution authority addressing a CCP in this financial condition could simply declare that the CCP will discontinue clearing and return any remaining assets to its clearing members, pro rata to unmet clearing obligations. This liquidation approach is more easily contemplated when continuity of clearing services can be provided by an alternative CCP handling the same classes of trades. During a wind-down, a CCP may need to haircut variation margin gains as a cash management strategy. (I will later discuss access to other forms of resolution liquidity.)

The alternatives to liquidating an insolvent CCP are:

1. Reorganizing the CCP through some combination of new capital injections and restructuring of its clearing obligations. The debt of the CCP can also be restructured, but in practice CCPs do not usually have much debt.
2. Transferring the clearing obligations of the CCP, if necessary after some restructuring, to another existing CCP or to a bridge CCP.

Under either approach, the legacy shareholders of the CCP should probably recover little or nothing for their equity, if indeed the CCP is even structured as a corporation with equity shareholders.[14]

---

14. For example, ICE Trust is an LLC trust company.

J. P. Morgan recently suggested that[15] capital for a successor CCP could be provided by the legacy clearing members and CCP operator through pre-committed funds held in escrow, for example in a trust fund. These prefunded contributions could be in the form of "bail-in" debt. If and when the CCP fails to meet its contractual obligations, or is otherwise undergoing a bankruptcy or other failure resolution process, the debt obligations of the trust to the clearing members and legacy CCP operator would be cancelled. The trust funds would then be used to meet the clearing members' new guarantee fund contributions to the bridge CCP. This is analogous to recent proposals for resolving systemically important financial institutions with a single-point-of-entry failure resolution or with the "quick sale" approach of Jackson (2015) under a proposed new Chapter 14 of the bankruptcy code. (The set of financial firms to which Chapter 14 would apply excludes CCPs.)

As previously emphasized, it is important to design any such legal framework so as to avoid the breakup of cross-silo netting sets. Further, there is a critical decision of when to trigger this form of resolution, balancing the harm caused by lack of access of the original CCP to additional default-fund contributions from clearing members that could prevent a CCP failure, relative to the harm caused by draining capital from systemically important clearing members without necessarily the prospect of emerging with a viable CCP.

Nothing rules out the prefunding of recapitalization funds from unrelated investors who may wish to earn rents associated with "insurance" of this form. For example, a large unrelated institutional investor could be a creditor to a CCP recapitalization trust fund, using a debt instrument that is "bailed in" at resolution in the manner suggested for clearing-member recapitalization bonds in the J. P. Morgan proposal. The advantage of wider loss-sharing is obvious. There would be an offsetting moral-hazard disadvantage of separating the loss-bearing from those who could discipline the risk management of the CCP. Some insurance firms have suggested that they would be willing to participate in CCP loss-sharing as a fee-based business, but as part of

---

15. See "What Is the Resolution Plan for CCPs?" J. P. Morgan Chase.

the CCP's contractual recovery default-management resources rather than as part of the failure-resolution recapitalization.[16] An additional concern is the benefit of leaving some significant element of control of the recapitalized CCP in the hands of equity owners who have a sophisticated working knowledge of CCPs.

Even if prefunded and escrowed funds are available to set up a new guarantee fund, the CCP (or its successor or bridge) may need additional capital to cover the cost of liquidating failed positions. Several approaches for this have been suggested, including tear-ups and variation margin gains haircutting, along the same lines that could be applied contractually in a recovery process.

If restructuring is an option, bankruptcy courts or failure resolution administration procedures could be given the legal authority to apply VMGH or tear-ups even if that option is not contractually recognized in clearing agreements. Under a US Title II failure administration procedure, the FDIC has the legal right to reject contracts, provided that rejection is not applied selectively across contracts with the same counterparty. It is not clear whether or how the FDIC could conduct VMGH or partial tear-ups. To this point, the FDIC has not described the failure-resolution strategies that it would use in the case of CCPs.

Stays on Clearing Agreements

Agreements between a CCP and its members may give clearing members the right to terminate their agreements at specified "default" events of the CCP. Under current US bankruptcy law, clearing agreements are exempt from automatic stays and from certain trustee-avoiding powers covering constructive fraud and preferences.[17] In order to allow

---

16. The insurance firm GSCA made such a proposal in its September 2013 comment on the "Consultative Report on the Recovery of Financial Market Infrastructure," http://gcsacapital.com/wp-content/uploads/2013/12/Consultative -Report-on-the-Recovery-of-Financial-market-Infrastructure.pdf.

17. Under interoperability agreements between CCPs, initial margin or its effective equivalent can be provided by one CCP to another or to a third-party custodian. These additional agreements would also need to be treated in a failure resolution.

an effective treatment of CCP failure, whether by a bankruptcy-style insolvency process or by an administrative failure resolution process, new legislation may be needed to enable a temporary stay on clearing agreements, as suggested by Duffie and Skeel (2012). A stay of clearing agreements is already possible in the United States under Title II of the Dodd Frank Act (assuming that Title II applies to CCPs), and is anticipated in the European Union.[18] The US Bankruptcy Code should now be amended to permit stays of clearing agreements for systemically important CCPs. In both the United States and Europe, there is a stated preference to use insolvency processes such as bankruptcy, and to resort to administrative failure resolutions only when an insolvency process is deemed to be ineffective.

One may consider the situation envisioned in the J. P. Morgan proposal to obtain continuity by setting up a recapitalized bridge CCP. In the event that a bankruptcy court or resolution administrator such as the FDIC wishes to resolve a CCP along these lines, it would first stay the clearing members' contractual rights to terminate (assuming a suitably enabling statutory amendment in the case of the bankruptcy code). In the case of an administered failure resolution process based on a bridge CCP, clearing agreements could then be transferred to the bridge CCP, along with the initial margin funds, residual guarantee funds, and new guarantee funds obtained from the pre-committed trust funds. Other necessary assets, including licenses and other intellectual property, would also be transferred to the bridge.

It is not clear whether clearing agreements will be amended along the lines of a new international protocol for ISDA derivatives contracts.[19] Under this approach, so long as a designated systemically important CCP undergoing a failure resolution process is meeting its payment obligations to clearing members, the clearing members would not have the right to terminate their clearing agreements and must continue to meet their own payment obligations to the CCP. If this approach were adopted, however, any non-contractual variation

---

18. See European Commission (2012).
19. See ISDA (2014).

margin haircuts or tear-ups would presumably trigger the rights of clearing members to terminate their clearing agreements, unless those rights are statutorily stayed by virtue of the appointment of a failure resolution administrator such as the FDIC.

The CPMI consultative paper on failure resolution of financial market infrastructure (FMI)[20] states that an FMI's "ability to continue to make payments is a fundamental part of the service" provided by the FMI and that a "resolution authority's decision to impose a moratorium to prevent outgoing payments by the FMI even for a short period is therefore likely to carry the risk of continuing or even amplifying systemic disruption."

Whether or not there is a stay, clearing members whose agreements with the CCP have not been rejected or otherwise terminated or modified by the process would continue to have an obligation to make replenishment payments to default guarantee funds.

How to resolve the cleared positions of clients of clearing members is beyond the scope of this chapter.

There is a potential for CCPs handling over-the-counter derivatives to "interoperate" with each other. This is rare in practice. Interoperability can be effected through various procedures, for example by allowing clearing members to port positions from one active CCP to another. This involves inter-CCP margins, which may be held in a third-party custodian. Inter-CCP agreements of this sort should not be stayed, if that can be avoided, because they are designed to protect against a domino-style sequence of CCP failures.

Sources of CCP Liquidity in Failure Resolution

In addition to its immediately available cash, a CCP could obtain liquidity through financing that is secured by non-cash assets. These include assets held in the default-management waterfall as initial margin (to the extent legally permitted) or paid-in guarantee fund contributions, and claims to future contributions to the default guarantee fund. A further potential source of liquidity is VMGH—to the extent legally permitted.

---

20. See CPSS-IOSCO (2012b).

Under conditions stated in the Dodd-Frank Act under Title VIII, a designated US CCP is eligible to receive secured financing from the Federal Reserve, provided that private-market sources of liquidity have been exhausted.[21] Similarly, the Bank of England gives CCPs access to its Discount Window Facility.[22] During insolvency, assuming that the CCP still meets the designation requirements, this is a potential supplement to other sources of liquidity, including any debtor-in-possession (DIP) financing that might be obtained in bankruptcy. If DIP financing or central bank liquidity is to be secured specifically by derivatives payables to the CCP, rather than by a general super-priority claim on the estate of the CCP, then the provider of financing might need some means to perfect an interest in those derivatives payables.

In the event of a Dodd-Frank Title II failure resolution procedure, there is also access to liquidity through the Orderly Liquidation Fund (OLF) of the US Treasury, subject to its legislative restrictions. Title II rules out OLF funding beyond 10 percent of the value of the pre-resolution assets of the covered institution, or 90 percent of its post-resolution value, as explained by Skeel (2015). Depending on the legal interpretation of "assets," a failed CCP may in some scenarios have a small amount of assets relative to the amount of liquidity necessary to provide continuity of clearing. Even healthy CCPs and their operators

---

21. "The Board of Governors may authorize a Federal Reserve bank under section 10B of the Federal Reserve Act (12 U.S.C. 347b) to provide to a designated financial market utility discount and borrowing privileges only in unusual or exigent circumstances, upon the affirmative vote of a majority of the Board of Governors then serving (or such other number in accordance with the provisions of section 11(r)(2) of the Federal Reserve Act (12 U.S.C. 248(r)(2)) after consultation with the Secretary, and upon a showing by the designated financial market utility that it is unable to secure adequate credit accommodations from other banking institutions. All such discounts and borrowing privileges shall be subject to such other limitations, restrictions, and regulations as the Board of Governors may prescribe. Access to discount and borrowing privileges under section 10B of the Federal Reserve Act as authorized in this section does not require a designated financial market utility to be or become a bank or bank holding company."

22. See paragraph 79 of the Bank of England's Red Book.

tend to have balance sheets that are tiny in comparison with potential losses, as we have discussed. The maximum extent of OLF funding for potential future CCP resolutions should be clarified.

Skeel (2015) offers a general analysis of sources of liquidity at the bankruptcy of a systemically important financial institution.

No Creditor Worse Off

An objective or requirement of some bankruptcy and failure resolution processes is that no creditor should be allocated greater losses than would have occurred in a counterfactual scenario in which the failing entity is simply liquidated. The philosophy, as explained for example by Davies and Dobler (2011), is that allowing the contractual loss allocation to run its course all the way to liquidation is a benchmark. Resolution processes that cause some creditors to lose more than they would have in a liquidation scenario, in order to reduce total social losses, would in this sense involve some sort of violation of property rights. If necessary, the principle of "no creditor worse off" could be supported in failure resolution through compensating payments to affected creditors.

In the case of a CCP, it is not clear what would be the most relevant counterfactual benchmark scenario, when judging whether some creditors are worse off than they would have been in that scenario. Failure resolution administrators have significant discretion over when the contractual default management process is to be interrupted by failure resolution, and also over which of various loss-allocation tools could be used in the counterfactual scenario. It is likely to be difficult to predict which of those tools would have been used.

How to apply the no-creditor-worse-off principle to CCPs therefore remains murky. The Treasury of the United Kingdom[23] summarized its views on this issue by writing: "It is anticipated that clearing house compensation orders would be made only in exceptional circumstances. That being the case, it is not considered necessary to prescribe the provision that should form part of any such order in advance."

---

23. See H. M. Treasury (2014).

Outline of a CCP Failure Resolution Process

Based on our discussion, an administrative CCP failure resolution process could have the following basic steps.

1. Verify the conditions for initiating a failure resolution process and initiate the process. Consult with relevant foreign authorities.
2. Stay the termination of clearing agreements and other contracts, with the likely exception of interoperability agreements with other CCPs.
3. Replace the senior CCP management if that is deemed appropriate, while taking steps to retain key personnel.
4. Assess the immediate cash needs of the CCP and the available sources of liquidity. Make a plan to access liquidity in priority order. Obtain the necessary cash, whether for orderly wind-down or for continuity of clearing.
5. In the event of insufficient cash, interrupt payments to clearing members as legally feasible under contracts or stays, and as appropriate to minimizing the aggregate losses of all parties, including unrelated market participants.
6. Enter claims on the estates of failed clearing members.
7. In a restructuring aimed at the continuation of clearing services:
   a. If the CCP undergoing resolution is not suitable for restructuring and continuation as a single entity, then transfer un-rejected clearing agreements and other CCP property and agreements to a bridge or other successor CCP.
   b. Replenish the default guarantee fund, using prefunded assets as available and additional replenishment contributions from clearing members to the extent permitted by contract and judged systemically safe from the viewpoint of contagion risk.
   c. Rebalance the derivatives positions of the CCP. For example, conduct tear-ups or allocate failed derivatives positions to surviving members, for example by auction.
   d. Assign the equity and any debt claims of the recapitalized or bridge CCP.

    e. Resume clearing new trades.

    f. Make appropriate changes to the CCP's rules, clearing agreements, and risk management procedures.

    g. Permit clearing member resignations after a cooling-off period.

8. In a liquidation and wind-down:

    a. Tear up remaining positions or novate them to other CCPs.

    b. Evaluate claims against the assets of the CCP held by clearing members and other creditors.

    c. Liquidate the CCP's remaining assets.

    d. Assign the liquidated assets of the CCP to claimants.

It is not clear whether a CCP should continue clearing new derivatives trades while undergoing resolution. This should presumably be determined by the circumstances at the time, with the objective of minimizing the total distress costs of clearing members and other market participants. An inability to clear new trades could present some difficulty to market participants who have come to rely on straight-through processing of trades (including clearing) and are attempting to quickly add or replace hedges. Moreover, US regulations may require that a designated clearing organization (DCO) continue to provide clearing services and (subject to exemptions) that market participants continue centrally clearing designated "standardized" derivatives. Whether waivers of these regulations can be obtained, and under what circumstances, is not clear. If a CCP is unable to clear during its reorganization, then regulatory clearing requirements should, if possible, be temporarily waived for those types of derivatives for which there are no alternative CCPs.

Cross-Border Issues

Most major CCPs have, or will soon have, administrative failure resolution processes under designated national authorities. In the United Kingdom, the Financial Services Act of 2012 established a resolution regime for central clearing parties under which the Bank of England acts as the resolution authority. In the United States, the FDIC may have the necessary legal authority for managing the resolution of systemically important CCPs, subject to interpretation of the Dodd-

Frank Act. Some CCPs are cross-border and some CCP operators manage CCPs in multiple jurisdictions.

In its submission to CPMI, the Global Financial Markets Association[24] wrote:

> To the extent key functions of the FMI are performed through an affiliated group of entities, some of which may be formed in jurisdictions other than the home jurisdiction of the FMI, it is essential that the resolution process encompass all such entities in a single process, and that all applicable jurisdictions agree to respect the determinations of the primary jurisdiction. During the financial crisis, we have seen circumstances in which courts in two jurisdictions claimed jurisdiction over a dispute, rendered conflicting judgments, and refused to enforce each other's judgments—leaving market participants with no clear form of redress. Where multiple resolution authorities may claim jurisdiction over a single FMI, including as a result of different jurisdictions of formation of its affiliates, these authorities should agree in advance as to which authority has primary jurisdiction and how to ensure that its determinations have finality in other jurisdictions.

Gleeson (2015) offers a general legal analysis of cross-border recognition of resolvency regimes, including the issue of whether a Title II resolution would be recognized by English courts as an "insolvency regime."

References

Bank of England. 2014. "The Bank of England's Sterling Monetary Framework," Bank of England, November, http://www.bankofengland.co.uk/markets/Documents/money/publications/redbook.pdf.

BlackRock. 2014. "Central Clearing Counterparties and Too Big to Fail," BlackRock Viewpoint, April.

CDS Default Management Working Group. 2011. "Principles and Best Practices for Managing a Defaulting Clearing Member's Remaining Portfolio and Shortfall in Available Funds," January.

---

24. See http://www.bis.org/cpmi/publ/comments/d103/theglobalfin.pdf.

The Clearinghouse. 2012. "Central Counterparties: Recommendations to Promote Financial Stability and Resilience," December, http://www.theclearing house.org/index.html?f=074643.

Committee on Payment and Settlement Systems, Board of the International Organization of Securities Commissions. 2012a. "Principles For Financial Market Infrastructure," Bank for International Settlements, April, http://www.bis.org/cpmi/publ/d101a.pdf.

Committee on Payment and Settlement Systems, Board of the International Organization of Securities Commissions. 2012b. "Recovery and Resolution of Financial Market Infrastructures," consultative report, July, http://www.bis.org/publ/cpss103.pdf; comments, http://www.bis.org/publ/cpss103/comments.htm.

Committee on Payment and Settlement Systems, Board of the International Organization of Securities Commissions. 2014. "Recovery of Financial Market Infrastructures," consultative report, October.

Davies, Geoffrey, and Marc Dobler. 2011. "Bank Resolution and Safeguarding the Creditors Left Behind," Research and Analysis, *Bank of England Quarterly Bulletin*, Q3: 213–23.

Dembo, Amir, Jean-Dominique Deuschel, and Darrell Duffie. 2004. "Large Portfolio Losses," *Finance and Stochastics* 8:3–16.

Duffie, Darrell, and David A. Skeel. 2012. "A Dialogue on the Costs and Benefits of Automatic Stays for Derivatives and Repurchase Agreements," in *Bankruptcy Not Bailout: A Special Chapter 14,* ed. K. E. Scott and J. B. Taylor (Stanford, CA: Hoover Press).

Elliott, David. 2013. "Central Counterparty Loss-Allocation Rules." Bank of England, Financial Stability Paper 20, April, http://www.bankofengland.co.uk/research/Documents/fspapers/fs_paper20.pdf.

European Commission. 2012. "Consultation on a Possible Recovery and Resolution Framework for Financial Institutions Other than Banks," Directorate General, Internal Markets and Services.

European Securities and Markets Authority. 2012. "Draft Technical Standards under the Regulation (EU) No 648/2012 of the European Parliament and of the Council of 4 July 2012 on OTC Derivatives, CCPs and Trade Repositories, Final Report," September, http://www.esma.europa.eu/system/files/2012-600_0.pdf.

European Union. 2012. "Regulation (EU) No 648/2012 of the European Parliament and of the Council of 4 July 2012 on OTC Derivatives, Central Counterparties and Trade Repositories," Official Journal of the European Union,

June 12, http://eurlex.europa.eu/LexUriServ/LexUriServ.do?uri =OJ:L:2012:201:0001:0059:EN:PDF.

European Union. 2014. "Directive 2014/59/EU of The European Parliament and of the Council of 15 May 2014, Establishing a Framework for the Recovery and Resolution of Credit Institutions and Investment Firms," Official Journal of the European Union, June 12, http://eur-lex.europa.eu/legal-content /ENTXT/?uri=uriserv:OJ.L_.2014.173.01.0190.01.ENG.

Financial Stability Board. 2014. "Key Attributes of Effective Resolution Regimes for Financial Institutions," Basel, October 15.

Gleeson, Simon. 2015. "The Consequences of Chapter 14 for International Recognition of US Bank Resolution Action," chapter 5 of this volume.

H. M. Treasury. 2014. "Secondary Legislation for Non-Bank Resolution Regimes," consultation outcome, June 9, https://www.gov.uk/government /consultations/secondary-legislation-for-non-bank-resolution-regimes /secondary-legislation-for-non-bank-resolution-regimes.

Huertas, Thomas. 2013. "Safe to Fail," Ernst & Young LLP, May 7.

ISDA. 2013. "CCP Loss Allocation at the End of the Waterfall," August.

ISDA. 2014. "Resolution Stay Protocol," November 4, http://assets.isda.org /media/f253b540-25/958e4aed.pdf/.

Jackson, Thomas H. 1982. "Bankruptcy, Non-Bankruptcy Entitlements, and the Creditors' Bargain." *Yale Law Journal* 91, no. 5: 857–907.

Jackson, Thomas H. 2015. "Building on Bankruptcy: A Revised Chapter 14 Proposal for the Recapitalization, Reorganization, or Liquidation of Large Financial Institutions," chapter 2 of this volume.

J. P. Morgan Chase & Company. 2014. "What Is the Resolution Plan for CCPs?" Office of Regulatory Affairs, September.

Singh, Manmohan. 2014. "Limiting Taxpayer 'Puts': An Example from Central Counterparties." International Monetary Fund Working Paper, October.

Skeel, David. 2015. "Financing Systemically Important Financial Institutions in Bankruptcy," chapter 3 in this volume.

Steigerwald, Robert, and David DeCarlo. 2014. "Resolving Central Counterparties after Dodd-Frank: Are CCPs Eligible for 'Orderly Liquidation,'" working paper, Federal Reserve Bank of Chicago, November.

CHAPTER 5

The Consequences of Chapter 14 for International Recognition of US Bank Resolution Action

Simon Gleeson

One of the most difficult issues in bank resolution is the question of how resolution measures in one country can be given effect under the laws of another. This debate has turned on two sets of issues. The first of these is whether resolution measures are properly regarded as "insolvency" measures, and should therefore be recognized using existing doctrines of recognition for giving effect to overseas bankruptcy proceedings. This takes us to a series of questions as to whether the way in which the resolution powers are characterized in the home jurisdiction (as bankruptcy or not) is determinative of the way in which courts of other jurisdictions should apply them. The second set of issues concerns whether, where a jurisdiction has an accepted doctrine on universality in bankruptcy, that doctrine should be applied in cases of bank resolution in the same way that it would be in normal bankruptcy. These debates highlight the fact that whereas cross-border recognition of resolution is new and untested territory, cross-border recognition of bankruptcy proceedings is well-trodden ground. The upshot of all of this is that replacing Title II with Chapter 14 could well have a positive impact on the enforceability in other jurisdictions of US resolution measures, since most courts find it easier to recognize foreign bankruptcy proceedings than unclassified administrative procedures which may bear little resemblance to anything in the home jurisdiction.

Most legal systems have mechanisms by which the insolvency regimes of other systems can be given effect. These are not always highly developed, but there can be very few legal systems anywhere in the world which have not had to grapple with the commercial consequences in their jurisdictions of the insolvency of firms established elsewhere. Thus cross-border recognition of insolvency procedures is an established fact of life. Cross-border recognition of bank resolution, by contrast, is even more embryonic than bank resolution itself—there are some ideas as to how it might be accomplished, but very little by way of hard law and nothing by way of precedent. This suggests that one of the issues to be considered in analyzing the Chapter 14 proposal is the extent to which, by using established cross-border insolvency recognition mechanics, it might make cross-border resolution more robust.

Generalizations across multiple legal systems are rarely of any great value, so for this purpose we will consider a specific example. Assume a US bank group company which has obligations owed under English law to English creditors. For this purpose, we will assume that we are dealing with a bank holding company which is capable of qualifying as a financial company under Title II as it currently stands. It has issued bonds which are governed by English law, some of which are held by English resident creditors. How will the English courts treat the intervention of (a) administrative action under Title II, compared with (b) court-ordered action under Chapter 14?

Choice of Law

The starting point for choice of law analysis in the United Kingdom is the Rome I Regulation,[1] which embeds the principle that as a matter of English law parties are free to choose the jurisdiction which governs their contracts, and that choice will be respected by the English courts. Article 3(3) sets out a partial derogation from this principle, in that "where all other elements relevant to the situation at the time of the choice are located in a country other than the country whose

---

1. See regulation (EC) No 593/2008 of the European Parliament and of the Council of June 17, 2008, on the law applicable to contractual obligations.

law has been chosen, the choice of the parties shall not prejudice the application of provisions of the law of that other country which cannot be derogated from by agreement."

Thus, if the situation were that the bond issuance was an entirely domestic US arrangement, and the only reason for the choice of English law was an express desire to avoid the application of US law, it is possible that an English court might be prepared to apply US resolution law on the basis that it would be considered by the US courts to be mandatory. However, in the more likely situation where the bond was offered to international investors in the London or other markets, it is very unlikely that this would apply.

Article 12(1)(d) of the Rome I Regulation also provides that the law chosen by the parties governs not only the rights arising between the parties, generally, but in particular "the various ways of extinguishing obligations, and prescription and limitation of actions."

As a result, it seems clear that the question of whether the obligations of the issuer of the bonds have been reduced or discharged will be a matter for the chosen law of the bond—in this case, English law.

Variation of Liabilities by Foreign Statute under English Law

The basic position under English law as regards the effect of foreign laws on an English law-governed contract is set out in *National Bank of Greece and Athens SA v. Metliss*.[2] In this case a Greek bank had issued English law bonds, whose terms had been purportedly varied by a Greek statute. The House of Lords held that the obligations concerned were contractual obligations, and could therefore not be varied by a law other than the law governing the contract. The Greek government responded to this by passing a new law which purported to be a corporate reorganization measure, but which included provisions that had the same effect as the variation. In general, corporate reorganization measures should be dealt with in accordance with the place of incorporation of the entity concerned, and on this basis the moratorium could have been held to be effective at English law. However, when this

---

2. [1958] AC 509 (House of Lords).

was litigated in *Adams v. National Bank of Greece*,[3] the House of Lords held that where a law structured as a reorganization measure had the effect of varying contractual rights, to that extent it was a contractual and not a reorganization measure, and could not take effect so as to vary existing contractual rights governed by a different law. These cases have recently been followed in *Global Distressed Alpha Fund 1 v. P. T. Bakrie*,[4] in which it was held that an Indonesian court-approved scheme of arrangement could not have the effect of varying obligations owed by a company under English law-governed notes. The reason that this is important in this case is that where a foreign law reorganization leaves an instrument intact but removes from the obligor under that instrument its ability to repay that debt (as would be the case if a bridge bank transfer had the effect of removing from the original obligor the resources which it would require to discharge those obligations), such a reorganization might well be considered as a variation of rights under this doctrine.

The application of these cases in the context of cross-border recognition of resolution actions taken directly under statute is clear. It also seems relatively clear that, confronted with a US issuer who had issued English law-governed bonds, the starting point for the English courts would be that any purported variation of the terms of the bonds by US statute—including variation of amounts due or substituting an obligor—would be ineffective to vary the obligations of the bank. It would therefore be possible for an English bondholder to obtain judgment in England for the amount due and to attach property in England in satisfaction of that debt.

Contractual Issues
It has been suggested by some commentators that the English courts could give effect to a US resolution law through an implied term theory. The best formulation of this is the observation of Ian Fletcher

---

3. [1961] AC 255 (House of Lords).
4. [2011] EWHC 256 (Commercial court).

in *Insolvency in Private International Law*[5] (cited with approval in *Bakrie*):

> In the case of a contractual obligation which happens to be governed by English law, a further rule should be developed whereby, if one of the parties to the contract is the subject of insolvency proceedings in a jurisdiction with which he has an established connection based on residence or ties of business, it should be recognised that the possibility of such proceedings must enter into the parties' reasonable expectations in entering their relationship, and as such may furnish a ground for the discharge to take effect under the applicable law.

The court suggested that this rule could be developed either as a rule of private international law (following Re *HIH Casualty and General Insurance Ltd.*[6]) or that such a provision might be implied as a term into the contract between the parties, following the argument that those who contract with regulated entities should be presumed to intend the regulated entity concerned to act in accordance with the regulations which apply to it. It is possible that English law may develop in this direction at some point in the future, but there is no authority for suggesting that an English court would follow this line of reasoning today.

Consequences of Variation of Debts

If a US bank entity subject to resolution had English law–governed debt in issue which did not include an express "recognition of resolution" clause, then the effect of a US statutory variation of obligations would be to leave the bank concerned liable to pay money under English law but prohibited from paying that money under US law. If the bank had no assets outside the United States, the English position probably would not matter, since even if a judgment against the US

---

5. Ian F. Fletcher, *Insolvency in Private International Law, Main Work (2nd Edition) and Supplement* (Oxford: Oxford University Press, 2005).

6. [008] UKHL 21 (House of Lords).

bank for the debt were obtained in the English courts, it is unlikely that the US courts would enforce it.

However, if the entity concerned had branches (and therefore, presumably, assets) in the United Kingdom, the real risk is that the English courts would attach assets held in the United Kingdom and apply them in satisfaction of the English law debt. There is no general English doctrine of comity which would suggest that the English courts should give effect to a mere administrative act of another sovereign. Thus, in the absence of any other proceedings, the English court would recognize the validity of the English debt and, in the event of non-payment, permit the assets in the United Kingdom to be attached and collected, to be applied in satisfaction of that debt. It is also likely that the English court would be prepared to grant injunctions restraining the removal of assets from the jurisdiction pending payment of the debts concerned.

There are broadly two routes by which the US government, or other US creditors, could seek to challenge this. One would be where ancillary English insolvency proceedings are opened in respect of the UK assets—in this case it would be possible to intervene in these proceedings to request that the US resolution process be recognized. The other would be to seek to take advantage of the existing mechanism whereby decisions in overseas insolvency proceedings may be given effect by the English courts.

Where UK Ancillary Proceedings Are Opened

It is very likely (although not inevitable) that the commencement of resolution proceedings under Title II in the United States would result in the commencement in the United Kingdom of insolvency proceedings resulting in the gathering in of the assets of the branch under the supervision of the insolvency courts. The question then becomes one of how the English insolvency courts would regard the US provisions.

The leading case in this regard is *Felixstowe Docks and Railways v. US Lines.*[7] This case concerned the behavior of the UK courts in exactly this situation where the insolvent entity was a US company

---

7. [1989] QB 360 (QBD).

which had entered into a Chapter 11 reorganization. The company argued that the assets collected should be passed to the company to be applied in accordance with the court-approved Chapter 11 plan for reorganization, whereas the UK creditors argued that the assets should be retained in the United Kingdom. The court found in favor of the UK creditors. However, it should be noted that the facts of *Felixstowe Docks* were somewhat unusual, in that the approved plan of reorganization for the entity involved its withdrawal from all non-US markets, and therefore a discriminatory treatment of UK creditors as compared with US creditors. It should also be noted that the policy of the English courts at the time was to regard any insolvency arrangement which did not ensure equal treatment of creditors as unfair (the United Kingdom only introduced an administration regime equivalent to the US Chapter 11 regime in 1985). In other decisions on similar facts, it was held in *Banque Indosuez v. Ferroment Resources*[8] that where there was no established discrimination against UK creditors, the UK creditors could represent themselves in the relevant US Chapter 11 proceedings, and the assets could therefore be dealt with in those proceedings. In *Re HIH Casualty and General Insurance,*[9] the court considered the position where the (Australian) overseas proceedings were based on an explicit discrimination between some creditors and others. It held that the assets should be dealt with under the Australian regime, and that the fact that that regime might be discriminatory between creditors (and therefore violate the principle of equal treatment) was not an obstacle to cooperating with the jurisdiction concerned.

It is therefore clear from this that in the circumstances described above, the English courts would be prepared to remit UK assets to the US authorities to be dealt with if they regarded the US resolution proceedings as insolvency proceedings and there was no explicit discrimination against non-US creditors in those US proceedings.[10]

---

8. [1993] BCLC 112 (CD).

9. [2008] UKHL 21 (House of Lords).

10. It should be emphasized at this point that we are considering the resolution of a US bank holding company. If the resolution were a direct resolution of a US bank deposit-taking entity, the rules granting insolvency preference to US

Is Title II an "Insolvency Regime"?

The key question, therefore, is whether Title II could be regarded for this purpose as an insolvency proceeding. It is clear from the Financial Stability Board (FSB) Key Attributes paper that there is no automatic answer to the question of whether resolution regimes are insolvency regimes or not. The paper explicitly provides for resolution to be a court-supervised process,[11] but this does not of itself constitute it as an insolvency process.

The starting point for the United Kingdom courts in considering whether a resolution power constituted an insolvency proceeding would almost certainly be to identify the equivalent UK powers, and ask whether those powers would be regarded as insolvency proceedings or not. In UK legislation the position is clear that they would not—the equivalent powers of the UK resolution authority[12] are conferred under part 1 of the Banking Act 2009, and that act makes a clear distinction between part 1 (bank resolution) and part 2 (bank insolvency).[13]

The court would then go on to consider the characterization of the relevant powers as a matter of their proper law—in this case, US law. If US law provided that Title II was an insolvency proceeding, the English courts would begin with a presumption that that was the case. However, that presumption is capable of being rebutted. In particular, the less similar the proceeding is to UK insolvency, the less likely it is that the proceeding will be accepted as an insolvency proceeding. To this end, important relevant characteristics will include similarity

---

depositors over non-US depositors would constitute clear discrimination against overseas creditors, and the situation would be much more complex. However, in general US resolution practice seeks to intervene at the holding company level, and this issue is therefore currently of only theoretical importance.

11. See, e.g., paragraph 1.13 of the Essential Elements of Recovery and Resolution Plans section of the Financial Stability Board's Key Attributes paper.

12. These powers would be exercised through a partial property transfer under Part 1 of the Banking Act 2009.

13. Sections 129 and 165 of the act make explicit that bank insolvency and bank administration are to be regarded as insolvency proceedings for the purpose of section 426.

to UK insolvency processes, court supervision, the existence of some administrative or similar procedure designed to weigh the competing claims of different creditors, and some commitment to procedural fairness. A procedure which does not have at least some element of each of these is unlikely to be recognized by the English courts as an insolvency procedure.[14]

It is hard to envisage a situation in which Chapter 14, if enacted, would not be regarded as an insolvency proceeding under any local law. As noted above, the characterization of proceedings under local law is not always completely determinative for this purpose. However, it seems very unlikely that any court-supervised proceeding under the US bankruptcy code would not be recognised as an insolvency proceeding by the UK courts.

Where UK Ancillary Proceedings Are Not Opened

Both at common law and as a matter of treaty, English courts may in certain circumstances give effect to the actions of foreign liquidators without the opening of formal ancillary proceedings.

The United Nations Commission on International Trade Law (UNCITRAL) model law on cross-border insolvency is incorporated into English law by the Cross-Border Insolvency Regulations 2006. It provides for English courts to cooperate with foreign courts in matters of foreign insolvency where the foreign court concerned has jurisdiction. The UK regulations do not apply to bank insolvencies, but do apply to insolvencies of bank holding companies. However, the definition of "proceedings" for this purpose is "a collective judicial or administrative proceeding in a foreign state . . . pursuant to a law relating to insolvency in which proceedings the assets and affairs of the debtor are subject to control or supervision by a foreign

---

14. There is a decision of the European Court of Justice (LBI hf v Kepler Capital Markets SA [2013], EUECJ C-85/12 [October 24, 2013]) which may cast some doubt on this conclusion. However, since the judgment is particularly confusing and difficult to follow (even by ECJ standards), and appears to be based on a strongly purposive construction of the EU directive relating to mutual recognition of bank winding-up proceedings within the EU, it is merely noted here.

court, for the purpose of reorganisation or liquidation." It is hard to see how a Title II OLA (Orderly Liquidation Authority) proceeding could be said to be "judicially supervised" for this purpose,[15] and it therefore seems that the UNCITRAL model would not be available for the purpose of giving effect to a Title II resolution in the United Kingdom.

The Consequences of Explicit Contractual Terms Recognizing Resolution

It is worth pausing at this point to enquire whether this is in fact an imaginary problem. Article 55 of the European Union (EU) Bank Recovery and Resolution Directive purports to address this issue by requiring EU banks to insert into the terms of any contract which they enter into under any non-EU law a provision to the effect that the contract may be varied in accordance with the relevant resolution law. Could the United States solve this issue simply with an equivalent requirement?

A preliminary issue which arises here is whether the effect of an explicit incorporation of US resolution powers into an English law-governed instrument would be (a) to subject the relevant provisions of the document to US governing law (thus creating a bifurcated governing law provision) or (b) to incorporate the relevant provisions as contractual terms. At English law this is not a relevant distinction, since both approaches would be legally robust, although it may raise issues in other jurisdictions. However, it is hard to see how the first view (implicit split governing law) can be supported—there is no part of the document which is explicitly subjected to a separate governing law, and the ordinary construction of such a provision would be that the parties are simply agreeing by contract that their obligations to each other shall be calculated as if the relevant US legislative provisions

---

15. See Stanford International Bank Ltd. [2010] 3 W.L.R. 941. For example, a scheme of arrangement under section 899 of the UK Companies Act 2006, which is proposed by the management of a company to its creditors and approved by them, is not an "insolvency proceeding" for this purpose, since it is not conducted under "insolvency law."

had applied to the document. This is no more than a variation of an English law obligation by agreement.

Once this is established, the validity of the contract term is prima facie established. The remaining question is whether there is any other doctrine of law which might invalidate it.

One possibility here would be the doctrine set out in *Government of India v. Taylor.*[16] This doctrine says that where a foreign government seeks to appropriate property by statute, that act should not be recognized in any other jurisdiction. Although primarily concerned with tax legislation, the case is sometimes taken as authority that statutory unilateral appropriation of property by a government should not be given extraterritorial effect. Even in the absence of an explicit provision, we do not believe that such a challenge could be successful, since a resolution does not constitute a simple appropriation of property. The inclusion of an express provision recognising the possibility of a variation of terms by administrative action removes this issue completely.

Allied to this, and potentially of slightly more concern, is the risk of challenge under the Human Rights Act. Strictly speaking, the UK Human Rights Act is irrelevant to an act of the United States, since it affects only UK authorities. However, it does embody a presumption that English law should be interpreted as far as possible in a way which is compatible with the European Convention on Human Rights. This could be relevant if it could be shown that the relevant resolution provisions were contrary to that convention.

The relevant part of the convention is the first protocol, which imposes an obligation on the state not to interfere with peaceful enjoyment of property, deprive a person of his possessions, or subject a person's possessions to control. For this purpose, the question has been raised in the United Kingdom as to whether the exercise of a resolution power could constitute an unlawful deprivation of a person's property.

The key issue here is that Protocol No. 1 is subject to a proviso that an act of state will not constitute a violation of this right if such interference, deprivation, or control is carried out lawfully and in the public interest. The question of what is in the public interest is

---

16. [1955] AC 491.

in general left to the state itself to determine, and the majority of the challenges to state action based on this protocol before the European Court of Human Rights have resulted in a finding that the act concerned was in the public interest. In general, only an act which constituted either a completely discretionary taking of property or a refusal to grant a property right previously contracted for would constitute a clear breach of this protocol. In the context of a bank resolution it is almost impossible to imagine a court taking the view that the exercise of the resolution power was so egregious that it could not constitute a legitimate manifestation of the public interest. This will particularly be the case where one of the considerations which is required to be taken into account in initiating the resolution is the preservation of systemic stability within the state concerned.

The most significant difficulty with an explicit contract term, however, is whether it could potentially be struck down as an attempt to contract out of the insolvency jurisdiction of the host country. It is a strong principle of English law that it is not possible to "contract out of insolvency,"[17] and any contractual provision which purports to vary the claims of a creditor of an insolvent entity so as to vitiate the principle of equality of treatment of creditors may be struck down as contrary to public policy.[18] Where branch insolvency proceedings have been commenced in the UK, the position of a contractual provision purporting to vary the creditors' claims in that insolvency would be at least questionable.

New Developments—Statutory Powers

The issues outlined above are, of course, extremely clear to the UK resolution authorities. Since those authorities have a strong interest in ensuring that a resolution of the UK operations of US banks is as

---

17. British Eagle International Air Lines Ltd v. Cie Nationale Air France [1975] 1 WLR 758 (Court of Appeal).

18. There are, of course, certain types of contractual provision which *are* effective to "contract out" of insolvency—subordination being the most commonly encountered. In practice, in deciding whether to give effect to a contractual provision of this kind, a court would almost certainly end up asking whether the provision was a species of subordination clause.

effective as possible, much thought has been given—on both sides of the Atlantic—as to how this can be achieved with minimum risk of subsequent litigation challenge.

The answer to this—in the United Kingdom at least—is that as regards physical operations in the United Kingdom, what is assumed is that ancillary insolvency proceedings will be commenced in the United Kingdom, and that the provisional liquidator appointed by the UK court will cooperate with the US resolution authority in effecting the bridge bank transfer, on the basis that this strategy is likely to provide the best outcome for creditors. This is almost certainly correct, both as a matter of law and as an analysis of the likely behavior of an insolvency office-holder. It does, however, somewhat emphasize the point that even though resolution may be a non-insolvency procedure in the country in which it is implemented, it is likely to be implemented through insolvency mechanisms in other jurisdictions.

The intervention of a court-appointed liquidator also has—for the UK authorities—the unwelcome consequence of introducing another actor into an already crowded field, and in particular one whose primary objective is not necessarily the preservation of systemic stability.[19] A power is therefore being introduced into UK law which will enable overseas resolution action to be "adopted" into UK law by a further UK administrative action.

As from January 1, 2015, the United Kingdom has a separate statutory regime intended to enable overseas resolution actions to be enforced at English law. This is contained in new Chapter 6 of Part 1 to the Banking Act 1989, sections 89H to 89J.[20] These provide for the Bank of England (as resolution authority), with the consent of the Treasury, to make an order recognizing the resolution action of any third-country resolution authority. The effect of such recognition

---

19. The United Kingdom does have a separate regime (the bank insolvency regime, created by part 2 of the Banking Act 1989), which permits an office-holder to be appointed in respect of bank insolvency proceedings whose statutory objectives do include a wider systemic objective, but such an appointment can only be made in respect of a UK bank.

20. Inserted by article 103 of the Bank Recovery and Resolution Order 2014.

is (per section 891(2)) that the third-country resolution action has "the same legal effects in . . . the United Kingdom as it would have produced had it been made . . . under the law of . . . the United Kingdom." The format of the provision is that the bank "must" make the order recognizing the foreign action, but has a wide discretion not to in a range of circumstances. Some of these are specific (thus, such an order may not be made if the third-country resolution action would disadvantage foreign creditors against domestic creditors[21]) but others are generally expressed (thus, no order should be made which "would have an adverse effect on financial stability in the United Kingdom or another EEA [European Economic Area] state"). It should also be noted that the making of such a recognition order is trumped by the commencement of UK insolvency proceedings (section 89H(5)). The meaning of this provision is far from clear, since it is copied directly out of the BRRD (European Bank Recovery and Resolution Directive) (Article 94(6)). However, at the very least it raises considerable uncertainty as to whether UK resolution authorities, even given the section 89H power, may not in the end be driven back on the approach of appointing provisional liquidators under the UK insolvency regime in preference to using this power, simply in order to avoid the power being challenged by a series of dissident creditors seeking to trump the power by seeking the appointment of such a liquidator.

UK Recognition of Overseas Insolvency Regimes

We turn now to the question of how different the position would be if, instead of the US authorities exercising their Title II powers, they were to proceed under the US Bankruptcy Code.

In general, the approach of the UK courts to insolvency proceedings is "modified universalism." Many legal commentators take the view that the UK courts flirted briefly with broad universalism,[22] but

---

21. It would therefore not be possible to make such an order to facilitate an FDIC conservatorship of an insured institution.

22. Cambridge Gas Transportation Corp v. Official Committee of Unsecured Creditors of Navigator Holdings Plc [2006] UKPC 26, [2007] 1 AC 508 (House of Lords).

have now retreated to the position where they will restrict the exercise of their powers to the narrow scope of English domestic law.[23] However, it should be emphasized that although the UK courts have rejected broad universalism to the extent of declining to assert an in personam jurisdiction which they would otherwise not possess arising purely out of a power to enforce third-country judgments, they have not budged in their fundamental adherence to what has been called the golden thread of English cross-border insolvency law: "The English courts should, so far as is consistent with justice and UK public policy, co-ordinate with the courts in the country of the principal liquidation to ensure that all the company's assets are distributed to its creditors under a single system of distribution."[24]

Thus, where the English courts are satisfied that a foreign court is in control of an insolvency procedure, it will take all necessary steps, without the necessity for governmental, administrative, or statutory activity, to ensure that assets are got in and distributed in accordance with that single scheme. The key point here is that cross-border cooperation between insolvency courts, in this regard at least, is automatic and self-executing.

It is, of course, by no means the case that an English court will mechanically implement any decision of an overseas court. In particular, where the UK court gets in assets and there are significant UK creditors,[25] the UK court is very likely to order that the UK rules of insolvency set-off are adhered to in dealing with those creditors,[26] although it has been said that in other cases the English court may remit assets to be distributed under the scheme of the home jurisdiction.[27]

---

23. Rubin v. Eurofinance [2012] UKSC 46 (Supreme Court).

24. Per Lord Hoffmann, HIH Casualty and General Insurance Ltd [2008] UKHL 21, [2008] 1 WLR 852, para. 30.

25. "Significant UK creditors" in this instance means creditors whose debts arose out of transactions conducted in England or who are otherwise closely connected with England, not merely creditors who have proved in the English proceedings.

26. Re BCCI (No 10) [1997] Ch 213.

27. Per Lord Hoffmann in *HIH*.

Finally, there is the fact that even a discharge by a New York insolvency court would not finally determine claims under an English law document. It is a principle of English law that where a person owes an obligation, the obligation is only discharged by an act which is legally effective under the law of the obligation. Thus, where a New York person owes an obligation under New York law, if that person is made bankrupt under New York law the discharge is recognised under English law, since the question is a question under New York law, and New York law has firmly answered it. The position is more complex, however, where the obligation is an obligation under English law, since no provision of New York law can in principle affect the position inter parties under an English law agreement. This point has arisen from time to time in UK litigation, where UK creditors of foreign bankrupts have sought to attach property of those bankrupts in England on the basis that their debt is not extinguished by the foreign bankruptcy court's decision. The English courts have in general responded to this by adopting a doctrine based on estoppel. There are two limbs to this doctrine: first, that a creditor should not be able to prefer himself over other creditors in any insolvency (including a foreign insolvency) by attaching property after the commencement of the insolvency proceedings;[28] and, second, that if a creditor participates in the overseas proceedings, and accepts a distribution in them, he is treated by the courts as being estopped from pursuing the English law claim which he still has.[29]

It should be noted that all of these difficulties would be equally present in the event of a UK ancillary liquidation proceeding conducted in support of a Title II resolution. In particular, the discharge question would become even more acute if the US resolution were not conducted under insolvency law, since it appears from the English authorities that the two principles relied on above would not apply in respect of an administrative non-judicial process, and it is therefore possible that in such a case the English law claims might be inextinguishable.

---

28. Galbraith v. Grimshaw [1910] AC 508 (House of Lords).
29. Phillips v. Allan (1828) 8 B&C 477, Seligman v. Huth (1877) 37 LT 488.

Conclusion

Cross-border recognition of bank resolution proceedings is a complex and difficult area, and it would be wrong to present Chapter 14 as a "magic bullet"—even in relatively straightforward cases, cross-border recognition of insolvency proceedings is not trouble-free. However, it is true that national courts around the world have established mechanisms for dealing with cross-border recognition of insolvency proceedings, and those mechanisms are generally familiar to insolvency judges. By positioning resolution within that intellectual construct, Chapter 14 makes the task of overseas courts charged with addressing the legal issues resulting from US resolution substantially easier, and significantly improves the predictability of the behavior of those courts in a resolution.

CHAPTER 6

A Resolvable Bank

Thomas F. Huertas

Making banks resolvable is a key component of the regulatory reform program enacted in response to the crisis. A resolvable bank is one that is "safe to fail": it can fail and be resolved without cost to the taxpayer and without significant disruption to the financial markets or the economy at large.

Much of the discussion on recovery and resolution focuses, quite understandably, on global systemically important financial institutions (G-SIFIs) in their current form. This chapter takes the opposite approach. It starts with a blank sheet of paper and designs a bank that will be resolvable, first for a bank in a single jurisdiction and then for a banking group with branches and/or subsidiaries in multiple jurisdictions.[1]

Separation of investor obligations from customer obligations at the operating bank holds the key to resolvability. Such a separation hinges on two factors:

- "Customer" or "operating" obligations, such as deposits and derivatives, are senior to, and distinct from, "investor" obligations, such

The Financial Markets Group of the London School of Economics distributed an earlier version of this chapter as a Special Paper, and parts of the paper are taken from the author's book, *Safe to Fail: How Resolution Will Revolutionise Banking* (2014). The author is grateful to David Schraa, Stefan Walter, Wilson Ervin, Markus Ronner, and John Whittaker for helpful comments on earlier drafts. The opinions expressed here are the author's personal views.

1. The paper takes a global perspective, as expressed in FSB (2011a) and abstracts from the situation in specific jurisdictions.

as the bank's capital instruments (common equity tier 1 [CET1], additional tier 1 [AT1] and tier 2 [T2] capital).

- "Investor" instruments are subject to "bail-in," i.e., to write-down or conversion into CET1 capital at the point of nonviability (PONV).

If the amount of investor obligations is large enough, the bail-in will replenish the common equity of the bank. This assures the solvency of the bank-in-resolution and provides the basis for the bank-in-resolution to obtain liquidity. Together, the recapitalization and the liquidity provision should go a long way toward stabilizing the bank-in-resolution, assuring that it is able to continue its customer operations and paving the way for the resolution authorities to restructure the bank. Overall, resolution can occur without cost to the taxpayer and without significant disruption to the financial markets or the economy at large.

Standards for Resolvability

A resolvable bank should be "safe to fail."[2] This calls for the bank and the resolution process to meet three conditions:

1. The bank can be readily recapitalized without recourse to taxpayer money.
2. The bank-in-resolution[3] can continue to conduct essential functions, such as executing payments for customers, ideally from the opening of business on the business day following the initiation of the resolution.
3. The resolution process itself does not significantly disrupt financial markets or the economy at large.

Resolution falls into three stages, (i) pulling the trigger, or initiating resolution, (ii) stabilizing the institution, and (iii) restructuring the institution (see figure 6.1). This paper focuses on the second, or

---

2. For a full discussion, see Huertas 2014a.

3. The term "bank-in-resolution" covers the period from the entry of the bank into resolution until the end of the restructuring period.

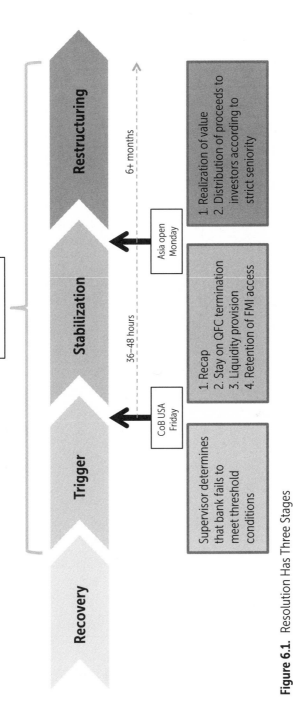

Figure 6.1. Resolution Has Three Stages

Source: Thomas F. Huertas, *Safe to Fail: How Resolution Will Revolutionise Banking* (London: Palgrave MacMillan, 2014)

stabilization, phase, under the assumption that the authorities initiate resolution as soon as the bank reaches the PONV. The key to stabilizing the bank is its prompt recapitalization, via write-down or conversion of investor liabilities such as subordinated debt into CET1 capital. The recapitalization sets the stage for the provision of liquidity to the bank-in-resolution, secured by a charge over the bank's unencumbered assets.

Resolution of a Unit Bank

We start with the case of a unit bank: a single bank in a single jurisdiction with no branches or subsidiaries. Assets consist of loans, securities, and other claims on customers such as derivatives. These assets are financed by capital instruments (CET1, AT1, and T2 capital); by customer obligations, such as deposits and derivatives; and by senior debt (see figure 6.2).

Capital instruments are plainly investor obligations. CET1 capital is the basis for capital requirements under the Basel III accord. It bears first loss and is the ultimate determinant of the bank's solvency. Under Basel III, AT1 and T2 capital must be subject to write-down or conversion into CET1 capital when the bank reaches the PONV. AT1 and T2 capital therefore contribute to what might be called "reserve capital," i.e., instruments that can be readily used to replenish CET1 capital, should CET1 capital be insufficient to maintain the bank's viability. Aggregate loss-absorbing capacity (ALAC) is therefore the sum of CET1 capital and the bank's "reserve capital."[4]

---

4. We have used the terms "reserve capital" and "aggregate loss-absorbing capacity" to avoid confusion with terms specifically used in legislation and/or policy proposals as well as to avoid framing the discussion in a vocabulary specific to any one jurisdiction. "Reserve capital" conforms in concept to gone-concern loss-absorbing capacity (GLAC)—instruments that are specifically subject to write-down or conversion at the PONV/entry of the bank into resolution. "Aggregate loss-absorbing capacity" conforms in concept to "total loss-absorbing capacity" (TLAC) and equals the sum of reserve capital and total CET1 capital. However, the details of ALAC do not necessarily conform to the term sheet proposed for TLAC in FSB (2014).

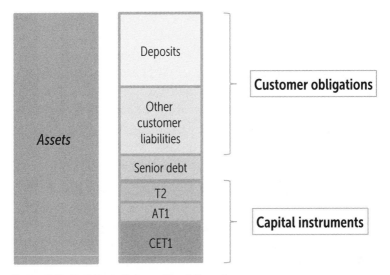

Figure 6.2. Unit Bank: Balance Sheet Overview

Senior debt is an investor obligation, but it is not clear that it should count toward reserve capital. Unlike AT1 and T2 capital, it is not generally subject to write-down or conversion at the PONV. Indeed, senior debt ranks on a par with other senior obligations, so that a default on senior debt would very likely trigger a default on customer obligations, such as derivatives, and compromise the bank's ability to continue to perform critical economic functions.

For senior debt to be counted toward reserve capital, it should be subordinated to customer/operating liabilities, such as deposits and derivatives. Although depositor preference and the collateralization

---

Note, however, that neither "reserve capital" nor ALAC encompasses the full scope of liabilities that would be subject to bail-in (i.e., subject to write-down or loss in the event of resolution). Should losses at the bank in resolution exceed ALAC, these losses would be imposed—in reverse order of seniority—on the remaining elements in the bank's liability structure. If losses were so severe as to reach insured deposits (the super-senior tranche of liabilities), losses attributed to that tranche would be borne by the deposit guarantee fund. For a summary of how this would work under the EU Banking Recovery and Resolution Directive (Directive 2014/59/EU, hereinafter "BRRD"), see BoE (2014, p. 14).

of the net exposure under derivatives contracts go a long way toward making senior debt subordinated in an economic sense, it would be preferable to make senior debt subordinate in a legal sense as well, so that it effectively becomes intermediate debt. Such intermediate debt could count toward reserve capital and ALAC.[5]

For a bank to be resolvable there has to be a reasonable assurance that the amount of reserve capital will be sufficient to replenish CET1 capital to a level where the bank is not only solvent but able, given sufficient access to liquidity, to continue operation whilst restructuring under the aegis of the resolution authorities. Determining the level of reserve capital therefore requires one to take a view on (i) what constitutes the correct target for CET1 capital after replenishment/recap; (ii) what is the likely state of CET1 capital at the point at which the authorities initiate resolution; and (iii) whether there should be provision for what might be called a reload capability (see figure 6.3).

As to the target for CET1 after recap, a conservative standard is to assume that CET1 should be replenished so that the bank-in-resolution meets not only the Basel III minimum requirement (4.5 percent of risk-weighted assets, or RWAs), but also fills the capital conservation buffer (2.5 percent of RWAs) and possibly some or all of the SIFI surcharge (currently 1 percent to 2.5 percent of RWAs). This would assure that the bank-in-resolution started the restructuring phase with CET1 capital at the threshold at which a bank outside resolution would be permitted to pay dividends or make distributions without restrictions.[6]

---

5. This is in fact the approach toward subordination taken in FSB (2014). Note, however, that the FSB proposes to require that intermediate debt have a remaining maturity of more than one year if it is to qualify as TLAC. This seems unduly restrictive (especially if the short-term intermediate debt remains *pari-passu* with the longer term intermediate debt) and consideration might be given to relaxing the maturity restriction and replacing this with a requirement for the bank to develop and be able to implement recovery options, should the weighted average maturity of the bank's issuance fall below two years.

6. According to the Bank of England (BoE 2014, p. 21), "The goal of ensuring that the firm can operate unsupported means that the firm must be recapitalised to a level that is sufficient to restore market confidence and allow the firm to access private funding markets. This means that the level of capital held by the

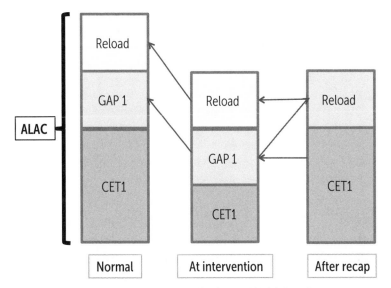

Figure 6.3. Determination of Reserve Capital and ALAC Requirements

The amount of replenishment required (GAP1 in figure 6.3) depends to a significant degree on whether the supervisor initiates resolution ("pulls the trigger") in a timely fashion. If it does, there is a greater probability that the bank still has positive net worth and positive CET1 capital. In contrast, if the supervisor and/or central bank exercises forbearance, by the time resolution is initiated CET1 capital may have slipped below the minimum of 4.5 percent of RWAs, possibly to zero or even below (so that the bank becomes balance-sheet insolvent).

To be very conservative, the ALAC standard could include what amounts to a reload component. This would assure that the bank maintained enough reserve capital to restore CET1 capital to its target level for a second time. The amount of the reload is accordingly equal to the GAP1 calculated above.

The total ALAC requirement therefore amounts to the bank's CET1 requirement plus the estimated GAP and any reload provision.

firm is likely to need to be higher than the minimum required for authorisation by the relevant supervisor." The European Banking Authority (EBA 2014) takes a similar approach.

Alternatively, one may posit a requirement for reserve capital either in lieu of, or as a supplement to, an ALAC requirement. Note that a reserve capital requirement targets much more exactly the problem at hand, namely assurance that there will be instruments available to convert into CET1 capital, in the event that the bank goes into resolution, but has the disadvantage of discouraging banks from holding equity in excess of minimum requirements (and so making failure more likely in the first place).[7]

Figure 6.4 illustrates how such an approach might work for a bank with a SIFI surcharge of 1 percent of RWAs. In normal times, the bank would have to maintain CET1 capital of 8 percent (the 4.5 percent minimum requirement, the 2.5 percent capital conservation buffer, and the 1 percent SIFI surcharge). We assume that losses deplete CET1 capital so that the buffers are exhausted at the point of intervention, that the bank reaches the PONV at 4.5 percent of RWAs, and that the authorities intervene promptly (do not exercise forbearance). This creates a gap of 3.5 percent of RWAs that must be filled and an equivalent provision for reload. The bank's ALAC in normal times (exclusive of the amount of CET1 capital in the buffers) is therefore 11.5 percent of RWAs (4.5 percent minimum CET1 capital plus 7 percent reserve capital).[8]

To assure that the bank can fill the recap gap at the PONV, the bank in normal times carries AT1 and T2 capital of 3.5 percent of RWAs. This also assures that the bank can meet its 8 percent total capital (CET1 + AT1 + T2) requirement without reliance on the CET1 capital contained in the buffers, both in normal times and after bail-in. To provide for the possibility that a reload might be required, the bank in normal times maintains intermediate debt equal to 3.5 percent of

---

7. The FSB TLAC proposal (FSB 2014) envisages that such "reserve capital" instruments would constitute at least one-third of TLAC.

8. Proposals to require higher levels of ALAC such as found in FSB (2014) therefore implicitly assume either (a) the bank-in-resolution will need much higher capital following stabilization or (b) the bank's CET1 capital ratio at the point of intervention will be lower than the 4.5 percent minimum, either as a result of deliberate forbearance or due to the difficulty in establishing a timely and accurate valuation of the bank's asset portfolio.

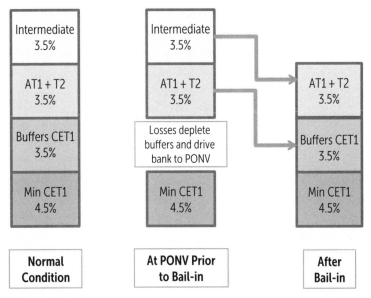

Figure 6.4. Prompt Corrective Action Limits the Need for Reserve Capital

RWAs. At the PONV, the AT1 and T2 capital is written down or converted into CET1 capital, and the intermediate debt is converted into AT1 or T2 capital.

This forms the basis for stabilizing the bank and should be supplemented by measures to assure the following:

- The bank-in-resolution has access to adequate liquidity (see below).
- The bail-in does not trigger close-out of qualified financial contracts (such as derivatives or repurchase agreements) or the liquidation of collateral held by counterparties in association with such contracts.[9]
- The bank-in-resolution retains access to financial market infrastructures (and such infrastructures remain robust).[10]

---

9. See "Other Considerations" below.
10. See "Other Considerations" below.

Do Branches Make a Bank Unresolvable?

We now extend the analysis to the case where the bank subsidiary has branches. This analysis certainly yields the same result where the branches are domestic, within the same jurisdiction as the parent, for the branch is an integral part of the bank as a whole.

It also yields the same result where the bank has foreign branches, provided the foreign jurisdiction takes a unitary approach to resolution. In this case the foreign jurisdiction also regards the foreign branch as being an integral part of the bank as a whole and the foreign jurisdiction accepts that the home country will run the resolution process. In this case the foreign jurisdiction recognizes that the assets of the foreign branch will be pooled with the assets of the rest of the bank. The foreign jurisdiction further accepts that the liabilities of the foreign branch will be paid in accordance with the rules of the home country. Effectively, the foreign jurisdiction recognizes the lead of the home country supervisor and home country resolution authority and accepts the decisions of the home country authorities.[11]

Things become more complex if the foreign jurisdiction takes a territorial approach to resolution and/or the home country institutes a preference for domestic liabilities such as deposits in head office and domestic branches. Although the motivation in each case is to preserve value for "their" creditors, the aggregate result is likely to be mutually assured fragmentation, possibly even liquidation, with significant costs to creditors as well as disruption to the financial markets and the economy at large.

---

11. The home country resolution authority also needs to follow the unitary principle. This involves an acceptance that the liabilities of the foreign branches are on a par with those of the bank's head office and domestic branches. Note that this commitment is easier to sustain if the bank has an ample amount of reserve capital that can be bailed-in in the event the bank enters resolution. Without such reserve capital in place, the home country resolution authority may elect or be directed to prefer the obligations of the bank's domestic branches over the bank's foreign branches. This is particularly likely to be the case (and was the case in Iceland in 2008) if the unitary approach to resolution would result in severe losses to domestic depositors and/or punitive levies on domestic banks under the domestic deposit guarantee scheme.

Under the territorial approach to bank resolution, the foreign jurisdiction resolves the foreign branch separately from the rest of the bank.[12] It uses the assets of the foreign branch to meet the obligations of the foreign branch to the creditors of that branch. Should any proceeds remain after the branch has fully met its obligations to its creditors, this excess would be remitted to the estate of the parent bank. Should a deficiency remain, the creditors of the foreign branch would have an unsecured claim on the estate of the parent bank. In effect, the territorial approach turns the liabilities of the foreign branch into what amounts to a covered bond, where the coverage constitutes the assets of the foreign branch. For this reason, the territorial approach is frequently reinforced by an asset maintenance requirement to assure that the foreign branch will have enough assets to cover its liabilities if the bank enters resolution.

The territorial approach to resolution is essentially a liquidation approach. It is likely to result in significantly greater costs to creditors and to society as a whole. In particular, if the foreign jurisdiction begins to liquidate the foreign branch, the home country will for all practical purposes have to liquidate the parent bank as well. That will almost certainly disrupt financial markets and the economy at large.

Foreign authorities are particularly likely to want the option to employ the territorial approach if the home country grants preference in resolution to creditors of the domestic offices of the bank, either generally or within a certain class of liabilities (e.g., deposits).[13] In such a case, the home country has the option to resolve the bank by transferring the obligations of the bank's domestic offices to a bridge bank along with the bank's best assets and leave the obligations of the bank's foreign branches (along with the bank's worst assets) behind in a rump bank. The bridge bank would continue in operation; the rump would not—it would be liquidated over time under the aegis of the home country resolution authority. As a result, creditors of the foreign branch would be likely to lose access to their funds for an extended

---

12. For a discussion of the US approach to branches of foreign banks, see Lee (2014, pp. 298–317).

13. See, for example, PRA (2014).

period of time and to suffer severe losses as and when the estate of the rump bank made a distribution. The territorial approach of the foreign jurisdiction counteracts this by placing the liquidation of the foreign branch under the administration of the foreign resolution authority. And, the asset maintenance requirement effectively collateralizes the obligations of the foreign branch and therefore counteracts the preference that the home country seeks to give to creditors of the bank's domestic offices.

Ideally, countries would change their legislation to adopt the unitary approach. But realistically, this is unlikely to happen in the near future. However, what authorities can do is to commit to these two principles:

A. The host country authorities will refrain from initiating the resolution of the branch in the host country without giving prior notice to the home country authority and giving the home country authority the opportunity to either cure the deficiency in the branch or initiate resolution of the bank as a whole.

B. If the home country authorities do initiate resolution of the bank as a whole, the host country authorities will refrain from initiating the territorial approach provided the home country authorities act to stabilize the bank-in-resolution via the bail-in of investor capital and the provision of liquidity facilities to the bank-in-resolution.[14]

Such a commitment offers the best hope of avoiding the "mutually assured fragmentation" that would result if home and/or host authorities were to actually implement the territorial approach to resolving a global systemically important bank.

---

14. The suggestions made here are a concrete example of the more general precept advanced by the Bank of England (2014, p. 9): "A host authority should not seek to take action with respect to subsidiaries or branches of foreign banks in its own jurisdiction which might frustrate the orderly resolution of the group being co-ordinated by the home authority."

Unit Bank with Parent Holding Company

We now turn to the case where the unit operating bank is owned by a parent holding company and both entities are incorporated or headquartered in the same jurisdiction (see figure 6.5). The parent holding company is not a bank, and has no license to conduct banking activities directly. We further assume that the parent holding company owns 100 percent of the equity in its bank subsidiary and subscribes to 100 percent of the reserve capital (AT1 and T2 capital plus intermediate debt) issued by the bank subsidiary.

The parent holding company's assets are restricted to investments in CET1 capital and reserve capital (AT1, T2, and intermediate debt) instruments issued by the bank subsidiary to the parent plus cash and marketable securities (such as government bonds). The liabilities of the parent holding company consist of common equity and debt (see figure 6.6). Note that the debt of the parent to investors is structurally subordinated to the obligations of the bank subsidiary. Cash flow from the operations of the bank subsidiary goes first to meet the bank's customer obligations, such as deposits and derivatives. Only after these have been met in full can the bank subsidiary pay interest (on intermediate debt or T2 capital), pay dividends, or make distributions.

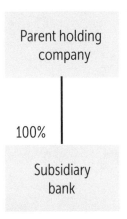

Parent holding company is an ordinary business corporation

Figure 6.5. Unit Bank with Parent Holding Company

Source: Thomas F. Huertas, *Safe to Fail: How Resolution Will Revolutionise Banking* (London: Palgrave MacMillan, 2014)

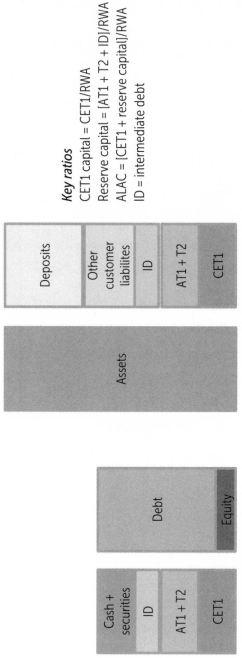

Key ratios
CET1 capital = CET1/RWA
Reserve capital = [AT1 + T2 + ID]/RWA
ALAC = [CET1 + reserve capital]/RWA
ID = intermediate debt

Parent holding company only

Cash + securities		Debt
ID		
AT1 + T2		
CET1		Equity

Bank subsidiary

Assets	Deposits
	Other customer liabilites
	ID
	AT1 + T2
	CET1

Figure 6.6. Parent Holding Company/Bank Sub: Balance Sheet Overview

Source: Thomas F. Huertas, *Safe to Fail: How Resolution Will Revolutionise Banking* (London: Palgrave MacMillan, 2014)

At the subsidiary bank, we assume that the bank conducts a full range of permissible banking activities (including securities trading, and derivatives) and that the bank has a standard balance sheet, with four significant exceptions:

1. The bank subsidiary may not invest in any obligation issued by the parent.

2. The subsidiary bank may not enter into contracts with cross-default clauses to the parent holding company. If the parent holding company defaults on its obligations to third-party investors, this shall not constitute an event of default for the subsidiary bank.[15]

3. The obligations of the bank subsidiary to its parent holding company are subordinated to the bank's obligations to third parties. This includes any payments due to the parent company under service contracts.

4. The bank subsidiary shall be subject to a requirement that it issue reserve capital in the same manner as described above for a unit bank. To satisfy this requirement, the bank subsidiary must issue reserve capital instruments to the parent holding company and the parent holding company must hold such reserve capital. Such instruments issued to the parent holding company are also subject to bail-in as a matter of contract between the parent holding company and the bank subsidiary. This contract shall be fully disclosed to supervisors of the bank and the parent holding company as well as to the creditors of the bank and of the parent holding company. As noted above, the bank subsidiary may pay interest and amortization on its reserve capital instruments, if and only if the bank has met its customer obligations on time and in full. Thus, cash flows like a waterfall, first to the holders of customer obligations at the bank level, and only then to the parent holding company as investor in the bank's reserve capital instruments and CET1 capital.

---

15. The ISDA (2014) Resolution Stay Protocol applies this principle on a temporary basis with respect to derivatives contracts.

We now examine the impact of varying levels of loss at the bank subsidiary (see table 6.1) and trace through the implications for recovery and resolution at the bank subsidiary, taking into account the bail-in/conversion of the reserve capital at the bank level into CET1 capital that would occur upon the subsidiary bank reaching the PONV/entering resolution.[16] We also trace the implications of losses at the bank level for the parent holding company.

We start with the case where the parent holding company's assets consist of marketable securities (50) as well as investments in and claims on its daughter bank subsidiary (CET1 capital [100], T2 capital [50], and intermediate debt [50]). These total assets of 250 are financed by third-party investors in the form of CET1 capital (100), T2 capital (50), and senior debt (100).

Now assume that the loan portfolio in the subsidiary bank has to be written down by 50 so that the CET1 capital of the bank subsidiary is reduced by 50. This in turn leads to a reduction of the same magnitude in the parent holding company's equity, or CET1 capital (see columns labelled "L" in table 1). In effect, losses at the subsidiary bank are borne by investors in the parent holding company's obligations.

To restore its equity to the prior level, the parent holding company bails-in the T2 and senior debt that it has issued to third-party investors. In a manner similar to that depicted in figure 6.4, the parent company converts 50 of T2 into CET1 capital (restoring this to 100) and converts 50 of senior debt into 50 of T2 capital (see columns headed "BP" in table 6.1).

But bail-in at the parent does not affect the balance sheet of the subsidiary bank (see table 6.1). The recapitalization of the parent has no impact whatsoever on the level of CET1 capital in the bank subsidiary. To recapitalize the bank subsidiary, it is necessary either to inject new equity into the bank subsidiary or to bail-in (via write-down or conversion) the bank subsidiary's reserve capital.

---

16. Alternatively, the bank itself may initiate the bail-in conversion at the bank level possibly upon demand by parent holding company creditors with longer remaining maturities who are time-subordinated to creditors with short remaining maturities. This would defer and possibly avoid resolution.

Table 6.1. Bail-in at Parent Does Not Recapitalize the Subsidiary Bank

Assets	I	L	BP	BB	Liabilities	I	L	BP	BB
Parent holding company only									
CET1 in bank sub	100	50	50		CET1	100	50	100	
Sub debt (T2) in sub	50	50	50		AT1	0	0	0	
Intermediate debt in sub	50	50	50		T2	50	50	50	
Marketable securities	50	50	50		Senior debt	100	100	50	
Total	250	200	200		Total	250	200	200	
Bank subsidiary									
Loans	1000	950	950		CET 1	100	50	50	
Investments	1000	1000	1000		Sub debt (T2) [AT1 = 0]	50	50	50	
					Intermediate debt	50	50	50	
					Other customer obligations	900	900	900	
					Deposits	900	900	900	
Total	2000	1950	1950		Total	2000	1950	1950	

Notes: I = initial condition; L = loss (50) in bank sub; BP = bail-in at parent; BB = bail-in at bank

To inject new equity into the bank subsidiary, the parent holding company would have to have recourse to other resources, such as cash or marketable securities. Note that the bail-in at the parent level cannot be the source of that cash, as the write-down or conversion of the parent's T2 capital and senior debt affects only the liability side of the parent-only balance sheet. It creates neither new cash nor new investments in marketable securities.

Consequently, if the parent holding company's cash and marketable securities are to be the source of funds for the recapitalization of the subsidiary bank, the parent will have had to take steps to assure that:

- The cash would in fact be available, when the bank subsidiary reached the PONV/entered resolution.
- The cash would indeed be used to recapitalize the failed bank subsidiary.

To assure that the cash and marketable securities would in fact be available at the PONV, the parent could place them into a segregated account pending the entry of the subsidiary bank into resolution. To assure that such cash would actually be used to recapitalize the subsidiary bank, a mechanism would have to be put in place to force the parent to make such an investment. This could, for example, take the form of an option that gives the bank subsidiary the right to sell (put) new CET1 capital to the parent holding and requires the parent holding to use the cash and marketable securities in the segregated account to buy the CET1 capital put to it by the subsidiary bank.

Conceptually, the parent could also raise new capital from third-party investors. However, such capital-raising will generally take time (unless the parent holding company has prearranged a contingent underwriting commitment from third-party investors) and will in any event depend on the condition of, and the prospects for, the bank subsidiary. Indeed, in the case outlined here, payments from the bank subsidiary (interest on debt, dividends, and distributions, plus any payments for services) are the primary and perhaps the only source of cash flow to the parent company.

Similarly, for bail-in to recapitalize the failed bank subsidiary, there must be enough reserve capital available (see discussion under "unit bank" above) and regulation must permit the resolution authority to execute this in a timely manner. This is most likely to be the case where the statutory provisions for bail-in are reinforced via the contract(s) governing the investment of the parent holding company in the reserve capital (AT1, T2, and intermediate debt) of the bank subsidiary.

In terms of our example, bail-in at the subsidiary bank (see column BB in table 6.2) converts 50 of T2 capital into CET1 capital at the subsidiary bank and 50 of intermediate debt into T2 capital. At the parent level, nothing changes on the liability side; all that changes is the composition of the asset side of the balance sheet, with the amount of CET1 capital rising from 50 to 100 and the amount of intermediate debt falling from 50 to zero.

This example brings out a number of issues. First, what counts in a resolution scenario is the asset side of the parent holding company's balance sheet, not in the first instance the capital structure of the parent holding company. If the parent holding company has endowed the bank subsidiary with reserve capital, the write-down or conversion of some or all of these instruments into CET1 capital is the source of strength that the parent has supplied in advance to the bank and upon which the bank can immediately and unequivocally draw. In contrast, the liability side of the parent only balance sheet cannot act as an immediate source of strength to the subsidiary bank (see above).

Second, the customer obligations of the operating bank subsidiary such as deposits and derivatives are considerably safer than the debt of the parent holding company. They have a much lower probability of default. The income of the bank goes first to service the claims of third-party creditors of the bank. Moreover, the rapid bail-in via write-off or conversion of the bank's reserve capital into CET1 capital (if the bank enters resolution) assures that deposits at the bank level enjoy what amounts to double protection (the bank's CET1 capital plus the bank's reserve capital or in total the amount of ALAC). Customers will only incur losses on their claims on the bank (e.g., via deposits or derivatives) if the losses at the bank level exceed the bank's ALAC and such claims are uncollateralized and uninsured.

Table 6.2. Bail-in at Subsidiary Bank Recapitalizes the Subsidiary Bank

Assets	I	L	BP	BB	Liabilities	I	L	BP	BB
Parent holding company only									
CET1 in bank sub	100	50	50	100	CET1	100	50	100	100
Sub debt (T2) in sub	50	50	50	50	AT1	0	0	0	0
Intermediate debt in sub	50	50	50	0	T2	50	50	50	50
Marketable securities	50	50	50	50	Senior debt	100	100	50	50
Total	250	200	200	200	Total	250	200	200	200
Bank subsidiary									
Loans	1000	950	950	950	CET 1	100	50	50	100
Investments	1000	1000	1000	1000	Sub debt (T2) [AT1 = 0]	50	50	50	50
					Intermediate debt	50	50	50	0
					Other customer obligations	900	900	900	900
					Deposits	900	900	900	900
Total	2000	1950	1950	1950	Total	2000	1950	1950	1950

Notes: I = initial condition; L = loss (50) in bank sub; BP = bail-in at parent; BB = bail-in at bank

In contrast, the parent receives cash flow from the subsidiary only if the subsidiary meets minimum requirements for CET1 and reserve capital. Consequently, the parent holding company has a much higher probability of default than the bank subsidiary and a much higher expected loss (see figure 6.7). For high levels of ALAC, the credit rating of customer obligations (e.g., deposits and derivatives) at the bank level will approach the AAAA standard that customers ideally want from their banks.[17]

Resolution of the Parent

A third issue concerns resolution at the parent and the degree to which this can be conducted using ordinary bankruptcy proceedings. Losses at the bank subsidiary directly reduce the equity of the parent holding company. If the losses are great enough, the parent holding company may not be able to service its debt to third parties in a timely fashion or it may become balance-sheet insolvent, so that the parent holding company has to enter some type of resolution proceedings.

Indeed, that threat is the whole point of the parent company superstructure and the attendant structural subordination of parent company debt to debt at the bank level. Such a superstructure effectively preserves the bank as a going concern for any loss less than the bank's ALAC and it forces parent company shareholders and creditors to absorb very significant amounts of first loss at the bank level (i.e., the total of the bank subsidiary's ALAC) before third-party creditors at the bank level would be called upon to bear loss.

Consequently, clarifying the process of resolution at the parent, including the rights of creditors during that process, is essential if investors in holding company debt are to understand the risks to which they would be exposed. Note that the clarification must cover cases where:

---

17. Merton and Perold (1993) make the point that customers acquire certain claims on banks in order to obtain a particular service (e.g., protection against a specific risk in the case of derivatives, or the ability to execute payments in the case of transaction accounts). Ideally, the bank should always be in a condition to provide the service in question. Counterparty risk should not be an issue—hence the reference to the AAAA standard.

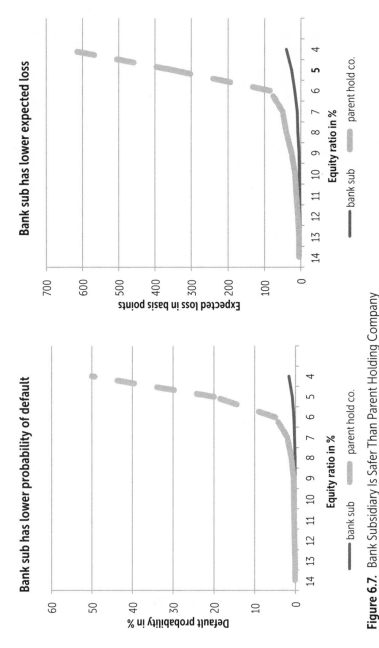

Figure 6.7. Bank Subsidiary Is Safer Than Parent Holding Company

Source: Thomas F. Huertas, *Safe to Fail: How Resolution Will Revolutionise Banking* (London: Palgrave MacMillan, 2014)

- The bank subsidiary has not entered resolution and continues to fulfill minimum capital and liquidity requirements.
- The bank subsidiary has entered resolution, but has become—as a result of the bail-in/conversion of the bank's reserve capital into CET1 capital—stabilized and is able to continue in operation while under administration of the resolution authority in the manner described above for a unit bank.[18]

The question is how resolution should proceed at the parent level and whether the proceeding at the parent level will adversely impact the ability of the bank subsidiary to continue operations.

The simple form of the parent—a pure holding company whose activities and assets are restricted to investments in the bank subsidiary plus holdings of cash and marketable securities—allows a very simple "pre-pack" restructuring process to be used (see figure 6.8).[19] This should be incorporated into the parent holding company's debt contracts and has two steps.

The first step is the creation of a solvent entity, Newco, that becomes the immediate parent of the subsidiary bank. Initially, at least, Newco is 100 percent equity financed. This equity represents the collective claims of the creditors of Oldco on the assets of the failed holding company. Newco's strong capital structure facilitates the ability of the bank subsidiary to meet regulatory requirements as well as satisfy concerns of creditors and supervisors of the bank subsidiary that the owner of the bank be in good financial condition. This lessens the danger of contagion, namely that the bankruptcy of the parent would infect the bank subsidiary.

---

18. Indeed, the parent holding company will almost certainly default on its obligations—almost regardless of its liability structure—as soon as the cash flow from the bank subsidiary is cut off, unless the parent has alternative sources of cash, such as investments in marketable securities.

19. This is essentially the approach advanced by Jackson (2015). This builds on an earlier proposal by the Bipartisan Policy Committee (Bovenzi, Guynn, and Jackson 2013) and is similar to the single-point-of-entry approach advanced by the FDIC (2013).

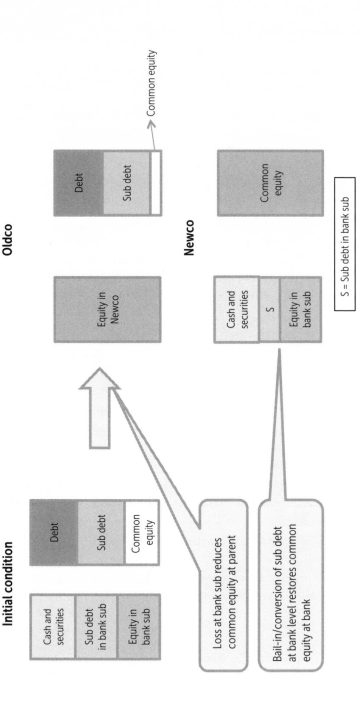

Figure 6.8. Resolution of Parent

Source: Thomas F. Huertas, *Safe to Fail: How Resolution Will Revolutionise Banking* (London: Palgrave MacMillan, 2014)

To create Newco, the estate of the parent in restructuring (Oldco) contributes its assets (investments in and advances to the bank subsidiary plus any remaining cash and marketable securities) to Newco in exchange for equity in Newco.

The second step is introduction of a stay on payments to creditors and investors in Oldco until such time as Oldco receives proceeds from Newco. Oldco's income is restricted to any dividends and distributions that Newco may make to Oldco over time, and Oldco is obligated to pass these payments onto creditors and investors according to strict priority.

There remain the questions of (i) who should exercise the decision rights over Newco (act as administrator) and therefore have decision rights over its bank subsidiary and (ii) what rights the creditors of Oldco should have during the restructuring process.

Take first the case where the parent holding enters resolution before the bank reaches the PONV/enters resolution. As noted above, this could happen as soon as the parent holding company stops receiving dividends and distributions from the subsidiary bank—an event that could happen, once losses at the bank start to deplete the bank's capital conservation buffer.[20]

In this case, there is no basis for putting the bank into resolution. The parent holding company should go into resolution, not necessarily the subsidiary bank. From the standpoint of bank regulation, this amounts, not to resolution, but to a change in control of the parent holding company (from equity owners in the parent holding company to investors in the parent company's debt). Effecting that change in control as promptly and smoothly as possible is the best way to prevent contagion (i.e., prevent the condition of the parent from adversely affecting the subsidiary bank).

In practical terms, the resolution of the parent should be handled via the pre-pack solution outlined above. This effectively transfers

---

20. Note that bail-in at the parent level (via write-down or conversion of debt to equity) may be an effective means for the parent to avoid default while the subsidiary bank continues to meet minimum conditions for authorization.

economic control of the parent holding company (and decision rights over the subsidiary bank) to the creditors of the parent holding company.[21]

---

21. Consideration might also be given to implementing in advance the "pre-pack" solution outlined above. In such a case, the immediate parent of the bank would be 100 percent equity financed. Thus, the parent would remain solvent (and remain outside of resolution proceedings) as long as the loss at the bank subsidiary was less than the bank's ALAC. This minimizes the risk of contagion from the parent to the bank subsidiary. As the owner of the bank, the 100 percent-equity financed parent would be regulated and supervised as a bank (or financial) holding company. However, the owner of the owner need not be so regulated (and indeed is not in cases where the bank is owned by a natural person or a non-financial company). In particular, the 100 percent-equity financed parent could be owned by another company, the "grandparent." The grandparent could potentially be an ordinary business corporation subject to ordinary bankruptcy proceedings. It would not be subject to capital requirements. In effect, there would be a "trade": the addition of a reserve capital requirement at the bank subsidiary level plus a requirement that the bank's immediate parent be 100 per-cent equity financed, in exchange for the removal of capital requirements at the grandparent level.

Under the structure we have outlined, the critical economic functions are exercised at the bank level. Consequently, it is the bank that needs to continue in operation, and the bank that needs to be able to meet its liabilities on an on-going basis. The parent assures that the bank can do this by acting as a source of strength up front via investments in the bank's common equity and reserve capital. By instituting a reserve or "gone concern" capital ratio, the regulator mandates the degree of back-up strength that the parent must provide. In effect, the parent has committed to what amounts to double liability.

The 100 percent-equity finance requirement at the parent level assures that the parent remains solvent until the entire amount of the bank's ALAC is exhausted. This simplifies resolution of the bank subsidiary. As emphasized above, the ability of the parent holding company to act as a source of strength to the bank in reso-lution does not depend on the parent's liability structure. It depends on the asset side of the parent company's balance sheet.

Removing capital regulation at the "grandparent" (this would require legisla-tion in jurisdictions such as the United States) also underlines that public concern is primarily at the bank level—with the safety of deposits, the operation of the pay-ments system, etc.—and secondarily at the parent level (the owner of the bank). Owners of the owner of a bank should be subject to market discipline; arguably, the removal of capital requirements on "grandparents" would underline that such

Creditors would be better placed to guard their interests and exercise their rights if they (or the banking group) were to set up a standing creditors' committee (or empower a trustee) in advance of any entry of the parent into resolution proceedings. Such a standing creditors' committee or trustee would monitor the banking group's condition as well as the group's observance of any covenants contained in the debt that the parent holding company issues to investors, including any provisions for write-down or conversion of parent company debt into parent company equity. The standing creditors' committee (or trustee) would also be empowered to exercise on behalf of creditors any remedies foreseen under the parent holding company's debt contracts, including the right, in the event that the parent defaults, to put the parent (but only the parent) into resolution proceedings.[22]

We now turn to the case where the subsidiary bank has entered resolution. In general, resolution regimes envision that the resolution authority should exercise control over the bank while it is in resolution. This allows the resolution authority to take the decisions necessary to stabilize the bank and assure continuity of essential functions. Such decisions include without limitation the bail-in of reserve capital at the bank level and the arrangement of any necessary liquidity facilities.

What implications should this have for the parent holding company and its creditors? We distinguish between two cases: first, where the resolution statute restricts the resolution authority's mandate to the subsidiary bank; and second, where the resolution statute empowers the resolution authority of the bank to put the parent holding company into resolution as well.

Where the resolution authority's mandate is limited to the subsidiary bank, the parent holding company would be resolved according to the pre-pack solution depicted in figure 8. Newco would own any

---

market discipline would indeed be applied to the investors in holding companies that were the owners of parents of banks.

22. Such arrangements for a standing creditors' committee or trustee might also help assure that the parent holding company discloses information to investors adequate to enable them to assess the risk of investment in holding company debt and capital instruments. For further discussion, see Huertas (2012).

equity in the subsidiary bank that remained after the losses had been written off and Newco's investments in the reserve capital of the subsidiary bank had been bailed in.

However, if the bail-in of the bank's reserve capital were insufficient to restore the subsidiary bank to positive net worth, Newco would no longer have any interest in the failed bank, and no responsibility, under the principle of limited liability, to make additional investments in the failed bank, even if Newco had the resources (such as cash and marketable securities) to enable it to do so. Creditors of the failed bank subsidiary (such as uninsured depositors) would have no right to "pierce the corporate veil" and attach the assets of Newco. From the standpoint of investors in the debt of the parent holding company, there would be a reasonable assurance that their exposure to losses at the subsidiary bank would be limited to the extent of their investment in the subsidiary bank.

It is not clear that such investors would enjoy such assurance in the case where the resolution statute empowers the resolution authority of the subsidiary bank to put the parent holding company into resolution alongside the subsidiary bank. In such a case it would be possible for the resolution authority to order the parent holding company in resolution to utilize other resources (if available) to absorb losses in the failed subsidiary bank in excess of the parent holding company's original investment in the equity and reserve capital of the bank subsidiary.[23]

Creditors of the parent holding company (Oldco), who are the shareholders in Newco, have very limited rights while the bank is in resolution. Instead, they are protected ex post by the "no creditor worse off" than under liquidation (NCWOL) clause. Should the

---

23. Although debt investors would enjoy protection under the NCWOL provision, they would have to bring, prove, and win such a case before they could receive compensation. This may be particularly difficult in the United States, as section 616 of the Dodd-Frank Act codifies the obligation of parent holding companies to act as a source of strength to domestic insured depository institutions. Note that this source-of-strength obligation does not necessarily extend to foreign subsidiaries—an additional reason why host country authorities would want to see parent holding companies inject reserve capital into such entities up front.

creditors in fact fare worse under resolution, they have a claim for compensation for the difference.[24]

This allocation of rights may be quite appropriate for situations where the bail-in of reserve capital fails to stabilize the bank (return the bank to compliance with minimum conditions for authorization). However, where the bail-in of reserve capital has stabilized the bank subsidiary (and thereby enabled it to meet again the minimum conditions for authorization), consideration might be given to granting the creditors of Oldco/shareholders of Newco[25] certain rights with respect to major decisions, such as the sale of the business to a third party. These might include the right of first refusal (right to match the third party's bid) and the right to bid in terms of debt forgiveness rather than be required to raise fresh cash to support their bid. Oldco creditors could also receive the right to present a reorganization plan for the parent holding company. Decisions taken by creditors would be by class, with the ability of a supermajority (e.g., 90 percent) to "cram down" its decision (force acceptance by the rest of the creditors in that class). Additionally, the creditors of a junior class could receive the right to buy out the claims of the next most immediately senior class at par plus accrued interest (see table 6.3).

Linking creditors' rights in a parent company bankruptcy to condition of the bank subsidiary after bail-in aligns the rights of the parent holding company creditors with the degree of strength that the parent has given the bank subsidiary up front. If the bail-in of reserve capital is sufficient to restore the bank subsidiary's ability to meet threshold conditions, the creditors of the parent holding should effectively have some say over the disposition of the bank subsidiary. If, however, the bank subsidiary fails to meet the minimum conditions for

---

24. The resolution regime should spell out how such a claim would be calculated/established and who would be responsible for paying such a claim. Note that the latter is often left unclear in resolution statutes.

25. Note that the shareholders in Oldco (the original parent) have no rights in resolution (even though resolution may have been initiated at a point where the bank had positive net worth). Although shareholders may receive warrants in recognition of their economic interest, they have no voting or control rights in the resolution/restructuring process.

Table 6.3. Decision Rights during Resolution Process

	Sub bank meets MC after bail-in		Sub bank fails MC after bail-in	
	Parent solvent	Parent in resolution	Parent solvent	Parent in resolution
a. Right to run subsidiary bank	Oldco equity	Resolution authority pending approval of (d)	Resolution authority	Resolution authority
b. Right of first refusal on sales	n.a.	Oldco creditors	Resolution authority	Resolution authority
c. Bid via debt forgiveness	n.a.	Oldco creditors	Resolution authority	Resolution authority
d. Right to present reorganization plan	n.a.	Oldco creditors	Resolution authority	Resolution authority
e. Safeguard	n.a.	NCWOL	NCWOL	NCWOL

Notes: MC = minimum conditions for authorization; NCOWL = no creditor worse off than under liquidation

Source: Thomas F. Huertas, *Safe to Fail: How Resolution Will Revolutionise Banking* (London: Palgrave MacMillan, 2014)

authorization even after the bail-in/conversion of the subordinated debt into CET1 capital, the parent company has either elected or been forced to walk away from the bank subsidiary and the decision rights over Newco should fall entirely to the resolution authority for the bank.

Finally, some consideration should be given to the question of double leverage (the ratio of CET1 capital at the bank subsidiary to CET1 capital at the parent holding company). For ratios greater than one, the parent holding company has effectively borrowed money from third-party investors and down-streamed the proceeds into the bank subsidiary as CET1 capital. This makes the bank subsidiary less likely to fail (than would be the case if its CET1 capital were limited to the amount of the parent's CET1 capital). Although double leverage increases the risk of debt at the parent holding company, in a world where resolution at the parent works smoothly, double leverage becomes a secondary consideration (as parent company debt effectively bears loss). Thus, from a public policy standpoint the far more relevant leverage ratio for the group as a whole is the ratio of ALAC to the total assets of the group.

Parent Holding Company with Domestic and Foreign Subsidiaries

We now turn to the case where the parent holding company has two subsidiaries, one in the same jurisdiction as the parent (the domestic bank) and one in a foreign or host-country jurisdiction (see figure 6.9). This introduces issues of (i) interaction and possible conflict between the laws of the home and host countries as well as (ii) coordination and cooperation between home and host authorities.

The resolution statutes in the respective countries set the framework—and pose the potential for conflict. Generally, the resolution statute mandates domestic authorities to act to promote financial stability in the domestic jurisdiction. This is the overriding objective, even if the statute mandates the domestic authorities to cooperate with their foreign counterparts.

Two approaches are under discussion. Under the first, single-point-of-entry (SPE) approach, resolution is a unified, global process

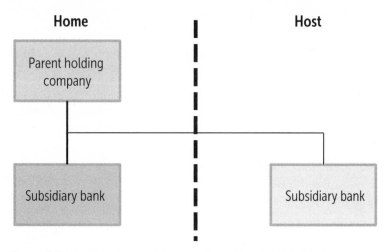

Figure 6.9. Banking Group with Domestic and Foreign Subsidiaries
Source: Thomas F. Huertas, *Safe to Fail: How Resolution Will Revolutionise Banking*
(London: Palgrave MacMillan, 2014)

under the aegis of the home country resolution authority. Under the SPE approach, the failure of one or more subsidiaries to meet minimum conditions for authorization triggers resolution of the group as a whole. The home country resolution authority takes control of the parent holding company and acts to recapitalize the failing bank(s). This stabilizes the banks in the group and the group as a whole, and serves as the basis for the provision of a liquidity facility (see below), so that "subsidiaries would remain open and continue operations."[26] The SPE approach therefore assures continuity and removes any need for the taxpayer to provide solvency support.

Under the second, multiple-point-of-entry (MPE) approach, subsidiaries are resolved separately within each jurisdiction. If a subsidiary bank reaches the PONV/enters resolution, the resolution authority for that subsidiary resolves it, while the rest of the group continues in operation. In effect, the MPE approach follows the principle of limited liability and allows the parent holding company to walk away from a failing subsidiary.

26. See FDIC (2013).

Who should make the choice between the two approaches, and when should the choice be made? Should the choice be left entirely to resolution authorities, and entirely until resolution is initiated? That would be consistent with a long-standing bias among policymakers, particularly central banks, in favor of "constructive ambiguity." But this doctrine refers to the creation of doubt as to whether there will or will not be a bailout.

What bail-in requires is "constructive certainty"—a method to assure that markets know that investors, not taxpayers, will bear the cost of bank failure. Although the authorities may prefer ambiguity, for it enables them to retain the option to decide based on the facts of a specific resolution case, more certainty as to the path the authorities would actually take is likely to enhance resolvability. Policymakers and firms need to map out in advance how an institution is likely to be resolved, and take steps—such as the institution-specific cooperation agreements advocated by the Financial Stability Board (FSB)—to anchor these commitments into what might be called a presumptive path.[27] Not only will such a presumptive path underline that holders of investor obligations will indeed be exposed to loss, but it will enable investors in such instruments to form a better idea of the losses that they could incur if resolution were required. That in turn will facilitate the sale of such instruments to investors and facilitate resolvability.

Today, no such certainty exists as to the presumptive path the authorities might follow. A firm can express a preference for resolution under an SPE approach, but there is no assurance that resolution authorities will respect or implement this choice. Alternatively, a firm can express a preference for an MPE approach, but there is no assurance that the resolution authorities will respect or implement this choice. There is a gap between theory and reality. In theory, all subsidiaries are equal. In practice, they are not. The bank subsidiary headquartered in the same jurisdiction as the parent holding company

---

27. There is also a timing consideration in favour of ex ante cooperation agreements. Waiting until resolution is initiated to start negotiation of international cooperation is impractical and raises the likelihood that resolution will result either in a bailout or in disorderly liquidation.

is plainly, in the eyes of the home country regulator, *primus inter pares*. This poses challenges to both the SPE and MPE approaches. Confronting those challenges holds the key to creating constructive certainty.

Single Point of Entry

The SPE approach is viable if, and only if, (i) the home country resolution authority is authorized, able, and willing to assume command of what amounts to a global resolution syndicate and (ii) the host countries are willing to accept such leadership by the home country resolution authority (see figure 6.10).

For the SPE approach to work, the home country resolution statute must authorize the home country resolution authority to take control of the parent holding company upon (i) the failure of the group to meet minimum conditions for authorization on a consolidated basis, or (ii) in the event that a subsidiary bank fails to meet minimum conditions and is placed into resolution.[28] However, seizing the parent due to losses at the subsidiary raises significant issues with respect to property rights, so that the authorization to take control of the holding company may be (i) subject to prior approval by the central bank, finance ministry, and/or head of government; (ii) restricted to certain resolution techniques, such as temporary public ownership, that involve the use of taxpayer funds (iii); and/or restricted to cases where the failing bank is headquartered in the home country.[29]

---

28. Note that the subsidiary bank in question must generally be a domestic subsidiary bank. There is no provision for the resolution authority of a host country subsidiary bank to put the parent holding company in the home jurisdiction into resolution, much less for the host country resolution authority to take responsibility for the resolution of the group.

29. In the United States, for example, the FDIC may employ the Orderly Liquidation Authority (the basis for the SPE approach) if—and only if—it can demonstrate that resolution under normal bankruptcy procedures (as called for under Title I) would be harmful to financial stability in the United States and this decision has the prior approval of the FDIC itself (two-thirds of its Board), the Board of Governors of the Federal Reserve System (with two-thirds majority), and the secretary of the treasury "in consultation with the President."

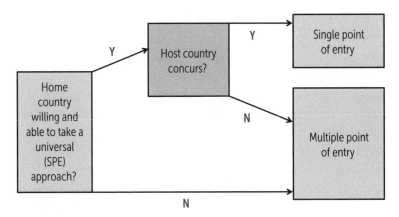

Figure 6.10. SPE Approach Demands Concurrence of Home and Host
Source: Thomas F. Huertas, *Safe to Fail: How Resolution Will Revolutionise Banking*
(London: Palgrave MacMillan, 2014)

From the standpoint of the host country authorities responsible for the home country's subsidiary in the host jurisdiction, this situation is not entirely satisfactory, as there is no guarantee the home country resolution authority can actually assume the role intended for it and assigned to it under the SPE approach. Not only does the home country resolution authority have to pass a test before it can implement the SPE approach, but the grades for that test are generally based on the impact that the failure of the global systemically important bank (G-SIB) would have on financial stability in the home country only. Hence, from the vantage point of the host country authorities, it is unclear that the home country resolution authorities could always implement the SPE path, particularly if the losses prompting the entry into resolution were concentrated in the group's foreign subsidiaries.

For this reason, it will be entirely rational for host countries to require—if they are to concur with the SPE approach—some greater assurance that the home country will actually implement the SPE approach regardless of the source of the loss and that the SPE approach will actually result in the stabilization of the subsidiary in the host country. Failing such reassurance, it is natural to expect host authorities to take measures to protect the creditors of the subsidiaries located within their jurisdictions.

Multiple Point of Entry

The central premise of the MPE approach is that resolution can take place at the level of each individual subsidiary according to the rules and procedures of that jurisdiction. For this to be the case, each of the subsidiaries should be self-sufficient, with separate funding and no inter-affiliate transactions. In particular, the bank subsidiaries should not invest in instruments issued by the parent holding company; should not hold cash balances with other entities within the group; and should refrain from using affiliates for services, such as cash management and/or custody that create a credit exposure to the affiliate. To the extent that the subsidiary obtains services from other affiliates within the group, the services should be provided from a separately capitalized central services subsidiary (rather than from another bank within the group) that can continue to provide services to the subsidiary in resolution for a transition period. In other words, each bank subsidiary should be handled in the manner outlined for a unit bank at the start of this paper.

Under the MPE approach, there is a premise that the holding company can walk away from a subsidiary in country A where losses have exhausted its equity investment in that subsidiary. But the terms on which this could occur need to be spelled out. First, is each bank subsidiary within an MPE group required to issue a minimum amount of reserve capital (see "unit bank" above)? Second, to the extent that a bank within an MPE group sells reserve capital instruments to third parties, is there a robust resolution process by which the holders of such instruments as a class can take control of the subsidiary bank-in-resolution? In particular, will the subsidiary bank be resolved on the unitary principle or the territorial principle (if the latter, the resolution process will in all likelihood result in liquidation rather than continuity—see above). Third, will all resolution authorities in the jurisdictions in which an MPE group does business confirm that they will not exercise what amounts to a cross-resolution provision, whereby country B takes the entry into resolution of the group's subsidiary in country A to put the group's subsidiary in country B into resolution and sell this subsidiary to a third party at a knock-down price?

Fourth, is the home country also willing to have the MPE process apply to the group's domestic bank, so that the parent could keep healthy foreign subsidiaries while limiting its liability for losses at the domestic bank to the amount of its investment? It is doubtful that this would be the case, especially where the domestic bank is systemically important in the domestic market and legislation in the home country allows the resolution authority to take control of the parent holding company upon entry of the domestic bank into resolution. Even though the owners of the parent holding may conclude that it would be economically rational for them to walk away from the domestic bank, the economics for the home resolution authority point in the direction of exercising its option to take over the holding company, employ a single-point-of-entry approach, provide a continuity guarantee to host countries with respect to the group's subsidiaries in the host country, and use proceeds from the sale of the group's healthy foreign subsidiaries to reduce losses to creditors of the domestic subsidiary bank.

This brings us full circle. Although the SPE approach is likely to be most effective from a global standpoint in terms of preserving financial stability, political pressures in the home country (as well as the terms of the home country legislation) may lead to the impression that the home country wishes to have the option to implement an SPE approach when the losses have occurred at the domestic bank subsidiary, but reserve the right to resort to an MPE approach when the losses are at the foreign subsidiary. To defend against this possibility, host countries will potentially want to ring-fence their bank up front, demand significant infusions of capital up front, and restrict inter-affiliate transactions.[30]

---

30. Recent policy proposals by the United States illustrate the differing perspectives of home and host. As home, the United States (FDIC 2013) advocates the SPE approach for US-headquartered institutions and proposes that the FDIC act as a global resolution authority in a manner that will assure that subsidiaries "remain open and continue operations." As host, the United States (FRB 2014) has expressed doubt regarding the ability of foreign banking organizations (FBOs) "to provide support to all parts of its organization." For this reason, the Federal Reserve Board, as the principal host regulator of FBOs in the United States, has

Constructive Certainty

Fragmentation is likely to be the end result. This will diminish efficiency without necessarily improving resolvability. What is needed is a presumptive path—call it constructive certainty—that both home and host authorities can follow.

One possible approach is a hybrid between the SPE and MPE approaches. This would be driven by who holds the reserve capital that all bank subsidiaries would be required to issue: the parent holding company or third-party investors. It is based on putting and keeping a certain amount of strength (either from the parent holding company or third-party investors) up front into the subsidiary banks within a group, rather than requiring the parent holding company to act as a source of strength after the subsidiary bank has failed.

For all groups designated as G-SIBs, this would entail the following steps:

1. Each bank subsidiary within a group must issue and keep outstanding reserve capital greater than or equal to the threshold level required for that bank under [3] or [4]. Such reserve capital shall be mandatorily convertible into CET1 capital in the bank immediately upon entry of the bank subsidiary into resolution.
2. The parent holding company may not pay dividends or make distributions unless all the group's bank subsidiaries—both domestic and foreign—meet both (i) their minimum CET1 capital requirement (7 percent of RWAs including the capital conservation buffer) and (ii) the reserve capital requirement outlined in [3] or [4].
3. Where the parent holding company does not own 100 percent of the reserve capital issued by the bank subsidiary,

---

imposed a rule requiring FBOs to establish intermediate holding companies that meet US standards. In the view of the Federal Reserve, this "reduces the need for an FBO to contribute additional capital and liquidity to its U.S. operations during times of home country or other international stresses, thereby reducing the likelihood that a banking organization that comes under stress in multiple jurisdictions will be required to choose which of its operations to support."

a. The threshold amount of reserve capital at the bank subsidiary shall be equal to the minimum required CET1 capital ratio (including capital conservation buffer) *plus* the SIFI surcharge. The terms and conditions for the conversion of such reserve capital into CET1 capital in the bank shall be established in advance, including the process by which the holders of such debt as a class could assume control of the subsidiary bank-in-resolution.[31]

b. The bank subsidiary shall fulfill what might be called an independence requirement so that the bank subsidiary could continue in operation, even if the parent holding company and/or a sister affiliate were to enter resolution. This independence requirement would include strict limits on inter-affiliate transactions. To the extent that the bank subsidiary obtained services from the rest of the group, contracts for such services should assure that such services could continue to be provided to the bank subsidiary for an extended transition period in the event that the bank subsidiary entered resolution, notwithstanding the possibility that such a subsidiary could cease to be part of the group.[32]

4. Where the parent holding company owns 100 percent of the reserve capital issued by the bank subsidiary,

a. The threshold amount of reserve capital at the bank subsidiary shall be equal to the minimum required CET1 capital ratio (i.e., 7 percent, including capital conservation buffer). The

---

31. In particular, such a process shall make clear that the original parent holding company has no claim on the subsidiary bank-in-resolution, but mandate that the original parent holding company provide a warranty and indemnity to the restructured bank-in-resolution for liabilities relating to misconduct at the subsidiary bank-in-resolution prior to the entry of the subsidiary bank into resolution.

32. To fulfill such an independence requirement, the banking group may find it advantageous to form a separately capitalized services subsidiary (OpCo) that is bankruptcy-remote from the entry of either the bank subsidiary or the parent holding company/sister affiliate. This would assure continuity of services to the subsidiary bank, even if the parent holding company or a sister affiliate entered resolution.

bank subsidiary shall be prohibited from paying interest and dividends or making distributions to the parent holding company unless the reserve capital issued to and held by the parent exceeds the threshold amount. Should the bank subsidiary not be permitted to pay interest in cash to the parent holding, it shall pay interest in kind (e.g., if the bank cannot pay interest on its T2 capital, the bank shall issue additional T2 capital to the parent on the same terms and conditions as the previous T2 capital in an amount equal to the interest payable).

b. Should such in-kind payments be insufficient to restore the reserve capital to the threshold 7 percent level, the subsidiary bank shall have the right to sell additional reserve capital to the parent holding company and the parent holding company shall have the obligation to subscribe to such capital. To help assure that the parent holding can meet such commitments, the parent holding shall maintain a reserve of cash and marketable securities at the parent level equal to the SIFI surcharge for the group as a whole on a consolidated basis.

Together, these measures would go a very long way to assure that each of the group's bank subsidiaries—domestic or foreign—could be recapitalized in the event that the subsidiary in question failed to meet minimum conditions for authorization. Moreover, the measures go a long way to establishing a presumptive path for resolution. Finally, the measures should help assure host country authorities that the subsidiary in their country could be resolved without recourse to their taxpayer and without significant disruption to their economy.

The Provision of Liquidity to the Bank in Resolution

As outlined above, recapitalization is necessary but insufficient to stabilize the bank-in-resolution. In addition to fresh capital, the bank-in-resolution will need access to liquidity. This will be especially true for G-SIBs. If a G-SIB were to enter resolution, it would in all likelihood require very significant amounts of liquidity, starting immediately upon the opening of business in Asia.

The bail-in/conversion of reserve capital creates the basis for such a provision of liquidity, for it assures that the "bank-in-resolution" remains solvent for any loss that is less than the ALAC of the bank. However, in addition to being solvent, the bank-in-resolution also has to have unencumbered assets that it can pledge as collateral to the liquidity provider. To prepare for such an eventuality, the bank should prepare and maintain what might be called a collateral budget that tracks the bank's unencumbered assets so that they can be readily pledged, if required during resolution, to the central bank or private lenders.[33]

For banking groups with domestic and foreign subsidiaries, it makes sense to think through in advance the arrangements that would be made to provide liquidity to the banks within the group, should one or more bank subsidiaries in the group reach the PONV and enter resolution. It would seem sensible to align the approach to liquidity provision to the overall (MPE or SPE) approach to resolution.

Under the MPE approach, the liquidity facility to each subsidiary would be based solely on that subsidiary's collateral as pledged to that bank's resolution authority/central bank as lender. In making this loan, the local resolution authority/central bank would act as principal and keep the home country (group) resolution authority/central bank informed that it had made the loan. Should the subsidiary bank fail to repay the credit and the collateral prove insufficient to extinguish the bank's obligations to the liquidity provider, the lender would have recourse against that subsidiary only and no claim on either the parent holding company or other subsidiaries within the group.

Under the SPE approach, it would potentially be advantageous for the home country resolution authority/central bank to arrange a global liquidity facility for the group as a whole. This would effectively

---

33. Proposed liquidity regulation (BCBS 2014) would in fact require banks to track unencumbered assets. The "collateral budget" (Huertas 2014a, p. 100) would take this a step further and look at sources (including borrowing of collateral) and prospective uses (including possible demands for the bank to post additional collateral, if the bank were to be downgraded). Such an analysis would help the bank and the supervisor/resolution authority estimate the amount and type of collateral that might be available to the bank-in-resolution.

allow collateral to be pooled across the group and funds to flow to the point at which they were most needed within the group. In practical terms, the global liquidity provider would take a fixed and floating charge over the parent holding company's assets as well as over any unencumbered assets that the subsidiary might currently have or obtain in the future. To the extent that local resolution authorities/central banks figured in such a facility, it would be as agents of the home resolution authority/central bank.

Other Considerations

Although recapitalization via bail-in of reserve capital and access to liquidity hold the key to making banks resolvable, there are a number of other considerations that the presumptive path should also take into account. These include:

1. Assuring that the bank-in-resolution can continue to obtain essential services, both from other affiliates within the group and from third parties.[34]
2. Assuring that counterparties to the failed bank's qualified financial contracts (e.g., repurchase agreements and derivatives) do not immediately terminate such contracts and liquidate the collateral that the bank-in-resolution had provided.[35]

---

34. This may require amendment of service level agreements and/or contracts with third parties to assure that the service provider continues its services without interruption to the bank-in-resolution. To facilitate this result, it may make sense, particularly where the banking group has multiple subsidiaries, for the group to form a so-called OpCo, or separately capitalized service subsidiary that would contract on behalf of the group with third parties and provide services to the bank subsidiaries within the group. For further details, see Huertas (2014a, 171).

35. Under qualified financial contracts (QFCs), the bank's counterparty is entitled to terminate the contract upon the entry into resolution of either the bank or its parent holding company (if the parent has guaranteed the obligations of the subsidiary bank). Upon termination the bank's counterparty has the right to sell any collateral provided by the bank and to use the proceeds to satisfy its claim on the bank (should the proceeds exceed the claim, the excess is returned to the bank; if the proceeds do not cover the claim, the counterparty has a claim

3. Assuring that the bank-in-resolution retains its authorization to operate as a bank.[36]

4. Assuring that the bank-in-resolution retains access to financial market infrastructures, such as payment systems, securities settlement systems, and central counterparties.[37]

Summary Assessment

In sum, resolving a G-SIB is a complex, multifaceted task. But it is a doable task, on which banks and the authorities have already made much progress.[38] What remains to be done are above all four things:

- Complete the reserve capital/bail-in regime so that banks can be readily recapitalized.
- Complete arrangements for provision of liquidity to the bank in resolution.
- Assure that resolution is not derailed by either derivatives counterparties or financial market infrastructures.

---

on the bank-in-resolution for the deficiency. This arrangement provides no incentive for the bank's counterparty to maximize proceeds from the sale (once the proceeds cover the debt due). Consequently, the so-called haircut (excess of collateral value over debt amount) may be at risk, if the bank's counterparty terminates the QFC.

In the case of derivatives, early termination would also very likely increase the amount due to the bank's counterparty. Under the ISDA master netting agreement underlying most OTC derivative transactions the non-defaulting counterparty has the right to close-out at its replacement cost (this includes the spread that it must pay to the dealer providing the replacement derivative). For further discussion of these points, see Roe (2011) and Huertas (2014a).

36. Formally, the entry into resolution brings about a change in control to the resolution authority and prospectively to the providers of reserve capital to the bank in resolution. Resolution planning should include steps to assure that this does not lead to revocation of the bank's license to operate, especially in foreign jurisdictions where the bank may have branches, subsidiaries, and/or affiliates.

37. For further discussion, see Huertas (2014b). It is also important that financial market infrastructures themselves remain robust. See CSS IOSCO (2013) and Duffie (2015).

38. For an assessment of progress toward resolvability, see Carney (2014) and IIF (2014).

- Conclude cooperation agreements among the G-SIB's supervisors and resolution authorities that create constructive certainty as to how the G-SIB would be resolved.

References

Bank of England. 2014. *The Bank of England's Approach to Resolution,* http://www.bankofengland.co.uk/financialstability/Documents/resolution/apr231014.pdf.

BCBS (Basel Committee on Banking Supervision). 2011a. *Basel Committee Issues Final Elements of the Reforms to Raise the Quality of Regulatory Capital,* http://www.bis.org/press/p110113.pdf.

BCBS (Basel Committee on Banking Supervision). 2011b. *Definition of Capital Disclosure Requirements,* http://www.bis.org/publ/bcbs212.pdf.

BCBS (Basel Committee on Banking Supervision). 2013a. *Liquidity Coverage Ratio Disclosure Standards,* http://www.bis.org/publ/bcbs259.pdf.

BCBS (Basel Committee on Banking Supervision). 2013b. *Revised Basel III Leverage Ratio Framework and Disclosure Requirements,* http://www.bis.org/publ/bcbs251.pdf.

BCBS (Basel Committee on Banking Supervision). 2014. *Basel III: The Net Stable Funding Ratio.* http://www.bis.org/publ/bcbs271.pdf.

Bovenzi, J., R. D. Guynn, and T. H. Jackson. 2013. *Too Big to Fail: The Path to a Solution. A Report of the Failure Resolution Task Force of the Financial Regulatory Reform Initiative of the Bipartisan Policy Center,* http://bipartisanpolicy.org/wp-content/uploads/sites/default/files/TooBigToFail.pdf.

Carney, M. 2014. *Statement before the International Financial and Monetary Committee, International Monetary Fund,* https://www.imf.org/External/AM/2014/imfc/statement/eng/FSB.pdf.

CPSS IOSCO. 2013. Committee on Payments and Securities Settlement Systems and Board of the International Organisation of Securities Commissions: Recovery of Financial Market Infrastructures, http://www.bis.org/publ/cpss109.pdf.

Committee on the Global Financial System. 2013. *Asset Encumbrance, Financial Reform and the Demand for Collateral Assets,*http://www.bis.org/publ/cgfs49.pdf.

Duffie, D. 2015. "Resolution of Failing Central Counterparties," chapter 4 in this volume.

Enhanced Disclosure Task Force. 2013. *Enhancing the Risk Disclosures of Banks (2nd Report),* http://www.financialstabilityboard.org/publications/r_130821b.pdf.

EBA (European Banking Authority). 2014. *Consultation Paper (EBA/CP/ 2014/41). Draft Regulatory Technical Standards on Criteria for Determining the Minimum Requirement for Own Funds and Eligible Liabilities under Directive 2014/59/EU,* http://www.eba.europa.eu/documents/10180/911034 /EBA+CP+2014+41+%28CP+on+draft+RTS+on+MREL%29.pdf.

FDIC (Federal Deposit Insurance Corporation). 2013. *Resolution of Systemically Important Financial Institutions: The Single Point of Entry Strategy,* http:// www.fdic.gov/news/board/2013/2013-12-10_notice_dis-b_fr.pdf.

FRB (Board of Governers of the Federal Reserve System). 2014. *Enhanced Prudential Standards for Bank Holding Companies and Foreign Banking Organizations,* http://www.federalreserve.gov/newsevents/press/bcreg /bcreg20140218a1.pdf.

FSB (Financial Stability Board). 2011a. *Key Attributes of Effective Resolution Regimes for Financial Institutions,* http://www.financialstabilityboard.org /publications/r_111104cc.pdf.

FSB (Financial Stability Board). 2011b. *Effective Resolution of Systemically Importnat Financial institutions: Recommendations and Timelines,* http:// www.financialstabilityboard.org/wp-content/uploads/r_110719.pdf.

FSB (Financial Stability Board). 2013a. *Thematic Review on Resolution Regimes: Peer Review Report.* http://www.financialstabilityboard.org/publications /r_130411a.pdf.

FSB (Financial Stability Board). 2013b. *Progress and Next Steps Towards Ending "Too-Big-To-Fail" (TBTF): Report of the Financial Stability Board to the G-20,* http://www.financialstabilityboard.org/publications/r_130902.pdf.

FSB (Financial Stability Board). 2014. *Adequacy of Loss-Absorbing Capacity Of Global Systemically Important Banks in Resolution. Consultative Document,* http://www.financialstabilityboard.org/wp-content/uploads/TLAC-Condoc -6-Nov-2014-FINAL.pdf.

Huertas, T. F. 2012. *A Race to the Top?* London School of Economics Financial Markets Group Special Paper 208, http://www.lse.ac.uk/fmg/workingPapers /specialPapers/PDF/SP208.pdf.

Huertas, T. F. 2014a. *Safe to Fail: How Resolution Will Revolutionise Banking.* London: Palgrave Macmillan.

Huertas, T. F. 2014b. "Financial Market Infrastructures: Their Critical Role during Recovery and Resolution." *Banking Perspective: The Quarterly Journal of the Clearing House,* 2 (1): 68–75, https://www.theclearinghouse.org/~ /media/Files/Banking%20Perspective/Q1_2014/011-certifying%20continuity .pdf.

IIF (Institute of International Finance). 2011. *Addressing Priority Issues in Cross-Border Resolution,* available at https://www.iif.com/publication /regulatory-report/iif-proposes-approaches-bail-and-resolution-planning.

IIF (Institute of International Finance). 2012. *Making Resolution Robust: Completing the Legal and Instiutional Frameworks for Effective Cross-Border Resolution of Financial Institutions.* Retrieved from hyperlink located at http:// www.iif.com/press/press+259.php.

IIF (Institute of International Finance, Cross-Border Working Group on Resolution). 2014. *Achieving Bank Resolution in Practice: Are We Nearly There Yet?* Retrieved from hyperlink located at http://www.iif.com/regulatory /article+1479.php.

ISDA (International Swaps and Derivatives Association). 2014. *Major Banks Agree to Sign ISDA Resolution Stay Protocol,* http://www2.isda.org/news /major-banks-agree-to-sign-isda-resolution-stay-protocol.

Jackson, T. H. 2015. "Building on Bankruptcy: A Revised Chapter 14 Proposal for the Recapitalization, Reorganization, or Liquidation of Large Financial Institutions," chapter 2 in this volume.

Lee, P. L. 2014. Cross-Border Resolution of Banking Groups: International Initiatives and US Perspectives, Part III. *Pratt's Journal of Bankruptcy Law,* June 2014, 291–335.

Merton, R. C., and A. Perold. 1993. "Theory of Risk Capital in Financial Firms," *Journal of Applied Corporate Finance* 6 (3): 16–32. Reprinted in *Corporate Risk Management,* ed. Donald H. Chew (New York: Columbia Business School, 2008), 131–61.

PRA. 2014. Bank of England Prudential Regulation Authority. *Supervising International Banks: The Prudential Regulation Authority's Approach to Branch Suprvision. Consultation Paper CP4/14,* http://www.bankofengland.co.uk/pra /Documents/publications/policy/2014/branchsupcp4-14.pdf.

Roe, M. 2011. "The Derivatives Market's Payment Priorities as Crisis Accelerator." *Stanford Law Review* 59 (3): 539–90.

Skeel, D. A. 2015. "Financing Systemically Important Financial Institutions in Bankruptcy," chapter 3 in this volume.

Strongin, S. H. 2013. "Does Being More Resolvable Make a Firm More Resilient? It Depends!" Presentation at Federal Reserve Bank of Richmond Conference on Resolution, Washington, D.C., October 18, 2013, https://www .richmondfed.org/conferences_and_events/banking/2013/pdf/resolution _conf_panel_5_strongin_doesbeingmoreresolvable.pdf.

CHAPTER 7

The Next Lehman Bankruptcy

Emily Kapur

Introduction

On Monday, September 15, 2008, Lehman Brothers filed for Chapter 11 bankruptcy and, according to some, "triggered a global financial crisis."[1] On Tuesday, the money market fund Reserve Primary deemed its claims on the Lehman Estate to be worthless and revalued its shares below $1.[2] Within a week, investors withdrew hundreds of billions from money-market funds, most funds in turn curtailed short-term lending, and ordinary corporations that relied on such funding found themselves at risk of failing to meet payroll or restock inventories. Some feared the consumer payment system would freeze.[3] As Federal Reserve Chairman Ben Bernanke later observed, "Of maybe the 13 . . . most important financial institutions in the United States, [all but

Many thanks are due to Tanya Beder, Timothy Bresnahan, John Cornish, Darrell Duffie, Wilson Ervin, Joseph Grundfest, Richard Herring, Thomas Huertas, Paul Kapur, Michael Klausner, William Kroener III, Thomas Jackson, Michael McConnell, Mitchell Polinsky, Steven Ray, David Skeel, Kenneth Scott, Kimberly Summe, John Taylor, and Phillip Warren, as well as participants in the Stanford University Economics PhD Seminar and the Stanford Law School Law and Economics Seminar, all of whom generously spent time with me discussing the issues in this article and offering comments on this and earlier drafts and presentations. All errors are my responsibility.

1. Joseph Checkler and Patrick Fitzgerald, "Lehman to Dole Out Additional $17.9 Billion to Creditors," *Wall Street Journal*, March 27, 2014.

2. Christopher Condon, "Reserve Primary Money Fund Falls Below $1 a Share," *Bloomberg*, September 16, 2008, http://www.bloomberg.com/apps/news?pid=newsarchive&sid=a5O2y1go1GRU.

3. FCIC (Financial Crisis Inquiry Commission), "The Financial Crisis Inquiry Report," 2011, 357–59.

J. P. Morgan] were at risk of failure within a period of a week or two."[4] Meanwhile, depositors began to withdraw deposits from "very, very strong banks," a classic measure of financial panic.[5]

Government interventions eventually halted these cascading runs. But the real economy fell "into an abyss from which it has not yet fully emerged."[6] One study estimates the crisis has cost the United States between $6 trillion and $14 trillion, or up to $120,000 per household.[7]

Scholars debate Lehman's exact responsibility for the crisis, but agree that its bankruptcy imposed immense systemic costs on the economy.[8] Unfortunately, even with much improved financial regulation, the failure of large financial institutions will continue to be a perennial problem. As I describe in part I, financial institutions and their short-term creditors are constantly at risk of falling into a prisoner's-dilemma dynamic that causes creditors to run and financial institutions to fail. These runs can easily spread and become extremely costly. The classic solution to runs on commercial banks has been to insure them, but large non-bank financial institutions like Lehman have never been insured because their creditors are not everyday taxpayers.

As a result, in 2008, there were two available alternatives for a failing firm like Lehman: file for Chapter 11 bankruptcy or be bailed out by the government.[9] Each option was problematic. As Lehman

---

4. Ibid., 354.

5. Ibid., 353–54 (quoting then treasury secretary Timothy Geithner).

6. Eduardo Porter, "Recession's True Cost Is Still Being Tallied," *New York Times*, January 21, 2014.

7. Tyler Atkinson, David Luttrell, and Harvey Rosenblum, "How Bad Was It?" Federal Reserve Bank of Dallas Staff Papers, no. 20, July 2013, 1.

8. Compare, e.g., Gary Becker, "Capitalism's Return from the Financial Crisis," *Becker Posner Blog*, September 16, 2013, http://www.becker-posner-blog.com/2013/09/capitalism-return-from-the-financial-crisis-becker.html, with John B. Taylor, "The Financial Crisis and the Policy Responses: An Empirical Analysis of What Went Wrong" (unpublished manuscript), November 2008: 15-18, http://www.stanford.edu/~johntayl/FCPR.pdf.

9. I define a bailout as a grant of public funds allowing creditors to receive more than they would in a liquid marketplace. See also Randall D. Guynn, "Are Bailouts Inevitable?" *Yale Journal on Regulation* 29 (2012): 125n17 (discussing bailout definitions).

illustrated, Chapter 11 bankruptcy risked contributing to a financial crisis because it failed to prevent runs. In Chapter 11, claimants' treatment depends upon their seniority in the debt structure, a ranking orthogonal to debt maturity. Unsecured short-term lenders therefore have strong incentives to run—by either recalling or refusing to renew debt obligations—before Chapter 11 begins. As we observed with Lehman, once the prospect of Chapter 11 bankruptcy became real, runs swept through the financial system, impacting institutions far removed from Lehman itself.[10] Bailouts, by contrast, help mitigate these immediate risks, but also generate long-term inefficiencies. In a typical bailout, shareholders sustain losses, but creditors are indemnified. This reduces creditors' incentives to run in the short term but, over the long term, it encourages them to offer financial institutions less expensive loans, which in turn encourages those institutions to structure themselves in a manner more prone to runs and therefore to failure. The costs of increasing the frequency of crises by making financial institutions more failure-prone could dwarf those of the 2008 financial crisis.

Three new recapitalization mechanisms—Chapter 14, the Federal Deposit Insurance Corporation's single-point-of-entry (SPOE) under Title II of the Dodd-Frank Act, and the European Union's Bank Recovery and Resolution Directive (BRRD)—all seek to address the problems of both Chapter 11 bankruptcy and bailouts in similar ways. The straightforward economic logic behind these proposals is that

---

10. There are of course many theories of how the financial crisis occurred, only some of which argue that Lehman's failure had any causal effect. For instance, one theory is that the crisis was caused by a common reassessment of the value of assets and that Lehman (and AIG) merely helped reveal that assets were mispriced. See, e.g., Kenneth Scott, "A Guide to the Resolution of Failed Financial Institutions," in *Bankruptcy Not Bailout: A Special Chapter 14*, ed. Kenneth E. Scott and John B. Taylor (Stanford, CA: Hoover Institution Press, 2012), 85–132. In all likelihood, many factors contributed. I mean only to ascribe some weight to the theory that Lehman's bankruptcy contributed in part by convincing markets that short-term lenders might bear losses. I do not mean to argue that Chapter 14—or, for that matter, SPOE—would have relieved the crisis through other channels that caused and perpetuated it.

swiftly recapitalizing an ailing financial institution will force losses onto shareholders and long-term creditors while maintaining operations and therefore forestalling runs. This is a compromise solution. Like bailouts, each of these mechanisms does indemnify short-term lenders. In conjunction with regulations requiring financial institutions to finance themselves with sufficient long-term relative to short-term debt, however, these mechanisms should substantially reduce the severity of bailouts' debt-subsidy problem. The upside of indemnifying short-term lenders is that, as with insurance, the probability of runs is far lower than with Chapter 11. Moreover, similar to insurance, each of these mechanisms also minimizes run risks by reducing uncertainty about the timing of resolution. Because regulators with better access to information about financial institutions' solvency play a substantial role in each mechanism, short-term creditors concerned that an institution may be on the edge of insolvency have less reason to run than in the case of Chapter 11, which gives managers an incentive to file for bankruptcy only after the firm becomes insolvent.

Building upon other chapters of this volume, part I briefly details how Chapter 14 solves both Chapter 11's tendency to induce runs and bailout's tendency to create moral hazard, at least for firms that fail due to insolvency. SPOE and BRRD can also solve these twin problems, though the moral hazard reduction achieved by Chapter 14 is likely to outweigh that of SPOE and the details of BRRD remain too murky for comparison.[11]

Part I is largely theoretical. It leaves open the question of whether various real-world obstacles will prevent Chapter 14 from working in practice. Would Lehman's case have turned out substantially better had it gone through Chapter 14 rather than Chapter 11?

The rest of the paper seeks to answer this question. Using previously unexplored discovery[12] and court documents available from Lehman's bankruptcy, it undertakes a counterfactual case-study analysis of how

---

11. See part I in this chapter.

12. All discovery documents referenced in this paper may be found at "Index of/lehman/docs," Jenner and Block, http://www.jenner.com/lehman/docs/.

and whether Chapter 14's section 1405 transfer would have worked had it been available in 2008. Part II analyzes Lehman's economic history and finds that perceived insolvency indeed drove Lehman's run. Lehman was therefore the type of case that Chapter 14 is best suited to address. Part III delineates the procedural aspects of a counterfactual Chapter 14 case for Lehman. It shows that, though the time frame to complete a Chapter 14 over-the-weekend asset-and-liability transfer is rushed, Chapter 14 places sufficiently minimal requirements on the courts so as to make this process feasible with the advance planning that the Dodd-Frank Act already requires.

Finally, part IV evaluates the prospects for a hypothetical post–Chapter 14 company called New Lehman. It assesses how new industry initiatives and US and EU laws and regulations would manage cross-border issues and considers the probability of market-provided funding. Part IV concludes that, in the counterfactual world, New Lehman's 19 percent book capital ratio eliminates insolvency-driven incentives to run. And even if lenders and counterparties run for other reasons, New Lehman can withstand a moderate drain on liquidity.

In the end, Chapter 14 improves outcomes for most parties at interest relative to Chapter 11: clients, counterparties, and most creditors face no losses. Unlike in a bailout, long-term lenders do face substantial losses, but still likely fare better than they did in Lehman's Chapter 11 case. As in Chapter 11, shareholders and subordinated debt holders likely receive nothing. Overall, the likelihood of systemic consequences is small and social welfare is much improved relative to Lehman's 2008 Chapter 11 case. Therefore, in Lehman's and in similar cases, Chapter 14 and similar mechanisms offer credible alternatives to bailouts and to Chapter 11. Part V concludes with a summary of findings.

Part I. The Logic of Chapter 14 for Insolvent Financial Firms

This part briefly addresses how Chapter 14 would solve the key problems of financial failure for those firms to which it applies. The Chapter 14 proposal would, among other supporting amendments, add a new Bankruptcy Code chapter exclusively for financial firms that would operate faster and with greater precision than does Chapter 11.[13] As detailed in other chapters of this book,[14] Chapter 14 may be used in a variety of ways for different types of financial institutions experiencing different types of failures. This paper analyzes only one application: a section 1405 transfer used for a systemically important financial institution. For brevity, the remainder of this paper uses the phrase "Chapter 14" to mean this particular application of the Chapter 14 provision.

Applied as a transfer, Chapter 14 would facilitate moving all of a parent holding company's assets and most of its liabilities into and out of bankruptcy over a weekend. Unlike Chapter 11, it would disallow business reorganization over the course of this brief bankruptcy and would leave all operating subsidiaries outside of bankruptcy entirely; instead, it would facilitate, in effect, only the reorganization of the parent company's balance sheet. Specifically, Chapter 14 would allow for the transfer of all of the parent company's assets and liabilities *except* long-term and subordinated debt to a new, non-bankrupt bridge financial holding company of which the bankruptcy estate would become sole owner. Long-term and subordinated debt and equity claims would remain with the estate while the new company would assume all good and bad assets as well as short-term debt, derivatives, and other contractual obligations. In addition, Chapter 14 would prevent counterparties and creditors of operating subsidiaries from terminating obligations. At the end of the process, the new company's balance sheet and contractual relationships would be nearly identical to the old company's *except* that equity would have taken the place of long-term and subordinated debt and, in this sense, the new company would be recapitalized.[15] In Lehman's

---

13. See Thomas H. Jackson, "Building on Bankruptcy: A Revised Chapter 14 Proposal for the Recapitalization, Reorganization, or Liquidation of Large Financial Institutions: Appendix," chapter 2 in this volume.

14. Kenneth Scott, "The Context for Bankruptcy Resolutions," chapter 1 in this volume; and Jackson, "Building on Bankruptcy: Revised Chapter 14," chapter 2 in this volume.

15. See part IV.A in this chapter.

case, this would have increased its book capital ratio from 5 percent to 19 percent.[16]

Before addressing the economic logic behind this process, it is important to note that Chapter 14 is only available for a subset of failing firms and therefore this logic applies only to this subset. At least when the Fed is filing the case,[17] to meet Chapter 14's legal standards: (1) the parent company of an ailing financial institution must provide adequate assurance of future performance on assumed contracts after it is recapitalized; and (2) Chapter 14 must be necessary to avoid serious adverse effects on US financial stability.[18] The first adequate-assurance standard largely excludes from Fed-initiated Chapter 14 both (i) failing firms that are already experiencing a severe run on liquidity; and (ii) firms that will remain insolvent even after converting all available long-term and subordinated debt into equity.[19] The second adverse-effects standard excludes firms for which a private-sector solution appears imminent or for which a Chapter 11 case would avoid systemic consequences. By comparison, the single-point-of-entry approach has a similar adverse-effects standard but lacks an adequate-assurance standard and could therefore be used

---

16. See discussion in part III.D of this chapter.

17. For firms in circumstances such as Lehman's, it makes sense to focus on this use of Chapter 14. As discussed in part III.A in this chapter, unlike Chapters 7 and 11, either the firm or the Fed can initiate Chapter 14. Jackson, "Building on Bankruptcy: Revised Chapter 14," section 2(4). A possibility of recovery will often remain even after Chapter 14 is warranted, however, leaving management and directors disinclined to file because their incentives are aligned with those of equity holders rather than creditors and, more generally, with the company rather than systemic welfare.

18. Jackson, "Building on Bankruptcy: Revised Chapter 14," sections 2(4), 2(13).

19. See also discussion in part III.B in this chapter. In some cases, firms in category (i) may use Chapter 14 if they can show that they will be able to secure new financing immediately following Chapter 14. Until markets are familiar with the Chapter 14 process, however, this is unlikely. Few firms will fit into category (ii) without already being in category (i). If one were to qualify, it could not use Chapter 14 because it would be expected to soon experience such a run due to ongoing insolvency.

for firms experiencing or about to experience a severe run that lacked any private-sector sources of additional liquidity or for firms that were already deeply insolvent.[20]

When available, Chapter 14 will be successful if it both generates social welfare gains relative to alternative policy options and offers a mechanism that policymakers in fact choose to use.[21] As explained below, these success benchmarks will predominantly be met when a firm is failing due to insolvency, rather than other causes.

The social welfare cost of bailouts comes largely through the moral hazard they engender by indemnifying creditors, which encourages instability in financial firms and thereby increases the frequency of financial crises. As a theoretical proposition, it is relatively uncontested that Chapter 14, like Chapter 11, will eliminate most moral hazard because, unlike bailouts, it will ensure that certain long-term creditors bear losses that the firm accrues beyond the value of equity. There is one caveat: Chapter 14 (like other recapitalization mechanisms) will prevent short-term creditors from bearing losses, encouraging eligible firms to use more short-term debt. Fortunately, this problem can be managed through straightforward regulatory rules. In part to address a similar incentive scheme generated by SPOE, regulators are already developing floors for the amount of long-term and subordinated debt that eligible firms must hold in the future.[22] These floors will ensure that a sufficient portion of financial firms' creditors are at risk and therefore

20. See SPOE Fed. Reg., "The Resolution of Systemically Important Financial Institutions: The Single Point of Entry Strategy," 78 Fed. Reg. 76,614.

21. See also Jacopo Carmassi and Richard Herring, "The Cross-Border Challenge in Resolving Global Systemically Important Banks," chapter 9 in this volume (discussing a longer but similar list of objectives propounded by the FSB and arguing, as I do here, that the most challenging objective is making resolution credible).

22. See, e.g., Stanley Fischer, "The Great Recession: Moving Ahead," speech at conference sponsored by the Swedish Ministry of Finance, Stockholm, August 11, 2014, http://www.federalreserve.gov/newsevents/speech/fischer20140811a.htm (stating that the United States is preparing requirements for systemically important US financial institutions to issue a certain amount of debt that could be left behind in a recapitalization).

reduce moral hazard relative to bailouts, where no creditors are at risk. Consequently, creditors will help to ensure that financial firms stay sufficiently far from the brink of failure. In the end, this will reduce the frequency of crises and thereby enhance long-term social welfare.

The analysis is similar for SPOE. The primary difference is that Chapter 14's provisions would be required by law whereas SPOE is only one possible manner in which the Federal Deposit Insurance Corporation (FDIC) could exercise its expansive powers under the Dodd-Frank Act. Under Chapter 14, all parties would know, in advance and in a clear and predictable manner, how and approximately when losses will be allocated. Under the Dodd-Frank Act, the FDIC retains substantial discretion to allocate losses as it sees fit. In particular, the act allows the FDIC to use the orderly liquidation fund (OLF) to loan taxpayer funds to a failing firm, funds which could ultimately be lost if the firm fails to recover (first by the firm, then by the industry).[23] The ongoing uncertainty as to precisely how, and to whose benefit, the FDIC's Title II powers will be used prevent SPOE from reducing moral hazard as much as would Chapter 14, though the more convinced the marketplace becomes of the FDIC's intent, the more similar the two proposals become in this respect.

Unfortunately, because clear details about the implementation of BRRD in EU member states will not emerge until 2016, it is too soon to say how it would compare to the SPOE and Chapter 14 options.[24]

---

23. See also David Skeel, "Financing Systemically Important Financial Institutions in Bankruptcy," chapter 3 in this volume, discussing the mechanics of the OLF and comparing it to alternative funding options.

24. Council and Parliament of the European Union, "Directive 2014/59/EU of the European Parliament and of the Council establishing a framework for the recovery and resolution of credit institutions and investment firms," May 15, 2014, Article 60a, sections 1–2, http://eur-lex.europa.eu/legal-content/EN/TXT /PDF/?uri=CELEX:32014L0059&from=EN. See Andreas Dombret and Patrick Kenadjian, eds., *The Bank Recovery and Resolution Directive: Europe's Solution for "Too Big to Fail"?* (Frankfurt am Main, Germany: Institute for Law and Finance, 2013); Pierre-Henri Conac, "Bank Resolution and 'Bail-In': The European Approach," (presentation August 8, 2014, on file with the author).

The more concerning question is not whether Chapter 14 will help to reduce moral hazard but rather whether policymakers will allow it to be used or will instead seek to invoke Title II (by finding bankruptcy to be insufficient to safeguard systemic risk) or to pass new legislation. Even if a failing firm has yet to experience a run, policymakers will fear that a run might occur after resolution, that such a run might turn into a cascade, and that such a cascade might cause systemic effects. Because the bailout alternative can generally prevent runs, policymakers will only use Chapter 14 if they are convinced it can forestall a run.

Runs occur for a variety of reasons. The most prominent, and the reason that best explains Lehman Brothers' case, is that the institution has become insolvent. Fortunately, it is these cases of insolvency-driven runs that Chapter 14 is best situated to address and prevent.

An insolvency-driven run occurs when depositors or short-term lenders believe a bank's assets are worth less than the cost of its liabilities. Figure 7.1 shows one way that insolvency can arise. The dealer bank in 7.1(A), whose balance sheet is modeled on Lehman's, has three kinds of assets: cash, encumbered assets backing secured loans, and unencumbered financial products, including other loans and investments. These are financed by repurchase agreements, other secured lending, deposits in commercial banking subsidiaries, long-term bonds (including some that are subordinated), and a small amount of equity. In 7.1(B), financial-product valuations fall sufficiently to cause the cost of liabilities to exceed the value of assets. 7.1(C) shows that this devaluation more than eliminates book equity, rendering the firm insolvent. If the firm can provide no private information that its assets are worth more than markets suspect, then it cannot obtain additional financing and will fail.

Insolvency drives runs by converting a bank's relationship with its creditors into the equivalent of a prisoner's dilemma. Consider the example of First Commercial Bank with two depositors, Anne and Bob, who have each deposited $10. With Anne and Bob's funds, First Commercial made a $20, 10 percent interest loan to Curly, for a total of $22 to be repaid. Anne and Bob come to believe Curly will default and pay only $18, rendering First Commercial insolvent. If

(A) Solvent Dealer Bank

(B) Severe Asset Devaluation

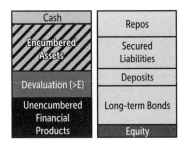

(C) Insolvency

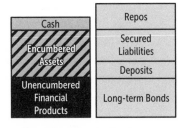

Figure 7.1. Insolvency Event for a Dealer Bank

First Commercial tries to sell the loan to Second Commercial, Second will want to conduct enough due diligence to be sure Curly will repay $18. If Second does not have time for due diligence before buying the loan, it will pay only the fire-sale price of $12 due to its uncertainty. Consistent with the classic prisoner's dilemma outcome, if Anne and Bob both stay and split the proceeds from the loan, each will get $9. If one runs while the other stays, the runner will be repaid at $10 while the one who stays will receive only $2. If both run, each will get $6.[25] Accordingly, in equilibrium both run and First Commercial fails. The

---

25. Graphically, the example looks as follows:

		Bob	
Payout		Stay	Run
Anne	Stay	$9, $9	$2, $10
	Run	$10, $2	$6, $6

same process plays out for dealer banks' more complex structures, particularly if investments become illiquid and then fall in value.

Chapter 14, invoked in a timely manner, solves this problem and prevents the insolvency-driven run from occurring. When long-term and subordinated debt exceeds the extent of insolvency by a substantial amount—a requirement for Chapter 14's use in the first place[26]—Chapter 14 will leave a formerly insolvent bank solvent, as in 7.2(B), and therefore eliminate incentives to run. Note that the ultimate value of equity in 7.2(B) is less than the value of long-term debt in 7.2(A) due to costs associated with the recapitalization, but the 7.2(B) bank is nonetheless solvent. The new regulations the Fed is developing should ensure this outcome in the majority of cases.

Moreover, when long-term debt and subordinated debt are sufficient to cover both the insolvency gap and international friction costs associated with Chapter 14,[27] not only do short-term lenders lack incentives to run after Chapter 14's use, but the expectation of its use reduces ex ante uncertainty about runs as well. As the firm proceeds toward insolvency, Chapter 14 acts similarly to deposit insurance. Because the Fed can access private information unavailable to the marketplace and because its incentives are aligned with creditors', its pledge to invoke Chapter 14 in a timely manner retains insurance's sovereign credibility, without putting taxpayers at risk or subsidizing debt financing. This feature of Chapter 14 also reduces the likelihood that the solvency gap will become so large through inaction as to exceed the available cushion of long-term and subordinated debt. If short-term unsecured lenders expect Chapter 14 to be invoked as soon as private information indicates an eligible firm is insolvent, then runs driven by concern about insolvency alone should be eliminated.

In summary, for firms that fail due to insolvency and that, due to regulation or choice, have more than enough long-term and subordi-

---

26. See discussion above noting that debt will almost always need to be sufficient to cover the depth of insolvency in order to meet Chapter 14's adequate-assurance standard.

27. See discussion in part IV.A.

(A) Insolvent Bank with Sufficient Long-Term Debt

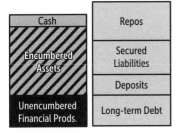

(B) After Recapitalization

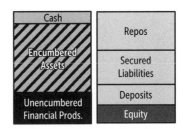

Figure 7.2. Recapitalization's Ability to Stop Runs Sparked by Insolvency

nated debt to cover their insolvency gap, Chapter 14 can be expected both significantly to reduce moral hazard relative to bailouts and significantly to reduce the risk of runs relative to Chapter 11. The next three parts address actual execution.

Part II. The Lehman Brothers Case

Many scholars have documented Lehman Brothers' demise,[28] but none have undertaken a precise analysis of its liquidity and balance-sheet

---

28. See, e.g., Anton R. Valukas, "Lehman Brothers Holdings Inc. Chapter 11 Proceedings Examiner's Report," 2010; James W. Giddens, "Trustee's Preliminary Investigation Report for the Securities Investors Protection Act (SIPA) Liquidation of Lehman Brothers, Inc.," 2010; Mark Roe and Stephen Adams, "Restructuring Failed Financial Firms in Bankruptcy: Learning from Lehman," *Yale Journal on Regulation* (forthcoming 2015), http://papers.ssrn.com/sol3/papers.cfm?abstract _id=2512490##; Kimberly Summe, "An Examination of Lehman Brothers' Derivatives Portfolio Postbankruptcy: Would Dodd-Frank Have Made a Difference?" in Scott and Taylor, *Bankruptcy Not Bailout*; David A. Skeel, *The New Financial Deal: Understanding the Dodd-Frank Act and Its (Unintended) Consequences* (Hoboken, NJ: John Wiley & Sons, 2011); Lawrence McDonald and Patrick Robinson, *A Colossal Failure of Common Sense: The Inside Story of the Collapse of Lehman Brothers* (New York: Three Rivers Press, 2010); Christopher Harress and Kathleen Caulderwood, "The Death of Lehman Brothers: What Went Wrong, Who Paid the Price and Who Remained Unscathed Through the Eyes of Former Vice-President," *International Business Times*, September 13, 2013.

challenges using the discovery and court documents available from Lehman's case. This part does so, focusing on those facts relevant to constructing a counterfactual Chapter 14 case in parts III and IV.

A. Lehman's Path to Failure and Structure upon Demise

In January 2008, Lehman Brothers was the fourth largest US investment bank and a highly respected global financial institution. It announced record revenues for 2007, had a $35 billion market capitalization, and held around $700 billion in assets.[29] Virtually no one expected a corporate default. Less than eight months later, on September 15, 2008, deemed insolvent and entirely out of cash, Lehman filed for bankruptcy. Market prices reflected around $54 billion of value losses relative to book as soon as the court proceedings began.[30]

Critically important to the workings of Chapter 14's section 1405 transfer and to SPOE is that, like most US-based large financial institutions, Lehman had a hub-and-spoke corporate structure. A holding company at the top, Lehman Brothers Holdings Inc. (Holdings), managed most long-term financing[31] while eight thousand operating subsidiaries around the globe ran business operations and managed short-term financing.[32] Key legal entities are shown in figure 7.4.

Though Lehman was predominantly a dealer-bank, its subsidiaries' legal identities varied widely. The two most important were Lehman Brothers Inc. (LBI) and Lehman Brothers International (Europe) (LBIE), Lehman's New York– and London-based broker-dealers. In addition, Lehman owned insured banks in Germany and the United States and many subsidiaries that specialized in real estate investments

---

29. Data from Bloomberg (on file with author); Lehman Brothers Holdings, Inc., Annual Report for 2007 (Form 10-K), February 28, 2008: 29, 33.

30. Calculated from data underlying figure 7.5.

31. Lehman Brothers, "Company Overview: Third Quarter 2007," Bates Stamp LBEX-LL 2165164: 2.

32. Statement by Harvey Miller, lead attorney for Lehman Bankruptcy Filing, at Federal Reserve Resolution Conference, October 18, 2013; Lehman Brothers, Liquidity Summary 091309 6pm.xls, Bates Stamp LBEX-DOCID 647325, 8 (noting LBI held 54.5 percent and LBIE 44 percent of all repo).

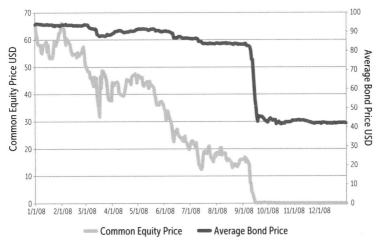

Figure 7.3. Lehman Stock and Bond Prices January–December 2008
Source: Based on data from Thomson Reuter's Datastream (on file with the author).
Bond prices reflect the average of all prices available as of April 2014 across all issuances
with pricing within 15 percent of par as of January 2008, to approximately capture most
issuances representing Lehman's outstanding long-term debt, while also excluding more
exotic instruments.

or derivatives trading.[33] The legal boundaries between these entities
did not, however, map to Lehman's primary business lines of investment banking, investment management, and capital markets.[34] Rather,
Lehman operated its businesses in a globally integrated manner that
left thousands of legal entities in dozens of jurisdictions intricately
intertwined from both profitability and operational standpoints. This
fact is partially responsible for the chaotic and expensive nature of Lehman's Chapter 11 bankruptcy;[35] in a Chapter 14 section 1405 transfer

---

33. Lehman, "Company Overview," 2; Lehman, "List of Subsidiaries" (Lehman
Brothers, "Exhibit 21.10: List of the Registrant's Subsidiaries,") in Lehman, 2007
10-K.

34. Lehman, 2007 10-K, 3. See also Carmassi and Herring, "Cross-Border
Challenge" (discussing the extent of complex mismatches between legal entities
and businesses in the industry as a whole).

35. Author interview with staff at the Lehman Estate, October 13, 2014 (notes
on file with the author).

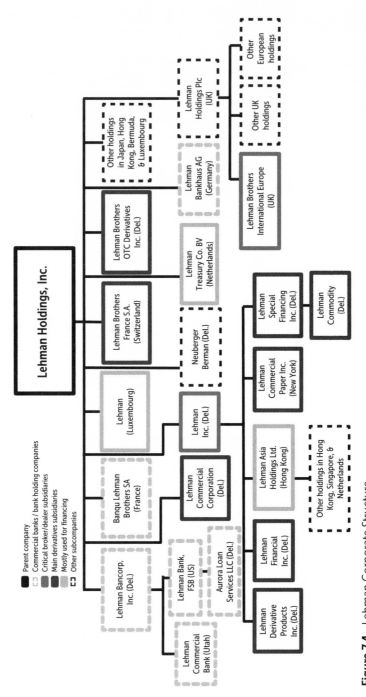

Figure 7.4. Lehman Corporate Structure

Source: Adapted from Lehman Brothers, "Company Overview: Third Quarter 2007," Bates Stamp LBEX-LL 2165164, 2.

proceeding, at least initially, none of these subsidiaries would go through bankruptcy.

Capital markets served as Lehman's primary financial intermediation segment, held 98 percent of Lehman's assets,[36] and was the underlying cause of Lehman's downfall. Most products with which capital markets worked were standard and relatively liquid, but its real estate–related investments became increasingly opaque and illiquid over 2007.[37] During that year, Lehman raised only $3 billion of equity[38] but added—both purposefully and accidentally[39]—around $89 billion of hard-to-value assets to its balance sheet,[40] far more proportionately than peer firms.[41] By early 2008, Lehman held hard-to-value assets that it marked at $265 billion against only $26 billion of equity.[42] A market determination that these assets were worth only 90 percent of what Lehman estimated would render the firm insolvent.

Market prices for Lehman's debt and equity over 2008 reveal that it took markets some time to determine how little Lehman's assets were

36. Lehman Brothers Holdings, Inc., "Quarterly Report for the Quarter Ending May 31, 2008 (Form 10-Q)," 22; Lehman, "2007 10-K," 102.

37. Lehman, "Q2 2008 10-Q," 21, 75.

38. Lehman, "2007 10-K," 30.

39. While Lehman's commercial real estate acquisitions were purposeful (Valukas Report, 103–17), its accumulation of residential mortgage-backed securities appears to have been accidental; ibid., 59–65. Lehman's banks originated many mortgages that Lehman planned to securitize and sell to third parties, but by the time it curtailed mortgage origination in Q2 2007 it had become very hard to sell the residential mortgage-backed securities it had accumulated; ibid., 82–95.

40. Author's analysis, counting assets likely later categorized as Level 2 and 3 that appear in Lehman, "Q2 Factbook," June 13, 2008, Bates Stamp LBHI_SEC07940_593047, 17; and Lehman, "2007 10-K," 107. The Level 2 and 3 categorization was not common practice until 2008.

41. See Barclays Bank, "Long Island Transaction Overview," September 12, 2008, Bates Stamp BCI-EX-(S)-00053306, 12, 14 (noting Barclays' concern with Lehman's accumulated assets); compare Goldman Sachs, "Quarterly Report (Form 10-Q)," February 28, 2007: 20.

42. Figures calculated from Lehman Brothers Holdings, Inc., "Quarterly Report for the Quarter Ending Feb. 29, 2008 (Form 10-Q)": 6, 19, 23. The $265 billion figure includes all Level 2 and 3 assets and all real estate held for sale as of February 2008.

worth. As the value of assets equals the sum of the values of liabilities and equity, markets implicitly value assets when they value debt and equity instruments. In figure 7.5, I have used this identity to chart Lehman's "solvency equity" value: the difference between the approximate market valuation of Lehman's assets and the par cost of Lehman's liabilities.[43] The other two series additionally show Lehman's book equity (top) and the difference between book equity and solvency equity (bottom), or the amount by which the market was implicitly discounting the value of Lehman's assets.

As the figure illustrates, on a solvency-equity basis, by June 2008 markets already believed Lehman's assets to be worth $18 billion less than Lehman claimed[44] and its equity to be worth less than 2 percent of the value of its assets,[45] the point known as "critical undercapitalization" in banking parlance.[46] But they did not yet believe Lehman to be insolvent. As the summer proceeded, lenders and investors became increasingly concerned by three factors: Lehman's first write-downs as a public company;[47] Lehman's inability to find a strategic partner who would make a large equity investment;[48] and continued uncertainty

---

43. The Valukas Report coined the phrase "solvency equity." See Valukas Report, Appendix 21.

44. See the market discount from book series in figure 7.5. Book equity was marked at $28 billion (see table 7.1) while solvency equity was only $10 billion, $18 billion less.

45. With June 2008 asset valuations of $639 billion, 2 percent would have been $13 billion.

46. See Federal Deposit Insurance Corporation, "2000—Rules and Regulations: Subpart B—Prompt Corrective Action section 325.103(b)(5)," FDIC Law, Regulations, Related Acts, June 30, 2014, http://www.fdic.gov/regulations/laws/rules/2000-4500.html.

47. Lehman, "Q2 2008 10-Q," 24; Jenny Anderson, "Shares of Lehman Brothers Take a Beating," *New York Times,* July 11, 2008 (noting that the write-downs left Lehman "struggling against a tide of rumors, none substantiated but all magnified by fears about the true value of its assets that cannot be easily sold and the bleak prospects for its business in a weak economy").

48. Valukas Report, 618–24. By then, discussions had already ended with the Kuwait Investment Authority and Berkshire Hathaway. Thereafter, Lehman failed

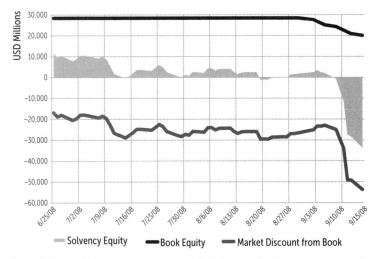

Figure 7.5. Market Valuation of Lehman's Solvency Equity

Source: Based on data from Thomson Reuter's Datastream and Bloomberg. Underlying calculations on file.

Note: The figure charts an approximation of the value $S \equiv (l_m + l_u) + (e_p + e_c) - L$ where l_m, is the market value of market-traded liabilities, l_u, is the book value of untraded liabilities, e_c, is the market value of common stock, e_p, is the estimated market value of preferred stock, and L is the par value of all liabilities. For market-traded liabilities, the figure uses representative bonds maturing over different time frames and a breakdown of the maturity schedule of all of Lehman's bonds to estimate an overall market valuation of all traded bonds and commercial paper. For preferred equity, the figure uses pricing from the February 2008 issuance, which was the most regularly traded of recent issuances, to price all outstanding preferred issuances accordingly.

about asset valuations.[49] The cumulative result of these concerns was a steady decline in markets' estimates of the value of Lehman's equity to near zero throughout late summer.

Lehman, of course, had a different view of the book value of its assets and equity. Due to their importance to part III below, it is useful to briefly review the latest-dated data about both Lehman's consolidated

---

to complete potential deals with MetLife and Investment Corp. of Dubai. On September 1, it rejected a deal from Korea Development Bank; ibid.

49. Barclays, "Long Island," 3–4, 12, 14; Giddens Report, Exhibit C 4 (discussing David Einhorn's allegations).

balance sheet and Holdings' portion of this consolidated whole. Table 7.1 summarizes the (incomplete) data available.

For Chapter 14's purposes, the most notable feature of this table is how columns (1) and (2) compare. Relative to Lehman as a whole, Holdings' balance sheet included almost no derivatives, repos (repurchase agreements), or reverse repos.[50] Rather, 83 percent of Holdings' assets were advances to and equity in subsidiaries; the remainder was mostly unencumbered financial instruments.[51] Holdings' balance-sheet liabilities were comprised of nearly all of Lehman's unsecured debt—$3 billion of commercial paper and $96 billion of long-term and subordinated debt[52]—as well as debts to subsidiaries. Though not reflected in the balance sheet, Holdings additionally guaranteed certain subsidiaries in their entirety[53] as well as individual subsidiary contracts with third parties. These guarantees ultimately comprised over one-third of the claims against Holdings.[54] In fact, allowed claims exclusive of guarantee claims were less than Holdings' balance sheet liabilities the day before Lehman's filing.[55]

B. The Insolvency-Driven Run on Lehman

As markets reduced valuations of Lehman's assets, Lehman experienced a slow drain on liquidity, but not an all-out run.[56] By the end

---

50. *De minimis* amounts of derivatives omitted from the table by rounding.

51. Lehman Brothers, "Liquidity Management at Lehman Brothers," Bates Stamp LBEX-DOCID008669, May 15, 2008: 31 (noting that Holdings' non-subsidiary funding assets were supported by cash capital; everything supported by cash capital was unencumbered).

52. Table 7.1. Long-term debt includes both long-term borrowings and current portion of long-term debt.

53. Lehman, "Company Overview," 2.

54. Author's calculation relying on Lehman's Third Plan Disclosure, "Lehman Brothers Holdings, Inc. and its Affiliated Debtors, Debtors' Disclosure Statement for Third Amended Joint Chapter 11 Plan," August 31, 2011: 499.

55. Compare table 7.1 with table 7.3.

56. Author's analysis, based on data from Lehman Brothers, "Liquidity Update," Bates Stamp LBEX-WGM 784543, September 11 2008: 86-87, 96; Lehman, "5/15/08 Liquidity," 82, 84, 85; Lehman Brothers, "2008 Q2 Liquidity Metrics," Bates Stamp LBHI_SEC07940_601022, 41, 42, 49.

of the third quarter, two weeks before its demise, Lehman marked its book equity at $28 billion.[57] As figure 7.5 shows, markets disagreed, valuing equity under $2 billion. In fact, information unavailable to markets, but available to regulators, indicated that Lehman was worth even less: the $2 billion valuation reflected expected third-quarter (Q3) common-stock losses of $2.3 billion.[58] As Lehman already knew and regulators could have known, Q3 common-stock losses were actually $4.1 billion,[59] a difference just large enough to eliminate market perceptions that Lehman was solvent.

Predictably, therefore, when on Wednesday, September 10, Lehman publicly announced its Q3 losses,[60] credit default swap spreads ballooned and ratings agencies threatened to downgrade Lehman if it did not arrange for an acquisition or capital injection over the weekend.[61] Over the course of the week in which this announcement was made, Lehman lost approximately $30 billion of liquidity and ended the week with $3 billion more debts due on Monday morning, September 15, than it had cash with which to pay them.[62] Lehman's story is entirely consistent with the theory that lenders stayed so long as they continued to believe the firm to be solvent, and then ran as soon as they learned otherwise.

Due to its relevance to assessing New Lehman's liquidity in part IV, it is helpful to review how Lehman lost $30 billion of liquidity in only a week. Figure 7.6 summarizes data drawn from Lehman's discovery documents.

57. Lehman Brothers Holdings, Inc., "Current Report (Form 8-K), Ex. 99.1," September 10, 2008.

58. Author's calculation, multiplying expected losses of $3.35 per share by shares outstanding. See Lehman Brothers, "Liquidity of Lehman Brothers," Bates Stamp LBEX-WGM 787681, October 7, 2008: 91 (noting expected losses per share).

59. Lehman, 9/10/08 8-K, Ex. 99.1, 1.

60. Ibid.

61. Lehman, "10/7/08 Liquidity," 91–92.

62. Author's calculation based on data from ibid., 90, 93, 94, 97, 99; Lehman, "9/13/08 Liquidity Summary," 25.

Table 7.1. Lehman's and Holdings' Balance Sheets

	(1) All Lehman 8/31/08		(2) Holdings 9/14/08	
	USD billions	% of total	USD billions	% of total
ASSETS				
Cash, equivalents, and segregated securities	20	3	103	5
Financial instruments & inventory positions	256	43	23	11
Liquid assets	47	8	6	3
Real estate–related assets	78	13	11	5
Corporate debt, equities, & loans	85	14	6	3
Derivatives and other contracts	46	8	0	0
Reverse repos and borrowed securities	273	46	0	0
All other	50	8	179	85
Receivables from subsidiaries	N/A		147	70
Equity in net assets of subsidiaries	N/A		26	13
Receivables from third parties	37	6	1	0
Other assets	9	2	2	1
Identifiable intangibles and goodwill	4	1	0	0
TOTAL ASSETS	598		209	
LIABILITIES & EQUITY				
Short-term & current long-term debt	26	4	19	9
Current portion of long-term debt	22	4	16*	
Commercial paper	4	1	3*	
Short positions	154	26	0	0
Repos	160	27	0	0
Accrued liabilities and payables	missing		1	0

(continued)

Table 7.1. (*continued*)

	(1) All Lehman 8/31/08		(2) Holdings 9/14/08	
	USD billions	% of total	USD billions	% of total
Owed to subsidiaries	N/A		88	42
Deposits at banks	29	5	0	0
Long-term borrowings	115	19	80	38
Senior notes	97	16	65	31
Subordinated notes	17	3	15	7
TOTAL LIABILITIES	569	95	189	90
Preferred equity	9	2	9	4
Common equity	19	3	11	5
TOTAL EQUITY	28	5	20	10
TOTAL LIABILITIES AND EQUITY	598		209	

Source: Based on data from Lehman Brothers, "Funding Lehman Brothers" (September 11, 2008), Bates Stamp LBEX-DOCID 008482, 7, 10, 15; In re Lehman Brothers Holdings, Inc, et al., Monthly Operating Report Balance Sheet as of September 14, 2008, available at www.sec.gov/Archives/edgar/data/806085/000090951809000059/mm01-3009_8ke991mor.htm; Lehman Brothers Holdings, Inc., Current Report (Form 8-K) (Sept. 10, 2008).

Note: Lehman went bankrupt before it released figures for its final quarter. The sources above fill most gaps, but imperfectly and sometimes in conflicting ways. Asterisks indicate approximations based on the author's analysis of source documents listed. Though no breakdown between commercial paper and the current portion of long-term debt was available, other discovery documents state that commercial paper stood at $3 billion at Lehman's demise.

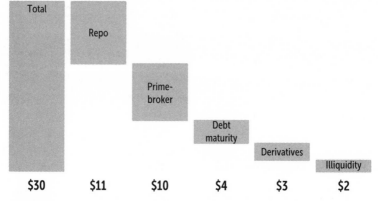

Figure 7.6. Liquidity Losses over Lehman's Final Week
Source: Based on data from Lehman Brothers, "Liquidity of Lehman Brothers," Bates Stamp LBEX-WGM 787681 (October 7, 2008), 90, 93, 94, 97, 99; Lehman Brothers, "Liquidity Summary 091309 6pm.xls," Bates Stamp LBEX-DOCID 647325, 25.

Lehman's most substantial drain on cash, approximately $11 billion, related to difficulties with its repo financing. Of this, $4.5 billion[63] went to address $48 billion of lending that failed to roll over.[64] (Lehman successfully used its overfunding policy[65] and collateral liquidation[66] to address the rest.) In addition, Lehman used $6.5 billion to meet haircut increases by tri-party lenders and collateral calls by clearing banks.[67]

---

63. Author's calculation based on data from Lehman, "10/7/08 Liquidity," 90, 97; Lehman, "9/13/08 Liquidity Summary," 2.

64. Author's calculation based on data from Lehman, "9/13/08 Liquidity Summary," 2.

65. Lehman borrowed hard-to-fund collateral and committed it to tri-party investors for cash, so that if investors in Lehman's own collateral began to run, Lehman could return the borrowed collateral and use the same commitments to fund its own collateral. It also secured contractual commitments exceeding what was lent. At the beginning of Q3, these two strategies left Lehman with a $27 billion "cushion" to absorb repo lender losses without needing to liquidate collateral. Lehman, "9/11/08 Funding Slides," 82.

66. Ibid., 91, 95.

67. Author's calculation based on data from Lehman, "10/7/08 Liquidity," 90, 93, 97; Lehman, "9/13/08 Liquidity Summary," 2.

The second largest drain came from London's prime broker operations, which caused $10 billion of losses.[68] Typically, UK prime brokerage generated excess cash because customers' trading positions could be pledged in the tri-party markets through rehypothecation.[69] LBIE generally relied on this cash to meet customer demands for withdrawals. Over the third quarter, however, UK clients limited rehypothecation to the point that LBIE had almost no cash left and then, in Lehman's final week, clients demanded the return of $23 billion.[70] Without cash to meet these demands at LBIE, Lehman drew $10 billion of liquidity from the general pool.

A variety of costs accounted for the remaining outflows. Lehman paid $3 billion to meet margin increases on derivatives.[71] Another $2 billion became hard to monetize due to Lehman's fleeing repo lenders.[72] And $4 billion more went to satisfy maturing debts as they came due, including commercial paper, bank funding, and long-term-debt maturities.[73] By September 12, Lehman was "essentially devoid of any liquidity for operations."[74] Holdings had only $1.4 billion remaining in its liquidity pool and LBIE ended the week with a $5 billion deficit.[75]

C. Systemic Effects after Lehman's Collapse

Though perceived insolvency drove its failure, Lehman's lack of financing proximately caused its filing. Without cash to pay its creditors on Monday morning, LBIE had to enter administration to avoid

---

68. Author's calculation based on data from Lehman, "10/7/08 Liquidity," 93, 97.

69. Lehman, "5/15/08 Liquidity," 16–17. This practice was not allowed in the United States. Ibid.

70. Lehman, "10/7/08 Liquidity," 85, 93, 97.

71. Ibid., 91.

72. Ibid., 90.

73. Ibid.

74. Harvey Miller and Maurice Horowitz, "Resolution Authority: Lessons from the Lehman Experience," conference presentation, April 11, 2013, slide 12, http://www.stern.nyu.edu/cons/groups/content/documents/webasset/con_041232.pdf.

75. Lehman, "10/7/08 Liquidity," 90.

criminal charges.[76] Once LBIE was in administration, Holdings would have faced claims by guaranteed derivatives counterparties— "a massive systemic risk"—that would quickly consume its remaining cash.[77] With no alternative, Holdings filed for Chapter 11 bankruptcy. Soon, Lehman operating entities entered more than eighty insolvency proceedings in sixteen jurisdictions around the world.[78] Lehman's financial information system broke down immediately, preventing Lehman from continuing to operate.[79]

Even today, there is no consensus as to Lehman's culpability for the ensuing financial crisis.[80] What is clear is that Lehman's filing helped to "sen[d] markets across the globe tumbling"[81] and was followed by a classic cascading run. Though many of Lehman's short-term lenders had run before bankruptcy, a few had rolled over commitments, including the Reserve Primary Fund.[82] On Tuesday, Reserve Primary determined its claim on the Lehman Estate to be worthless and revalued its assets as worth less than its liabilities, breaking the buck.[83] Money-market investors ran and, as one Fed economist stated, "[i]t was overwhelmingly clear that we were staring into the abyss—that

---

76. Insolvency Act 1986, c. 45 section 214 (UK) (creating personal liability for directors who allow trading if they "knew or ought to have concluded that there was no reasonable prospect that the company would avoid going into insolvent liquidation").

77. Lehman Brothers, "Minutes of the Board of Directors," Bates Stamp LBEX-AM 003932, September 14, 2008: 2.

78. Miller and Horowitz, "Lessons."

79. Ibid.

80. See discussion in Introduction, this chapter.

81. Susanne Craig, Jeffrey McCracken, Jon Hilsenrath, and Deborah Solomon, "AIG, Lehman Shock Hits World Markets," *Wall Street Journal*, September 16, 2008.

82. The Fund's investment manager later said that he rolled over because "like many other investors . . . I assumed that the federal government would [as with Bear Stearns] save the day if Lehman or one of the other investment banks, which were much larger and posed greater apparent systemic risks, ran into trouble." FCIC, "The Financial Crisis Inquiry Report," 356.

83. See Condon, "Reserve Primary Money Fund Falls Below $1 a Share." Ex post, it is clear this was an overreaction. See table 7.3.

there wasn't a bottom to this—as the outflows picked up steam on Wednesday and Thursday."[84] Within a week prime funds had lost $349 billion and stopped financing commercial paper in efforts to preserve their ability to meet redemptions.[85] Consequently, many non-financial corporations who had relied on short-term unsecured funding markets lost the financing they needed to meet payroll and restock inventories.[86]

An outflow at prime brokers mirrored that at money markets. In the week after Lehman's filing, hedge funds pulled $86 billion out of Morgan Stanley and only slightly less out of Goldman Sachs, in part due to concerns about bankruptcy treatment.[87] The run also spread to insured commercial banks. The two least stable fell quickly. On September 25, the FDIC seized Washington Mutual and sold most operations to J. P. Morgan.[88] The weekend after, the FDIC estimated Wachovia would face $115 billion of withdrawals. Wells Fargo bought it the next Friday.[89]

The threat to commercial banks and the skyrocketing cost of commercial paper caused the panic to soon endanger ordinary consumers' ability to use credit and debit cards.[90] In response, Congress passed the $700 billion Troubled Asset Relief Program and undertook other measures to allow the government to increase insurance for commercial deposits, directly fund commercial paper, guarantee banks' long-term debt, and take equity stakes in nine institutions holding 75 percent of US bank assets.[91] These and related measures ultimately halted the cas-

---

84. FCIC, "The Financial Crisis Inquiry Report," 357 (quoting Fed economist Patrick McCabe).

85. Ibid., 357–59.

86. Ibid., 358–59.

87. Bradley Keon, "Morgan Stanley at Brink of Collapse Got $107 Billion from Fed," *Bloomberg*, August 22, 2011, http://www.bloomberg.com/news/2011-08-22 /morgan-stanley-at-brink-of-collapse-got-107b-from-fed.html.

88. Robin Sidel, David Enrich, and Dan FitzPatrick, *"WaMu Is Seized, Sold Off to J. P. Morgan, In Largest Failure in U.S. Banking History,"* Wall Street Journal, September 26, 2008.

89. FCIC, "The Financial Crisis Inquiry Report," 367–70.

90. Ibid., 358–59.

91. Ibid., 372-75. The nine institutions were Citigroup ($25 billion), JP Morgan ($25 billion), Wells Fargo ($25 billion), Bank of America ($15 billion), Goldman

cading run across the shadow and commercial bank systems. But by the end of 2008, many policymakers believed that allowing any more "systemically important" firms to go bankrupt would generate costs exceeding those of bailouts, at least in the near term. As one official described the government's thinking about Citigroup in November 2008: "The main point is to let the world know that we will not pull a Lehman."[92]

Part III: How a Chapter 14 Counterfactual Could Have Proceeded

Taking the facts above as given, this part explores how a counterfactual Lehman case in Chapter 14 might have proceeded, had Chapter 14 and other reforms been available back in 2008. I have chosen the assumptions below to reflect the most likely legal and regulatory environment that large financial institutions will face in the coming few years, while also recognizing that it is impossible to construct a counterfactual incorporating all second-order pricing and structural changes that will emerge in response to these new regimes.

A. Structure of the Counterfactual World

I assume that the US legal environment includes both Chapter 14 and the Dodd-Frank Act. Pursuant to Dodd-Frank, the Fed regulates Lehman and Lehman describes in a living will how best to resolve itself under Chapter 14.[93] Also pursuant to Dodd-Frank, SPOE backstops Chapter 14, but can only be used if regulators certify that Chapter 14 will fail to prevent systemic consequences.[94] The Dodd-Frank-

---

Sachs ($10 billion), Morgan Stanley ($10 billion), Merrill Lynch ($10 billion), Bank of New York Mellon ($3 billion), and State Street ($3 billion). Ibid., 373–74.

92. Ibid., 380.

93. As Chapter 14 would be the applicable Bankruptcy Code chapter, Dodd-Frank's requirement that living wills describe bankruptcy resolution, Dodd-Frank Act section 5311(a)(4)(D), (d)(4), would require planning for a Chapter 14 case. See also William Kroener, "Revised Chapter 14 2.0 and Living Will Requirements Under the Dodd-Frank Act," chapter 8 in this volume.

94. Dodd-Frank Act, section 203(b).

amended Federal Reserve Act section 13(3) disallows firm-specific lending but allows lending programs "with broad based eligibility."[95]

In addition to this legal framework, I assume that forthcoming Fed regulations consider all subordinated debt and all long-term debt with an original maturity of at least one year to be eligible to be left behind and effectively converted to an equity interest in the event of failure. As with other chapters in this volume, I refer to this eligible debt as capital-structure debt.[96] I also assume Fed regulations require firms like Lehman to hold debt qualifying as capital structure debt in an amount equal to 20 percent of the book value of their assets, approximately what Lehman owed in 2008.[97] Notably, this is a similar figure to the total loss-absorbing capacity that Lehman would have to hold

---

95. Dodd-Frank Act, section 716.

96. See Jackson, "Building on Bankruptcy: Revised Chapter 14," section 2(6), defining "capital structure debt" to include, more specifically, "unsecured debt (including the under-secured portion of secured debt that would otherwise constitute capital structure debt), other than a qualified financial contract, of the debtor for borrowed money with an original maturity of at least one year that is either (a) of a kind required by the Board or other applicable government agency, (b) contractually subordinated to other unsecured debt, or (c) convertible upon specified financial events or conditions to a security that would have a lower priority in bankruptcy than unsecured debt." Ibid., section 2(3). For simplicity, I ignore under-secured debt and eligible convertibles.

97. In arriving at this estimate, I assume first that regulators will set a capital-structure-debt floor as high as politics allow. The starting point for this debate is likely to be the levels observed in 2008, around 20 percent. Though raising capital-structure debt requirements will be difficult, it will also be hard to argue for a lower figure without conceding that financial institutions' long-term debt is subsidized. In Lehman's bankruptcy, senior bondholders will receive a 27 percent payout; see Lehman Brothers Holdings, Inc. and Its Affiliated Debtors, "Notice Regarding Fifth Distribution Pursuant to the Modified Third Amended Joint Chapter 11 Plan, Exhibit A," March 27, 2014, whereas in a counterfactual Chapter 14 case, deeming all long-term debt to be left behind in resolution should return above 27 percent for these debt-holders. See part IV.E. Expectations of a greater than 27 percent recovery rate should make borrowing less expensive than expectations of a 27 percent recovery, implying that a 20 percent capital-structure-debt floor will only make debt more expensive if the current expectation is for a bailout.

under new Financial Stability Board regulations. These regulations will require institutions like Lehman to hold a total amount of capital and debt that would qualify as capital-structure debt equal to around 21–25 percent of the risk-weighted value of assets.[98] Finally, I assume that the Fed initiates and manages Lehman's Chapter 14 filing, though this need not always be the case.[99]

Internationally, I assume that Lehman and the large majority of its counterparties have signed the International Swaps and Derivatives Association (ISDA) Resolution Stay Protocol.[100] I also assume that BRRD Article 60a has been implemented in Europe and that Chapter 14 is considered a crisis management measure under that article.[101] Furthermore, I assume that foreign regulators choose not to place subsidiaries into separate resolution proceedings or to ring-fence foreign-held assets. This could follow from foreign regulators agreeing with the Fed that Chapter 14 should forestall systemic costs globally. But, it is also a significant assumption; many are rightly concerned that international authorities undertaking opposing actions in the event of a financial resolution will undermine any ability to maintain a firm's operations.[102]

---

98. See Financial Stability Board, "Adequacy of loss-absorbing capacity of global systemically important banks in resolution," November 10, 2014. Note, however, that the GLAC requirements are not directly comparable to the assumption of 20 percent capital-structure debt in addition to existing capital. On the one hand, GLAC requires more debt, because long-term debt with a remaining maturity less than one year is excluded from the total. On the other, it requires less because the 21–25 percent figure is relative to risk-weighted and not total assets.

99. Most often, management will be disinclined to file in a timely manner. This was certainly true in Lehman's actual case. See Miller and Horowitz, "Lessons": "There was absolutely no intention on the part of Lehman to consider the possibility of bankruptcy . . . [for] any part of the Lehman enterprise." In other cases, the disinclination to file may be outweighed by Chapter 14's perceived benefits.

100. International Swaps and Derivatives Association, "ISDA 2014 Resolution Stay Protocol," November 4, 2014, http://assets.isda.org/media/f253b540 -25/958e4aed.pdf/.

101. BRRD, Article 60a, sections 1–2.

102. In an effort to encourage the adoption of regimes of mutual recognition for foreign resolution proceedings, the Hoover Institution's Chapter 14 proposal

Despite the changes in the legal and regulatory environment, I assume that parties nonetheless find themselves with the same information, balance sheets, contractual relationships, operational systems, and market conditions as existed in the fall of 2008. Though the only feasible assumption, this is unrealistic. Among other issues, Lehman's lenders expected to be bailed out.[103] Had they expected greater chances of bearing losses in the event that Lehman's assets fell in value, they would have charged higher rates of interest, cut exposure, or both. More expensive financing might, in turn, have diminished Lehman's risk-taking and reduced the chances of failure. In addition, much higher capital and liquidity requirements would have made it far less likely that regulators would have allowed Lehman to find itself with the balance sheet and liquidity structure that it did.[104] Nevertheless, a firm with a balance sheet similar to Lehman's in September 2008 may well use Chapter 14. For this reason and simply because Lehman is the only large financial institution to have gone through bankruptcy, this exercise remains valuable.

B. Meeting the Standards for a Chapter 14 Filing

Like Chapter 11, Chapter 14 will be most successful when prepared for in advance. In the counterfactual world, Lehman's living will describes

---

includes a proposal to amend Section 1506 of the US Bankruptcy Code to provide that a Chapter 14 judge would only be obligated to enforce foreign home-country stay orders or to issue orders barring US ring-fencing if the foreign jurisdiction had already adopted comparable provisions respecting US ancillary proceedings. See Jackson, "Building on Bankruptcy: Revised Chapter 14," section 1(5). Though I assume that this amendment has been made along with all other Chapter 14 Bankruptcy Code amendments, I also assume for the purposes of the counterfactual that no foreign jurisdiction has adopted such provisions and that therefore this amendment has little practical impact. See also discussions in Thomas Huertas, "A Resolvable Bank," chapter 6 in this volume, and Carmassi and Herring, "Cross-Border Challenge."

103. See discussion of Reserve Primary's expectations in part III.C.

104. See Skeel, "Financing SIFIs," discussing the new reforms, which will require institutions like Lehman to, in the future, maintain around a 10.5 percent consolidated capital ratio and cash sufficient to cover all needs during a thirty-day stress period.

its resolution under Chapter 14.[105] In accordance with that plan, as markets lose confidence in Lehman's assets the Fed and Lehman staff develop three options. They prefer a private acquisition or recapitalization.[106] But, they also plan for Chapter 14 and SPOE.[107] Between the latter two, Chapter 14 is the statutory presumption.[108]

The Fed must consult the Treasury and FDIC as it considers filing a Chapter 14 case.[109] In addition, it may involve other domestic and international regulators if doing so is worth the risk of further sapping market confidence. The Fed may also notify members of the special Article III court that will hear the Chapter 14 case, preselected special masters,[110] and select private-market participants, if doing so is necessary to prepare the courts for a filing.

The Fed may file for Chapter 14 on Lehman's behalf once it gains sufficient evidence to meet the two Chapter 14 standards.[111] To begin a case, the Fed must certify that Chapter 14 is necessary to avoid serious adverse effects on US financial stability.[112] Additionally, the Fed must be prepared to certify within twenty-four hours that a recapitalized bridge company will provide adequate assurance of future performance on assumed contracts.

To make an adequate-assurance finding, the Fed must assess (a) whether Lehman has enough cash to continue in business following

---

105. See discussion in part III.A.

106. This preference was notable in Lehman's actual case, as recounted in the Valukas Report, 1516–22. Because neither Chapter 14 nor Title II was available, developing a private-sector option consumed all attention. When that failed, Chapter 11 was the only option left. Ibid., 1523–36.

107. Lehman is eligible for Chapter 14 as a corporation with assets over $50 billion whose business is the provision of financial services and products. Jackson, "Building on Bankruptcy: Revised Chapter 14," section 1(1).

108. See discussion in part III.A.

109. Jackson, "Building on Bankruptcy: Revised Chapter 14," section 2(4).

110. Ibid., section 3(1).

111. As Chapter 14 allows ex-post damages suits, the Fed must be confident that it has sufficient evidence to later defend both certifications in court, if necessary. Jackson, "Building on Bankruptcy: Revised Chapter 14," section 2(4).

112. Ibid.

Chapter 14;[113] and (b) whether New Lehman will be solvent after the Chapter 14 process is completed. Such an assessment of the Lehman facts indicates that, by the last Friday Lehman operated, September 12, it probably would have been too late to initiate a Chapter 14 filing because Lehman was already devoid of liquidity. As discussed in part II, Lehman had $3 billion more in debts due on Monday, September 15, than it had cash available[114] and expected to be short billions of dollars of cash each day of the coming week.[115] Rather, Lehman had enough liquidity to file only through Sunday, September 7. At that point, Lehman still had $34 billion of cash in its parent liquidity pool,[116] CDS spreads were around 300,[117] repo capacity had scarcely changed over the past week,[118] and commercial paper was continuing

---

113. In some cases, a liquidity-poor institution may be able to expect substantial private-sector financing following the Chapter 14 process, either independently or using Chapter 14's debtor-in-possession provisions. Lehman's facts indicate it would have had substantial trouble accessing private financing immediately. During Lehman weekend, assembled banks offered $20 billion of equity financing to facilitate Barclays' acquisition, but on the condition that Barclays guarantee Lehman's trading liabilities, which UK regulators barred Barclays from doing. See Valukas Report, 1528–29. In the counterfactual world, New Lehman would not have such a guarantee. This does not rule out the possibility of Lehman securing financing through debtor-in-possession funding, but to be conservative I assume here that Lehman and the Fed expect it to need to rely on existing liquidity for at least some time.

114. See discussion in part II.B.

115. Author's calculations based on Lehman, "9/13/08 Liquidity Summary," 3; Robert Azerad, "E-mail to Ian Lowitt, et al.," Bates Stamp LBEX-DOCID 717430, September 13, 2008; Lehman, "10/7/08 Liquidity," 99. Analysis of Lehman's liquidity projections also reveals that even if Lehman had deferred payments on maturing long-term debt and foregone buybacks and even if the Fed had accepted all repo unwound by the street, stepped into J. P. Morgan's shoes as clearing bank, and returned $7 billion of collateral—even then, Lehman would not have made it through Tuesday. Ibid.

116. Lehman, "9/13/08 Liquidity Summary," 25.

117. Lehman, "10/7/08 Liquidity," 92.

118. Ibid., 93.

to roll over.[119] Most importantly, this is the last date before which the market perceived Lehman to be insolvent.[120]

The second adequate-assurance inquiry is relatively straightforward to meet through September 7 because Lehman held $96 billion of capital-structure debt, far more than any estimate of the extent of its insolvency. Some, including both Fed staffers and Barclays, thought Lehman was solvent on September 15.[121] Others, including Fed management, thought Lehman was insolvent, but by far less than $96 billion. For instance, Bank of America had identified about $65 billion of real estate assets that it was unwilling to acquire without loss protection, which the FDIC later estimated might have incurred losses of $40 billion,[122] leaving Lehman insolvent by about $12 billion.[123]

While the two prongs of the adequate-assurance standard demarcate the latest possible filing, the earliest depends upon when the Fed can certify that Chapter 14 is necessary to avoid serious adverse effects on US financial stability. At the latest, the Fed can argue that Chapter 14 is necessary once markets will imminently perceive Lehman to be insolvent. Referring again to figure 7.5, the first date at which the markets adjudge Lehman to be insolvent is July 14. This dip would have justified certifying adverse effects on any of eight weekends between July 19–20 and September 6–7. Less conservatively, the Fed might have relied on traditional banking safety-and-soundness regulation, which deems a 2 percent capital ratio to be critically undercapitalized.[124] From a market-solvency standpoint, Lehman was consistently

---

119. Lehman, "9/13/08 Liquidity Summary," 1.

120. See figure 7.5.

121. James B. Stewart and Peter Eavis, "Revisiting the Lehman Brothers Bailout That Never Was," *New York Times*, September 29, 2014; FDIC (Federal Deposit Insurance Corporation), "The Orderly Liquidation of Lehman Brothers Holdings, Inc. Under the Dodd-Frank Act," *FDIC Quarterly* 5, no. 2: 1, 14 (noting that Barclays found only $20 billion of problematic assets, less than Lehman's book equity).

122. FDIC, "Orderly Liquidation of Lehman," 2.

123. Lehman had $28 billion of book equity at this point. See table 7.1.

124. See discussion in part II.A.

critically undercapitalized from June onward,[125] offering the Fed a possible additional five weekends earlier in the summer during which it could have filed.

Ideally, Chapter 14 cases will be filed early, particularly in fragile market environments. Though filing earlier than necessary risks imposing additional losses upon capital-structure-debt holders relative to no filing, it also minimizes their losses relative to later filings. Moreover, if Chapter 14 is used early enough to allow equity to absorb all losses, then it can be used to issue preferred shares or restructured debt instruments to capital-structure-debt holders with terms equal to those of the original debt instruments. This could make capital-structure-debt holders whole, imposing only *de minimis* losses while also staving off systemic risk concerns.

Realistically, though, regulators will resist triggering Chapter 14 until its use appears critical. I therefore assume that the counterfactual filing occurs on Friday, September 5, the last Friday before Lehman's liquidity fell critically low. By this point, in addition to the strong indications of insolvency, regulators could have demanded Lehman's Q3 results, which would have clearly shown that markets would imminently be convinced of insolvency.[126]

C. Filing Lehman's Chapter 14 Case

In the counterfactual world described above, on or before the evening of Friday, September 5, the Fed informs Lehman's directors that Holdings can file for Chapter 14 or else the Fed will file on Holdings' behalf. Though the Fed's ability to file is critical to ensuring a sufficiently early filing, who files is procedurally immaterial as any filing immediately begins the case.[127] Crucially, only Holdings enters bankruptcy;[128] all subsidiaries continue operating as usual and the Estate consists only of

---

125. Figure 7.5.

126. See part II.B.

127. See Jackson, "Building on Bankruptcy: Revised Chapter 14," section 2(4). By contrast, in an involuntary Chapter 11 case, there is first a period in which the debtor may dispute the filing.

128. Ibid., section 3.

Holdings' own balance sheet. Figure 7.7 illustrates Holdings' balance sheet and how it is connected to subsidiary funding, though note that figures therein (all USD billions) are mostly from September 14, the closest-dated to September 5 data available.

The Chapter 14 filing operates as an expanded automatic stay with four facets. In addition to the typical features of a Section 362 stay,[129] Chapter 14 also stays all US-law creditors of all Lehman entities (including non-filing subsidiaries such as the New York broker-dealer LBI and the main US derivatives subsidiary LBSF) from terminating, accelerating, or modifying any contract.[130] Second, it stays all contractual rights and obligations contingent upon a Chapter 14 filing.[131] Third, it overrides safe-harbor provisions to stay qualified financial contract counterparties' termination rights for up to forty-eight hours.[132] Finally, it permanently stays the rights of subsidiaries' creditors and counterparties to terminate contracts due to a change in control.[133] The second and third of these stay provisions require qualified financial contract counterparties of all Lehman companies to continue to perform payment and delivery obligations under US contracts. Therefore, even though Lehman's subsidiaries are not in bankruptcy, the stay prevents their counterparties to around $55 billion of US-law term repo agreements[134] and around $25 billion of US-law derivatives[135] from terminating on the basis of Holdings' filing, though it does allow maturing repurchase agreements to expire in due course.

---

129. 11 USC, section 362.

130. Jackson, "Building on Bankruptcy: Revised Chapter 14," section 2(9).

131. Ibid., section 2(7).

132. Ibid., section 2(8).

133. Ibid., section 2(9).

134. Lehman, "9/13/08 Liquidity Summary," 7–8. The figure comes from adding traditional repo in use ($90.4) and nontraditional shells booked ($93.2), subtracting all overnight and open repo in use ($82.1), then multiplying by the proportion of repo that was US-based (.54). Also see statement by Harvey Miller, Federal Reserve Resolution Conference, October 18, 2013.

135. Author's calculations from Disclosure Statement for First Amended Plan, Exhibit 11, April 14, 2010. Full derivation on file with author.

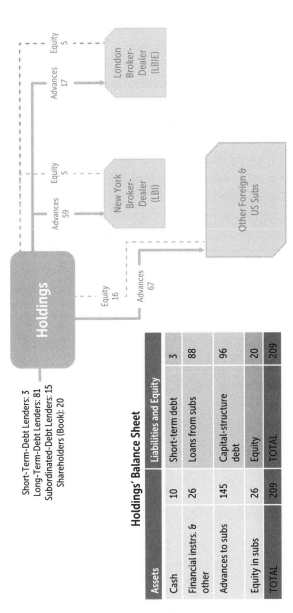

Figure 7.7. Only Holdings Files

Source: Based on data from "Lehman Brothers Holdings, Inc. and Its Affiliated Debtors, Debtors' Disclosure Statement for Joint Chapter 11 Plan," exhibits 9-4, 9-5, 9-6 (Apr. 14, 2010); Lehman Brothers, exhibit 21.10: "List of the Registrant's Subsidiaries," in Lehman, 2007 10-K (disclosing ownership structure of various intermediate holding companies); and table 7.1.

Naturally, Lehman's many European-law contracts are outside this stay's jurisdiction. Nothing in Chapter 14 prevents counterparties to around $45 billion of UK-law term repo agreements[136] and $17 billion of derivatives[137] from terminating their contracts. Nothing in Chapter 14 prevents foreign regulators from ring-fencing assets in their jurisdictions, nor does it prevent them from placing into administration subsidiaries domiciled in their jurisdictions.

Fortunately, few master repo agreements contain the same types of cross-default provisions as master derivatives agreements, and the ISDA Resolution Stay Protocol and BRRD article 60a go a long way in addressing the latter problem. Under the ISDA Protocol, any derivatives master agreement between Lehman and another Protocol party disallows cross-default and early termination rights on the basis of the Chapter 14 filing alone. Article 60a imposes a similar stay that likewise prevents counterparties from exercising termination rights.[138] Therefore, counterparties to the very large majority of contracts held by subsidiaries are stayed from accelerating or terminating their obligations. For the purposes of the counterfactual, I assume foreign regulators cooperate in the administration of Chapter 14, but I return to this issue in part IV.

D. Moving for a Section 1405 Transfer

On Friday evening, ideally at least forty-eight hours before Asian markets reopen on Monday, the Fed moves for a section 1405 transfer. This is the specific legal mechanism by which the Fed will move all assets and liabilities except for capital-structure debt to the bridge holding company, New Holdings. Concurrently, the Fed provides electronic notice that Holdings has filed for Chapter 14 and that a hearing will be held in twenty-four hours on its motion.[139] Figure 7.8 depicts a chronology for the weekend.

---

136. See note 134 (same sum times proportion of nontraditional UK-based (.44)).

137. Author's calculations from "Disclosure Statement for First Amended Plan Exhibit 11," April 14, 2010. Full derivation on file with author.

138. BRRD, Article 60a, sections 1–2.

139. Jackson, "Building on Bankruptcy: Revised Chapter 14," section 2(6).

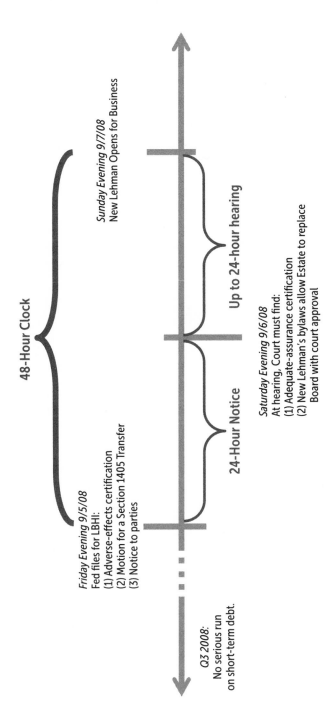

Figure 7.8. Counterfactual Timeline of Chapter 14 Section 1405 Transfer

48-Hour Clock

Friday Evening 9/5/08
Fed files for LBHI:
(1) Adverse-effects certification
(2) Motion for a Section 1405 Transfer
(3) Notice to parties

24-Hour Notice

Saturday Evening 9/6/08
At hearing, Court must find:
(1) Adequate-assurance certification
(2) New Lehman's bylaws allow Estate to replace
Board with court approval

Up to 24-hour hearing

Sunday Evening 9/7/08
New Lehman Opens for Business

Q3 2008:
No serious run
on short-term debt.

Chapter 14 requires the Fed to notify Holdings' twenty largest unsecured creditors,[140] the FDIC, and the primary regulators of each subsidiary whose equity may be transferred.[141] Holdings directly owns thirty-five material subsidiaries[142] which have eight primary regulators: the Fed, Securities and Exchange Commission, Commodity Futures Trading Commission, Commission Bancaire in France, Monetary Authority of Singapore, Australian Securities and Investments Commission, Commission de Surveillance du Secteur Financier, and German Federal Supervisory Authority for the Financial Services Industry.[143] As all other Lehman affiliates are owned by Holdings' subsidiaries, the Fed is not required to notify their regulators. Nonetheless, the Fed most likely provides courtesy notice to regulators of large indirect subsidiaries including the Office of the Comptroller of the Currency and Office of Thrift Supervision (still in existence back in 2008) in the United States, the Financial Services Authority in the United Kingdom, Swiss Federal Banking Commission, and Financial Services Agency in Japan.[144]

The transfer itself will allow New Holdings to step into Holdings' shoes. Specifically, the Estate will transfer to New Holdings all cash, financial instruments, advances to and equity in subsidiaries, and other miscellaneous assets.[145] These include a few qualified financial contracts and assets subject to secured creditors' liens, all of which can

---

140. Some of these were affiliates. See table 7.1 (showing that 47 percent of Holdings liabilities were owed to affiliates); Lehman, "First Disclosure" (Lehman Brothers Holdings, Inc. and Its Affiliated Debtors, Debtors' Disclosure Statement for Joint Chapter 11 Plan), Exhibit 9-5, April 14, 2010 (showing Holdings owed $33 billion to LB Treasury alone). Others may have been Lehman's largest third-party bondholders (owed another 42 percent of Holdings' liabilities, table 7.1), nearly all of whom were foreign. Lehman Brothers Holdings, Inc., "Chapter 11 Petition," September 15, 2008, 7–12.

141. Jackson, "Building on Bankruptcy: Revised Chapter 14," section 2(6).

142. Lehman, "List of Subsidiaries" (accounting as of November 30, 2007).

143. See Lehman Brothers Holdings, Inc., "Annual Report for 2007" (Form 10-K), 10–12.

144. Ibid. (discussing these regulators' roles in overseeing Lehman).

145. See table 7.1.

be transferred under the Chapter 14 provisions.[146] As consideration, New Holdings will issue to the Estate a 100 percent equity stake and will assume all of Holdings' liabilities except for its capital-structure debt. These liabilities include debt agreements with subsidiaries, structured debt agreements with third parties, qualified financial contract liabilities, and guarantees of subsidiaries and subsidiaries' contracts.[147] All transferred debts will be non-recourse.[148] In sum, the *only* assets and liabilities on Holdings' balance sheet that will not be transferred are capital-structure debt instruments. Figure 7.9 illustrates.

If approved, this transfer will cause New Lehman—the consolidated company led by New Holdings—to have a consolidated capital ratio of 19 percent.[149] As shown, Holdings' former shareholders and long-term-debt holders will continue to own claims on Holdings' Estate. Holdings' Estate will, in turn, own all equity in New Holdings. Other claimants will hold debt contracts on which New Holdings will be obliged to perform. New Holdings will own all thirty-five subsidiaries formerly owned by Holdings, it will guarantee those subsidiaries that were guaranteed by Holdings, and it will support subsidiary contracts that were guaranteed or otherwise supported by Holdings.

Additional elements of the transfer motion will clarify details regarding licenses for New Holdings, the structure of the relationship between the Estate and the directors of New Holdings, and initial management of New Holdings. One provision of Chapter 14 allows for the transfer of all licenses, permits, and registrations from Holdings

---

146. Notwithstanding the Bankruptcy Code's safe harbor, Chapter 14 allows the court to override anti-transfer provisions in QFC contracts in order to effectuate such a transfer. Jackson, "Building on Bankruptcy: Revised Chapter 14," section 2(8).

147. In the few cases where a non-qualified-financial-contract creditor is under-secured, that creditor's claim will be bifurcated. Jackson, "Building on Bankruptcy: Revised Chapter 14." The collateral and security interest will be transferred non-recourse and the deficiency claim will remain with the Estate as a general unsecured claim.

148. Jackson, "Building on Bankruptcy: Revised Chapter 14," section 2(3).

149. $116 billion book equity at New Holdings divided by $598 consolidated assets, table 7.1, gives a capital ratio of 19 percent.

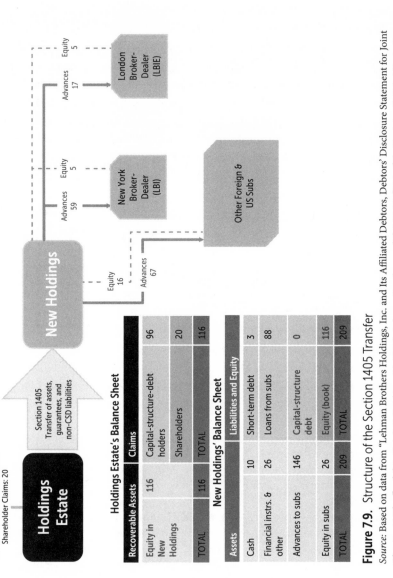

Figure 7.9. Structure of the Section 1405 Transfer

Source: Based on data from "Lehman Brothers Holdings, Inc. and Its Affiliated Debtors, Debtors' Disclosure Statement for Joint Chapter 11 Plan," exhibits 9-4, 9-5, 9-6 (Apr. 14, 2010); Lehman Brothers, exhibit 21.10: "List of the Registrant's Subsidiaries," in Lehman, 2007 10-K (disclosing ownership structure of various intermediate holding companies); and table 7.1.

to New Holdings.[150] Another requires that a trustee be selected from a pre-approved list to represent the Estate before the Chapter 14 judge, together with other committees representing parties in interest.[151] Within thirty days after the transfer, this trustee, together with the creditors' and shareholders' committees, will have an opportunity to replace the board of New Holdings.[152] No provisions, however, specifically constrain the Fed's discretion in determining whom among Lehman's managers and directors to propose to retain in order to maximize value for the estate, and whom to propose to let go. To help retention, the Fed also proposes a key employee retention policy upfront, as is typical for many bankruptcy filings.

Twenty-four hours after the Fed moves for the section 1405 transfer, the court holds a hearing to give shareholders, creditors, counterparties, and regulators opportunities to object. Chapter 14 allows the court only twenty-four additional hours in which to complete this hearing, for forty-eight hours total between filing and sale consummation. This tight time frame is not without precedent. In Lehman's actual bankruptcy case, Judge James Peck—taking into account the urgency and sensitivity of the situation—approved LBI's sale to Barclays in only twenty-four hours.[153]

Unlike Lehman's actual case, however, in a Chapter 14 case, the ex ante development and use of living wills focused on a Chapter 14 proceeding will enormously reduce the pressure involved in the short time frame.[154] Moreover, Chapter 14 is structured to mitigate the burden of the twenty-four-hour time frame. The Chapter 14 judge is a member of a preselected panel with financial services expertise who can also rely upon preselected special masters with additional expertise.[155] Most importantly, there is little upon which the court must rule. By the end of the hearing, the court needs only:

---

150. Jackson, "Building on Bankruptcy: Revised Chapter 14," section 2(10).
151. Ibid., section 2(15).
152. Ibid., section 2(6).
153. Lehman, "First Disclosure," 46.
154. See discussion in part III.A.
155. Thomas Jackson, "Bankruptcy Code Chapter 14: A Proposal," in *Bankruptcy Not Bailout*, 26–27.

1. To find that the Fed does not propose to transfer capital structure debt;
2. To find that New Holdings' bylaws allow for a thirty-day period in which the Estate, after notice and a hearing before the Chapter 14 judge, will choose New Holdings' board of directors; and
3. Either to find itself, or to note that the Fed had certified, that New Holdings will provide adequate assurance of future performance on each liability assumed.

The Fed's proposed transfer is structured to satisfy the first and second of these provisions by design. Consequently, the *only* provision at issue is the third. In the counterfactual, the Fed files early enough to make this certification itself. Therefore, the primary challenge the Chapter 14 judge faces is ensuring parties at interest receive an opportunity to be heard in the course of the twenty-four-hour hearing.

There may be few objections to the transfer. If Chapter 14 is credible and filed early, all parties should expect to be at least as well off with it than without it.[156] Nonetheless, creditors or regulators may object to their claims or regulated subsidiaries being transferred without their consent. They may not halt the sale if performance is adequately assured, but they may argue that the certification is unwarranted. Additionally, capital-structure-debt holders may object to the transfer of assets, though it will be challenging for them to show expected harm. It is highly likely that Holdings' assets—83 percent of which are equity in or debts due from subsidiaries[157]—will return more value if transferred to the bridge company than if retained with the Estate.[158] Furthermore, public policy reasons motivate the transfer; approving it over objections therefore likely satisfies due process under *Matthews v. Eldridge*.[159] If a court later concludes otherwise, the remedy is an ex-post damages action as specified in Chapter 14.[160]

---

156. See part IV.E.
157. Table 7.1.
158. See part IV.E.
159. 424 U.S. 319, 332–35 (1976).
160. Jackson, "Building on Bankruptcy: Revised Chapter 14," section 2(4).

Other objections may be more likely. Parties can object to New Holdings' proposed management, the New Holdings charter and bylaws, or provisions governing how the Estate will choose new management and directors of New Holdings after an interregnum period. Parties can also move to propose alternative management structures, trustees, procedures, or sale details. Ideally, the living-will process will have been used to address many such issues ahead of time.

So long as the court makes the findings above within twenty-four hours, a version of the sale outlined here, an interim management team and structure for New Holdings, a charter and bylaws, a list of trustees for the Holdings Estate, and an agreement governing Estate-Holdings relations are approved on Sunday evening, just before Asian markets open.

Part IV: Business after Chapter 14

This part asks two hard questions of the Lehman facts. Given New Lehman's state after Chapter 14, can it finance itself? And, would the social welfare outcomes exceed those of a bailout? With some conditions, it answers each question in the affirmative.

A. Managing the Business and Recapitalizing Subsidiaries

In the counterfactual world, New Holdings opens on Sunday evening, September 7, 2008, as a normal holding company neither directly controlled by regulators nor in bankruptcy. It receives no Bankruptcy Code protections nor is it subject to debtor-in-possession requirements, such as court approval for financing or for pursuing non-ordinary-course activities. New Holdings immediately assumes all responsibilities formerly borne by Holdings, particularly its cash-management and treasury roles. Operational systems are unchanged from those at Holdings; they merely have a different legal employer and owner.

The interim Board, CEO, and managers are immediately responsible for making all decisions to maximize value for New Holdings' single shareholder, Holdings' Estate.[161] Management has a volumi-

---

161. By contrast, under SPOE, the FDIC retains discretion to make these decisions. See SPOE Fed. Reg., 76617.

nous list of tasks. It needs to assess and administer Lehman's liquidity and generate strategies to obtain short-term cash, including asset sales and new debt or equity funding. It needs to address runs on the prime-broker business, derivatives novations, and potential runs on Lehman's banks. Though it has an exemption from meeting applicable debt and capital requirements for up to one year,[162] it needs to evaluate long-term restructuring and liquidation options for broad asset classes and business lines and develop a strategy to return to compliance with these regulations. It needs to communicate with regulatory bodies all over the world and thousands of counterparties. And fleeing employees or a ratings downgrade may hamper these efforts.

Yet, financial markets have a track record of absorbing stress and structuring unprecedented workouts when circumstances require. In the past couple of decades, such workouts have minimized losses associated with Bear Stearns in 2008, Long-Term Capital Management in 1998, Salomon Brothers in 1991, and Drexel Burnham in 1989–90, among others. Thus, though these challenges are immense, they are ones with which the private sector is familiar.

At the subsidiary level, several legal events have safeguarded businesses and contractual relationships from resolution. First, Chapter 14, the ISDA Resolution Stay Protocol, and BRRD article 60a together have disallowed subsidiary creditors and counterparties from terminating or altering obligations on the basis of Holdings' filing. The Chapter 14 stay lifts after the section 1405 sale, but, as no subsidiary has defaulted on obligations, counterparties must thereafter continue to perform all pre-sale obligations. By Sunday night, these parties are in the same legal positions as they were Friday afternoon.

Second, Holdings-owned subsidiaries such as New York broker-dealer LBI have experienced a change of control, as their ownership interests are now held by New Holdings. Chapter 14 permanently stays contractual provisions allowing these subsidiaries' creditors or counterparties to terminate on this basis.[163] Similarly, provisions allowing

---

162. Jackson, "Building on Bankruptcy: Revised Chapter 14," section 2(11).
163. See discussion in part III.C.

termination due to a change in the parent's or a subsidiary's credit rating are stayed for ninety days.[164]

Third, subsidiaries formerly guaranteed by Holdings, whether in full or with respect to certain contracts, are now guaranteed by New Holdings. In Lehman's actual case, the importance of these guarantees is illustrated by $94 billion of guarantee claims that subsidiaries filed against the parent.[165] These guarantees were integral to the pre–Chapter 14 debt pricing that creditors and counterparties offered subsidiaries and therefore their re-extension is imperative to ensure continued access to private financing and to reassure clients and foreign regulators.

Fourth, subsidiary contracts that implicated Holdings—such as ISDA Master Agreements listing Holdings as a credit support provider or specified entity—are deemed post-sale to instead implicate New Holdings. Once more, these provisions ensure that no creditor or counterparty with ongoing pre-sale obligations to subsidiaries under US law is able to terminate or alter those obligations on the basis of the Chapter 14 filing and its immediate consequences.

In Lehman's actual case, many of the most challenging legal issues related to foreign subsidiaries, foreign assets, and non-US law contracts. As discussed above, however, the ISDA Protocol and article 60a solve many of the foreign challenges observed. Nevertheless, some creditors and counterparties under non-US-law contracts may retain rights to accelerate or terminate obligations on the basis of the Chapter 14 filing and transfer.[166] Of even greater concern is that foreign regulators could intervene in the Chapter 14 process. Public data do

---

164. Jackson, "Building on Bankruptcy: Revised Chapter 14," section 2(7).

165. Author's calculations from Lehman, "First Disclosure," exhibit 4.

166. For example, Article 60a does not address change-of-control provisions. This might mean that counterparties to non-US-law contracts held by Holdings' thirty-five subsidiaries could accelerate or terminate their obligations on the basis of the transfer. This is most likely to be a problem for Holdings' ten foreign-domiciled direct subsidiaries, including its French and German banks. See Lehman, "List of Subsidiaries," 10–12. Other contracts might additionally contain provisions stating that, on the basis of this acceleration or termination, they too may accelerate or terminate.

not fully clarify the extent to which foreign contractual issues would have hindered New Lehman's ability to continue business,[167] and it is impossible to know how foreign regulators would have reacted and how costly their interventions might have been. For the purposes of the counterfactual, I must assume that the Fed and Lehman, through the living-will process, know ahead of time that these costs will be small enough not to threaten New Lehman's solvency. In subparts IV.B and IV.D below, however, I assume New Lehman may need to manage what I generically call "international friction" costs of $10 billion.

Even though subsidiaries have mostly been safeguarded from Chapter 14's effects, New Holdings may want to take steps to reassure funders, counterparties, and regulators of subsidiaries' sound footing. As illustrated in figure 7.10, New Holdings can recapitalize subsidiaries by altering its internal intra-company ledgers to convert debt owed by subsidiaries to New Holdings into equity New Holdings owns in subsidiaries. This increases key Lehman entities' capital ratios, reducing the likelihood of regulatory intervention and increasing the expected payout to creditors should New Holdings' management determine that some subsidiaries should enter their own resolution proceedings.

B. Lehman's Solvency and Financing after Recapitalization

The two factors most determinative of New Lehman's success—and Chapter 14's ability to prevent systemic costs—are its ability to obtain financing and the extent to which the marketplace is confident about its solvency. If New Lehman fails in either dimension and therefore experiences and is unable to weather a severe post–Chapter 14 run, the run could cascade and affect other firms, just as knock-on effects followed Lehman's Chapter 11 filing.[168] And unless policymakers believe a run is avoidable, they will forgo Chapter 14 entirely.

---

167. Because micro data on individual contracts have not been disclosed, it is impossible to know with precision what proportion of which subsidiaries' obligations were governed by non-US law and, of these, how many and in what amounts included provisions that could have been triggered by a Chapter 14 filing.

168. See part II.C.

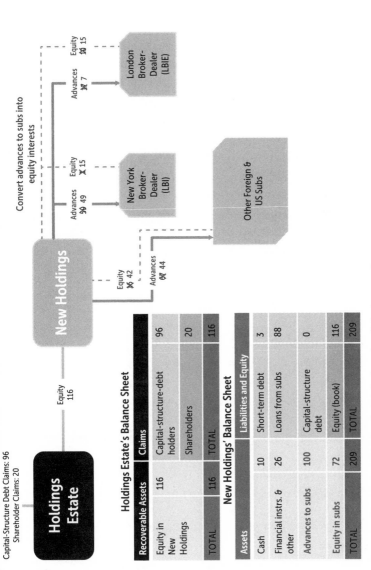

Convert advances to subs into equity interests

Capital-Structure Debt Claims: 96
Shareholder Claims: 20

Holdings Estate

Equity 116

New Holdings

Advances $49 — Equity $15 → New York Broker-Dealer (LBI)

Advances $7 — Equity $15 → London Broker-Dealer (LBIE)

Equity $42 — Advances $44 → Other Foreign & US Subs

Holdings Estate's Balance Sheet

Recoverable Assets		Claims	
Equity in New Holdings	116	Capital-structure-debt holders	96
		Shareholders	20
TOTAL	116	TOTAL	116

New Holdings' Balance Sheet

Assets		Liabilities and Equity	
Cash	10	Short-term debt	3
Financial instrs. & other	26	Loans from subs	88
Advances to subs	100	Capital-structure debt	0
Equity in subs	72	Equity (book)	116
TOTAL	209	TOTAL	209

Figure 7.10. Recapitalizing Subsidiaries after Sale Approval

Source: Based on data from "Lehman Brothers Holdings, Inc. and Its Affiliated Debtors, Debtors' Disclosure Statement for Joint Chapter 11 Plan," exhibits 9-4, 9-5, 9-6 (Apr. 14, 2010); Lehman Brothers, exhibit 21.10: "List of the Registrant's Subsidiaries," in Lehman, 2007 10-K (disclosing ownership structure of various intermediate holding companies); and table 7.1.

After Chapter 14, New Lehman has a 19 percent consolidated capital ratio, three to four times that of comparable institutions.[169] On a book basis it has $116 billion of equity supporting only $78 billion of questionable real estate–related assets.[170] As indicated in figure 7.5, though markets were concerned about the value of these assets, they did not perceive them to be worthless. Rather, until September 8, markets discounted the value of Lehman's assets by almost exactly their book-equity value. Even in Lehman's final days, market-implied losses relative to book peaked at $54 billion.[171] Assume that, in addition to this $54 billion figure, New Lehman faces liabilities related to international frictions of $10 billion and financing costs of another $10 billion. In total, this places losses at $74 billion, $42 billion less than New Lehman's book equity. Lenders who believe figures in this general ballpark have no incentive to run on the basis of insolvency. Figure 7.11 illustrates the impact that asset devaluations and increases to liabilities would have on New Lehman, showing that, even after devaluations of a magnitude never before seen, New Lehman remains solvent.

Nonetheless, creditors and counterparties might run for other reasons. In particular, New Lehman could experience a shock that might cause existing lenders to increase asset encumbrances or the market could—either independently or because of Chapter 14—become severely illiquid. Chapter 14 helps ameliorate run risks in these cases, but will be less successful than in the insolvency case.

A careful analysis of Lehman's liquidity position and liquidity risks as of September 5 (the Friday before the counterfactual filing) indicates that New Lehman is able to withstand a moderate liquidity crisis.[172] To

---

169. See part III.D.

170. Lehman, "9/11/08 Funding Slides," 82.

171. Book equity of $20 billion plus approximately $34 billion negative solvency equity. See figure 7.5.

172. Lehman had experience doing so by late 2008. Over the week beginning March 17, 2008, after Bear Stearns was sold to J. P. Morgan, Lehman lost $7 billion of repo funding, $4 billion of prime brokerage accounts, and $3 billion of commercial paper and had to handle $1 billion of derivatives novations. Relying on its ability to pledge affiliate collateral to the European Central Bank, the broker-dealers'

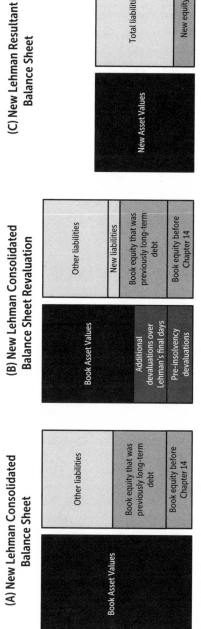

(A) New Lehman Consolidated Balance Sheet

(B) New Lehman Consolidated Balance Sheet Revaluation

(C) New Lehman Resultant Balance Sheet

Figure 7.11. Post–Chapter 14 Asset Devaluations Short of Insolvency

test this proposition, I developed a three-week stress test using data available in Lehman's discovery documents that mimics the run Lehman actually experienced the week of September 8–12 (the first week after the counterfactual filing) and Lehman's own projected outflows for the weeks of September 15–26 (the second and third weeks after the counterfactual filing).[173]

I derived estimates for outflows related to unsecured funding maturities, operating cash flows, and other contractual commitments and liabilities using data on what Lehman experienced in fact between September 8 and September 12, which is likely more severe than what New Lehman can be expected to face. With regards to secured funding, I was less conservative and assumed New Lehman can renew all of Lehman's maturing repo funding, but can do so only at the lower of haircuts that were either (a) charged by LBI counterparties during the week of September 8–12 or (b) charged by the Fed while LBI used the PDCF the week of September 15–19.

Table 7.2 displays the results. As shown, under these assumptions, New Lehman can weather a moderate three-week liquidity crisis and still have $18 billion of liquidity remaining at the end of September. If New Lehman additionally pays $10 billion to manage international frictions, the figure falls to $8 billion, but remains positive.

Only a driver other than insolvency, such as market-wide illiquidity, would cause a substantial run on New Lehman such as that reflected

---

trapped liquidity pools, cushions built into the structure of the repo book, and the newly available PDCF, Lehman weathered this event. Lehman, "5/15/08 Liquidity," 25. But success in the face of a liquidity crisis is far from assured. In May and June 2008, the Fed determined that, under certain assumptions, Lehman would have been short of liquidity if 35 percent of repo funding failed to turn over, 35 percent of prime broker clients pulled out, derivative margin requirements increased 35 percent, and 35 percent of derivatives counterparties experienced delays meeting payment obligations. Federal Reserve Bank of New York, "Primary Dealer Monitoring: Initial Assessment of CSEs," Bates Stamp FRBNY to Exam 000017-36, May 12, 2008.

173. If anything, these outflow estimates may be less conservative than the mean, as these were the figures that Lehman used to try to convince regulators to provide financing over Lehman weekend. See Azerad, "E-mail."

in table 7.2. As noted in the assumptions, New Lehman will need central bank assistance to fund some of the $109 billion of repo loans that were maturing in early September.[174] But market-wide illiquidity will also justify the Fed opening a facility to accept all dealer-bank collateral generally acceptable to tri-party lenders at higher haircuts, as the Fed's Primary Dealer Credit Facility (PDCF) did after September 15, 2008.[175] Figure 7.12 illustrates the peak and average amounts borrowed by a selection of Lehman peers between 2008 and 2010 as well as the number of days that each firm borrowed from the Fed. Given the amount of lending the Fed provided then, it is not hard to imagine a firm like New Lehman relying for some time on considerable central-bank support.[176]

On balance, the scenario explored in table 7.2 is near the center of a wide distribution of possible outcomes. If markets remain liquid, then it may too conservatively rule out additional unsecured financing. Even with $74 billion of losses,[177] New Lehman would remain well capitalized relative to its peers, with an 8 percent capital ratio.[178] This might well allow it to issue bonds or secure new lines of bank funding at high interest rates. On the other hand, if New Lehman experiences a run of greater magnitude than described in table 7.2 or if it uniquely faces challenging market conditions too narrowly tailored to justify a PDCF-type facility, then policymakers may be forced to turn to Title II in order to access the OLF.

---

174. Lehman, "9/11/08 Liquidity," 43–52.

175. A PDCF-type facility would be allowed by the new Dodd-Frank amended section 13(3). See Darrell Duffie, "Replumbing Our Financial System: Uneven Progress," presentation at conference of the Board of Governors of the Federal Reserve System, "Central Banking: Before, During, and After the Crisis," March 23–24, 2012, Washington DC; Brian D. Christiansen, "Federal Reserve Emergency Credit," *Skadden Commentary on the Dodd-Frank Act*, July 9, 2010, http://www.skadden.com/insights/federal-reserve-emergency-credit.

176. See also Skeel, "Financing SIFIs," arguing that the Federal Reserve Act should be amended to allow firms like New Lehman to access the discount window even outside of a program with broad-based eligibility. Such a reform would most likely have assured New Lehman's stability given the figures presented here.

177. See beginning of part IV.B.

178. (116-74)/(598-74).

Table 7.2. Post–Chapter 14 Hypothetical Liquidity Stress Test 9/8–9/26

Liquidity Available	Assumptions	USD Bil
TOTAL		50
Parent liquidity pool	As stated on 9/5 less assets pledged as intraday collateral	34
Broker-dealers' liquidity	As stated on 9/8	1
Affiliate bank sources	As estimated in Fed stress tests	4
Committed bank facilities	As reported on 9/15	5
Asset sales	As estimated in Fed stress tests	6
Liquidity Loss Categories	**Assumptions**	**Resultant Losses**
Secured Funding		(12)
Week of 9/8–9/12	Re-funds collateral for which Lehman in fact lost funding—either on the street or through a central bank—but only at haircuts that were charged by the street in Lehman's final week or by the PDCF after 9/15; clearing banks do not make collateral calls.	(4)
Week of 9/15–9/26	Renews all maturing repo—either on the street or through a central bank—but only at haircuts actually charged by the street in Lehman's final week or by the PDCF after 9/15.	(8)
Assumed haircut increases:	2%: Treasuries, Municipal Bonds, G10 Bonds	(1)
	4%: US Agency-Issued Securities	(2)
	6%: Asset-Backed Securities	(0)
	10%: Corporate Bonds and Commercial Paper	(1)

	15%: Equities	(1)
	20%: International Agency Securities, Agency & Private-Label Collateralized Mortgage Obligations	(3)
Unsecured Funding		**(5)**
Commercial paper and short-term debt	50% fails to roll, as occurred in fact between 9/8 and 9/12	(4)
Short-term bank loan maturities	Draw-downs offset 75% of maturities, as occurred in fact between 9/8 and 9/12	(0)
Deposit outflows	No maturing deposits turn over	(1)
Commitments and other liabilities	Must meet 100% of loan and conduit funding plus another $2 billion of on-boarding commitments, average of what occurred in fact and what was used in Fed stress tests.	(4)
Operating cash flows		**(11)**
Prime brokerage	75% loss of existing cash margins	(8)
Non-terminated derivatives	As occurred in fact between 9/8 and 9/12 and as estimated for 9/15–9/26	(3)
Total Liquidity Losses		(32)
Liquidity Available—Losses		18

Source: Author's analysis based on data from Lehman Brothers, Liquidity Summary 091309 6pm.xls, Bates Stamp LBEX-DOCID 647325, 1–3; Lehman Brothers, "Liquidity of Lehman Brothers," Bates Stamp LBEX-WGM 787681 (Oct. 7, 2008), 93–99; Lehman Brothers, *Liquidity Update*, Bates Stamp LBEX-WGM 784543 (Sept. 11 2008), 43–52; Federal Reserve Bank of New York, "Primary Dealer Monitoring: Liquidity Stress Analysis," Bates Stamp FRBNY to Exam 000033-37 (June 25, 2008); analysis of 9/8–9/12 funding losses in part II.B.

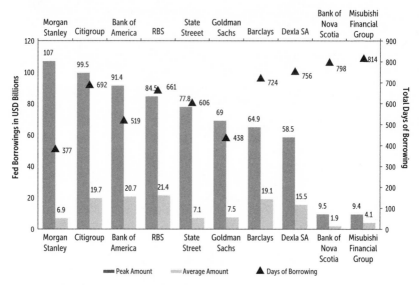

Figure 7.12. G-Reliance on Fed Funding during the Financial Crisis

Source: Based on data from Bradley Keoun et al., "The Fed's Secret Liquidity Lifelines," *Bloomberg,* http://www.bloomberg.com/data-visualization/federal-reserve-emergency -lending/.

Assuming New Lehman does successfully manage its liquidity, New Holdings and all Lehman subsidiaries meet all of the firm's debts as they come due. This results in dramatically different outcomes relative to Lehman's actual case. Commercial paper lenders such as the Reserve Primary Fund are paid in full at maturity, forestalling the entire chain of events that created a crisis in the commercial paper markets in 2008. Hedge fund clients who found themselves caught up in insolvency proceedings in the actual case are safeguarded. The legal entities that hold their assets have not themselves gone through insolvency proceedings. For those in London, LBIE has not even experienced a change of control. Counterparties to US-law contracts briefly have their contractual rights stayed but are otherwise unaffected. Lehman derivatives affiliates have continued to meet all obligations when due. Any parent-company creditors holding other non-capital-structure debt have been paid at maturity.

Consequently, there is no reason to expect a repeat of the systemic consequences observed as a result of Lehman's actual 2008 case.[179] There would be no reason for investors to run on money-market funds, no reason for those funds to in turn curtail lending to ordinary corporations, and no reason for depositors to respond to a money-market-fund crisis by pulling out of commercial banks. There would be no reason for hedge funds to flee their prime brokers or for investment banks to turn to the Fed for financing. And, there would be much less reason for legislation to inject hundreds of billions into the banking sector.[180]

C. Options for Reorganizing the Business

Assuming New Lehman does successfully manage its liquidity after opening for business, it spends the subsequent months restructuring the business and preparing to raise equity. In 2008, Lehman recognized that its "concentration of positions in commercial real estate–related assets ha[d] become a significant concern for investors and creditors,"[181] and had already developed plans to spin off to shareholders $25–$30 billion of its $33 billion in commercial real estate positions when it released its Q3 2008 losses. Though shareholders' dislike for this plan helped drive Lehman's crashing stock price the week of September 8,[182] the plan was not inherently a bad one. After Chapter 14, consummating all or part of such a plan is relatively straightforward.

New Lehman's real estate assets are owned by a wide variety of legal entities. Over a third are held at New Lehman's banks, New Holdings itself owns another portion, and the New York broker-dealer and its subsidiaries own another.[183] Assuming the commercial real estate assets that New Holdings does not own directly are held by legal

---

179. See part II.C.

180. Of course, to whatever extent these outcomes were caused by drivers other than Lehman Brothers, Chapter 14's use might have left them unaffected.

181. Lehman, 9/10/08 8-K, Ex. 99.1, 3.

182. See, e.g., Lehman, "10/7/08 Liquidity," 11. ("Lack of immediate actions around asset disposal [in September 9, 2008, earnings release] further dampened market sentiment.")

183. Author's calculations from Lehman, "9/11/08 Funding Slides," 82; Lehman, "First Disclosure," 49.

entities with sufficient debts to New Holdings,[184] New Holdings can simply "purchase" the relevant assets by forgiving these subsidiaries' receivables in amounts comparable to its book valuations of the assets in question. Having taken ownership of the assets, Holdings can transfer them to a separate vehicle with equity-only funding.[185] The Estate will then own two assets rather than one: 100 percent of the equity value of New Lehman, stripped of its questionable real estate assets, and 100 percent of the equity value of the spin-off vehicle.

New Lehman can also undertake other actions to partially liquidate and reorganize. For instance, Lehman had plans to sell a majority stake in its Investment Management Division, which remained profitable over the course of 2008.[186] As of August 31, it managed $273 billion in assets, had experienced no customer withdrawals over the summer, and included Neuberger Bermann, which had a reputation separate from Lehman Brothers.[187] By September 12, multiple parties had already undertaken due diligence and neared agreement on a price for the division.[188] Therefore, New Lehman can sell the division at a decent price and raise cash in the process.

---

184. Lehman, "First Disclosure," exhibit 4 offers traction on this issue, but without more granular data it is not possible to know whether the existing advances would have been sufficient.

185. This scheme allows the Estate to "retain upside in the commercial real estate portfolio" while also "leav[ing] the firm with limited commercial real estate exposure." Lehman, 9/10/08 8-K, Ex. 99.1, 2. The spin-off firm, which Lehman planned to call REI Global, is "appropriately capitalized to hold the [commercial real estate] assets;" "able to account for its assets on a hold-to-maturity basis"; and able, therefore, to "manage the assets without the pressure of mark-to-market volatility." That is, REI Global can wait out the "current economic cycle" until bids return to the assets' "intrinsic value." Ibid., 3.

186. Lehman, Q2 2008 10-Q, 22–23; Lehman, 9/10/08 8-K, Ex. 99.1, 1, 9; see also Valukas Report, 1966–67.

187. Lehman, 9/10/08 8-K, Ex. 99.1, 6.

188. "Debtors' Motion To (A) Establish Sales Procedures; (B) Approve A Seller Termination Fee And A Reimbursement Amount; And (C) Approve The Sale Of The Purchased Assets And The Assumption And Assignment Of Contracts Relating To The Purchased Assets," October 6, 2008, 7.

Finally, New Lehman may place subsidiaries into Chapters 7, 11, or 14 (the portion thereof meant for large operating subsidiaries) in the United States, or into relevant administration proceedings abroad, as circumstances warrant. In some cases this might be done in conjunction with proposals above. For instance, it might be easier to sell the Investment Management Division in a Chapter 11 363 sale in order to allow it to go through free and clear of liens and encumbrances. Critically, New Lehman's management and board, not the FDIC, Fed or bankruptcy court, make all of these decisions.

D. Procedures for Terminating the Chapter 14 Case

During its first months of operation, New Lehman looks like a typical financial services company except that Holdings' Estate continues to own it until the Chapter 14 case is terminated. In order to terminate the case, New Lehman's management, in consultation with the Estate, needs to determine that the firm is sufficiently stable so as to allow the marketplace to value its equity. Ideally, this occurs within a few months, though timing depends on market conditions.

The valuation occurs through an initial public offering of New Lehman stock,[189] which New Holdings undertakes similarly to a debtor in Chapter 11, that is, without complying with many applicable securities laws.[190] Before the Chapter 14 plan is approved, New Lehman first offers a small portion of its equity. As shown in figure 7.13, suppose New Lehman issues 100 million shares comprising a 10 percent stake at $70 per share and the price remains stable at issuance. This price implies losses of $46 billion relative to pre–Chapter 14 book values.[191] To reflect these losses on the balance sheet, New Holdings also writes down its equity stakes in subsidiaries.

---

189. By contrast, SPOE would rely on expert valuations of the company. See SPOE, Fed. Reg., 76617.

190. Jackson, "Building on Bankruptcy: Revised Chapter 14," section 2(13).

191. New Holdings' book equity is $116 billion. See figure 7.9. If a 10 percent stake sells for $7 billion (100 million shares times $70 per share), this implies total equity is worth $70 billion, or $46 billion less than the $116 billion book valuation.

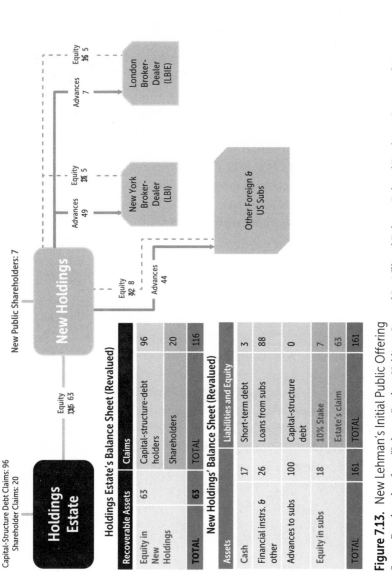

Capital-Structure Debt Claims: 96
Shareholder Claims: 20

New Public Shareholders: 7

Holdings Estate's Balance Sheet (Revalued)

Recoverable Assets		Claims	
Equity in New Holdings	63	Capital-structure-debt holders	96
		Shareholders	20
TOTAL	**63**	**TOTAL**	**116**

New Holdings' Balance Sheet (Revalued)

Assets		Liabilities and Equity	
Cash	17	Short-term debt	3
Financial instrs. & other	26	Loans from subs	88
Advances to subs	100	Capital-structure debt	0
Equity in subs	18	10% Stake	7
		Estate's claim	63
TOTAL	**161**	**TOTAL**	**161**

Figure 7.13. New Lehman's Initial Public Offering

Source: Based on data from "Lehman Brothers Holdings, Inc. and Its Affiliated Debtors, Debtors' Disclosure Statement for Joint Chapter 11 Plan," exhibits 9-4, 9-5, 9-6 (Apr. 14, 2010); Lehman Brothers, exhibit 21.10: "List of the Registrant's Subsidiaries," in Lehman, 2007 10-K (disclosing ownership structure of various intermediate holding companies); and table 7.1.

The $7 billion price for a 10 percent equity stake implies that the remaining 90 percent equity stake owned by the Estate is worth $63 billion. With this valuation, the Estate can now distribute the value of its single asset to claimants either by selling its equity stake for cash or by simply distributing shares using the Chapter 11 plan process, as shown in figure 7.14.

The Bankruptcy Code's restrictions on plans dictate exactly what occurs.[192] There are three classes of claimants: former general long-term debt holders, former subordinated debt holders, and former shareholders. The value of the single asset is worth less than the aggregate claims of the general long-term-debt holders, who are the most senior claimants. Therefore, absolute priority requires that they receive all of the Estate's value and that former subordinated-debt holders and shareholders receive nothing. Since the Estate's equity stake is worth $63 billion, general long-term debt holders each receive $0.78 on the dollar.

E. Outcomes for Social Welfare, Clients, Counterparties, and Creditors

At the close of the Chapter 14 case, it is clear that all parties have done at least as well as in Lehman's Chapter 11 case. Table 7.3 details outcomes in Holdings' actual case, as of early 2014. As shown, Chapter 11 has resulted in Holdings recovering only 22 percent of value relative to book on its assets. Though secured creditors have been paid in full, unsecured creditors have received payouts well under $0.30 on the dollar, largely because of the huge claims made on guarantees that Holdings extended over subsidiaries. Clients, though largely paid in full, have in some cases been embroiled for years in litigation with the Lehman Estate.

In Chapter 14, by contrast, both clients and counterparties have been entirely unaffected by the Chapter 14 process. Creditors other than holders of capital-structure or subordinated debt do decidedly better than in Lehman's Chapter 11 case: like clients and counterparties, they are essentially unaffected, as New Lehman assumes and

---

192. By contrast, SPOE would grant the FDIC discretion to prefer some creditors over others of equal rank. See SPOE, Fed. Reg., 76616-18.

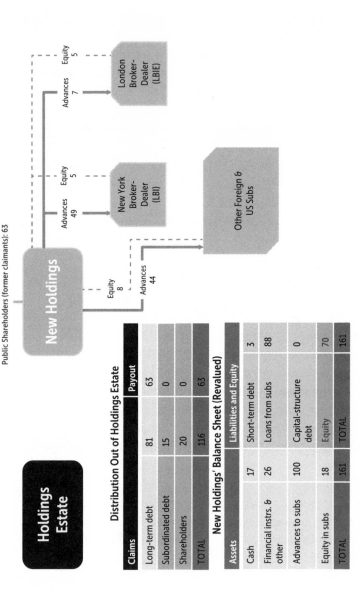

New Public Shareholders: 7
Public Shareholders (former claimants): 63

Distribution Out of Holdings Estate

Claims		Payout
Long-term debt	81	63
Subordinated debt	15	0
Shareholders	20	0
TOTAL	116	63

New Holdings' Balance Sheet (Revalued)

Assets		Liabilities and Equity	
Cash	17	Short-term debt	3
Financial instrs. & other	26	Loans from subs	88
Advances to subs	100	Capital-structure debt	0
Equity in subs	18	Equity	70
TOTAL	161	TOTAL	161

Figure 7.14. Approving a Plan and Paying Claimants

Source: Based on data from "Lehman Brothers Holdings, Inc. and Its Affiliated Debtors, Debtors' Disclosure Statement for Joint Chapter 11 Plan," exhibits 9-4, 9-5, 9-6 (Apr. 14, 2010); Lehman Brothers, exhibit 21.10: "List of the Registrant's Subsidiaries," in Lehman, 2007 10-K (disclosing ownership structure of various intermediate holding companies); and table 7.1.

meets all obligations to them. Shareholders and subordinated debt holders, by contrast, lose everything, at least under the assumptions used here. This, however, is precisely equal to how each group fared in Lehman's Chapter 11 case.

The one group that receives between zero and 100 percent are long-term creditors. In Chapter 11, this group expects to receive payouts of $0.27 on the dollar. It is highly unlikely that losses would be near as large under Chapter 14. For that to occur, the market needs to value New Lehman's $116 billion of book equity as worth only $22 billion, or $78 billion less than markets thought Lehman's long-term debt and equity was worth in July 2008.[193] Though markets were skeptical of the value of Lehman's $78 billion of real estate assets,[194] there is no evidence that they believed they were worth nothing.

A more realistic estimate could be obtained as follows. Suppose embedded balance-sheet losses are as large as markets implicitly estimated on September 15: $34 billion beyond Lehman's (by that point) $20 billion of book equity, or $54 billion total.[195] And, suppose that various financing obligations the firm takes on in its first months to relieve liquidity pressure carry high interest rates that cause another $10 billion in losses, international frictions cause an additional $10 billion in losses, and legal and administrative costs come to $6 billion. Even these assumptions yield total losses to be borne by equity and capital-structure debt of only $80 billion, $35 billion of which are borne by shareholders and subordinated debt-holders. Thus, even under this scenario, senior long-term-debt holders receive $0.55 on the dollar, double their receipts in Lehman's Chapter 11 case.[196]

---

193. In early July, markets valued Lehman's equity at about $18 billion (author's calculation from share price and shares outstanding, data from Bloomberg), and implicitly valued its long-term debt at 85 percent of par, or $82 billion, figure 7.3; $18 + $82 – $22 gives the figure cited.

194. Lehman, 9/11/08 Funding Slides, 82.

195. See figure 7.5; table 7.1.

196. $20 + $34 + $10 + $10 + $6 = $80 billion. The first $35 billion of this is borne by shareholders and subordinated-debt holders, see figure 7.14, leaving $45 billion to be borne by general long-term-debt holders. $45/$80 = $0.55 payout.

Table 7.3. Holdings' Balance Sheet, Recoveries, and Claims

ASSETS & RECOVERIES	(1) Holdings' Assets 9/14/08 in USD Billions	(2) Holdings' Recoveries 2010 in USD Billions	(3) Recoveries as % of Book
Cash, equivalents, and segregated securities	$10	$6	61%
Financial instruments & inventory positions	23	7	28%
Liquid assets	6	missing	
Real estate–related assets	11	4	40%
Corporate debt, equities, & loans	6	2	35%
All Other	179	34	19%
Receivable from subsidiaries	147	26	18%
Equity in net assets of subsidiaries	26	3	10%
Receivables from third parties	2	3	327%
Other assets	2	2	123%
TOTAL ASSETS	$209	$47	22%

LIABILITIES, EQUITY, & CLAIMS	(1) Holdings' Liabilities 9/14/08 in USD Billions	(2) Holdings' Allowed Claims 2011 in USD Billions	(3) Payout as % of Claim 2014
Short-term & current long-term debt	$19	Included in LT borrowings, general unsecured	
Collateralized financing	0	2	100%

		General unsecured	
Accrued liabilities and payables	1	65	25%
Owed to subsidiaries	88	99	21%
Long-term borrowings	80	84	23%
Senior notes	65	15	27%
Subordinated notes	15	11	0%
General unsecured claims	N/A	6	25%
Admin, priority & convenience claims	N/A		99%
Guarantee claims	N/A	95	16%
TOTAL LIABILITIES / CLAIMS	189	278	22%
Preferred equity	9		0%
Common equity	11		0%
TOTAL STOCKHOLDERS' EQUITY	20		0%
TOTAL LIABILITIES AND STOCKHOLDERS' EQUITY	209		

Source: Based on data from In re Lehman Brothers Holdings, Inc, et al., Monthly Operating Report Balance Sheet as of September 14, 2008; Lehman Brothers Holdings, Inc. and its Affiliated Debtors, Debtors' Disclosure Statement for Third Amended Joint Chapter 11 Plan, 499 (Aug. 31, 2011), Lehman Brothers Holdings, Inc. and Its Affiliated Debtors, Notice Regarding Fifth Distribution Pursuant to the Modified Third Amended Joint Chapter 11 Plan, Exhibit A (Mar. 27, 2014). Numbers do not sum due to rounding.

Finally, social welfare is also substantially improved relative to Lehman's Chapter 11 case. If this analysis is credible and markets believe it to be so, then the conviction that there is a rules-driven and systematic way to undergo resolution and to allocate losses will further reduce incentives for any parties at interest to run, either before or after a financial institution undergoes Chapter 14. These reduced incentives will, in turn, lower the overall expected costs of Chapter 14, increasing the likelihood that policymakers actually use Chapter 14, rather than passing new legislation in a crisis. In this way, Chapter 14 also avoids the time-inconsistency problem of bailouts. Policymakers who believe they have an existing legal option that will sufficiently minimize any risks of systemic consequences will have no incentive to respond to a possible crisis by passing new legislation to re-allow bailouts. Overall, these effects reduce moral hazard, without increasing systemic risks.

Conclusion

This paper began with a brief recapitulation of the financial turmoil of the fall of 2008 and the impacts that Lehman Brothers' bankruptcy may have had on that turmoil. In part I, I argued that Chapter 14 can address the problems of Chapter 11 and bailouts by avoiding the threat of a run cascade while imposing losses onto a substantial portion of creditors. As preparation for parts III and IV, part II described important details of Lehman's demise from the perspective of a Chapter 14 counterfactual, most importantly that Lehman failed due to insolvency and therefore was a strong candidate for the solutions Chapter 14 offers.

Part III began by laying out the structure of the counterfactual world. Importantly, it assumed that Dodd Frank and Chapter 14 exist in tandem and that international authorities agree to neither place foreign subsidiaries into resolution nor ring-fence foreign assets. It then argued that Chapter 14's requirements for certifications of both systemic risk and adequate assurance of future performance indicate that a Chapter 14 case could have been filed for Lehman between mid-July 2008 and September 5, 2008. Using the latter as the hypothetical counterfactual filing date, part III then walked through how a Chapter 14 Lehman weekend would have worked and showed that, though the time frame to effectuate a section 1405 transfer is short, it would have been relatively straightforward—at least with planning in a living will—to make the necessary legal findings quickly.

Part IV analyzed the consequences of a Chapter 14 case. Given the amount of capital-structure debt that would be left behind, even fairly extreme estimates of losses suggest that New Lehman would be solvent and would have a variety of options for reorganizing the business in order to minimize losses for the Estate. And under newly proposed gone-concern loss-absorbing capacity (GLAC) requirements, the amount of capital-structure debt left behind would have been even greater.

The more challenging question than whether New Lehman would be solvent is whether there would be a run on New Lehman, how large such a run might be, and whether New Lehman would withstand such a run. Subpart IV.B contended that though there would have been almost no reason to run for fear of insolvency, some creditors might have run anyway. It then argued that a counterfactual stress test of New Lehman's liquidity position shows that New Lehman would have withstood a moderate run if central banks had been willing to offer secured liquidity. Lehman's case therefore underscores David Skeel's argument in this volume that concerns about financing a large financial firm in a quick sale may be overblown. Part IV closed with an assessment of the losses that would have arisen for various parties out of this process and noted that, though capital-structure-debt holders would bear greater losses than any other creditors, even they would do at least as well under Chapter 14 as they did in Lehman's actual case.

Had these outcomes been expected, a rational assessment of the costs of using Chapter 14 for Lehman would have shown it to be a legitimate alternative to a bailout that not only offered a social welfare improvement but also provided an attractive option to policymakers. In conjunction with other critical measures such as capital requirements and safety and soundness regulation, Chapter 14 offers a way forward toward reduced moral hazard without increasing the risk of systemic effects from bank resolution. It may not solve the problem of "too big to fail," but it does reinstitute bankruptcy as the legal procedure of first resort for failing corporations.

CHAPTER 8

Revised Chapter 14 2.0 and Living Will Requirements under the Dodd-Frank Act

William F. Kroener III

The purpose of this brief chapter is to demonstrate that, if enacted and made part of US bankruptcy law, Chapter 14 2.0[1] as proposed will facilitate compliance by large financial companies with the provisions in Title I of the Dodd-Frank Act, 21 USC section165 (d), requiring the submission of credible resolution plans (so-called living wills). At the outset, it should be noted that the resolution plans required by Title I of Dodd-Frank are tested against bankruptcy law rather than orderly liquidation authority (OLA) under Title II in assessments of their credibility. Thus, as noted by Tom Jackson, "the effectiveness of bankruptcy law in being able to resolve SIFIs is critically important to the development of credible resolution plans under Title I."[2]

While bankruptcy thus remains the preferred option for resolution under Dodd-Frank, there are substantial impediments to the resolution of a nonbank financial company under existing bankruptcy law. Many of these are addressed by Chapter 14 2.0. This chapter provides a short, relevant summary of Chapter 14 2.0 as recently revised;

---

1. The nomenclature "Chapter 14 2.0" is used for consistency. Variations, with somewhat different features and different names, were introduced in the Senate and passed by the House in the 113th Congress. The House version identified the proposal as subchapter V to Chapter 11 of the Bankruptcy Code, while the Senate version created a separate Chapter 14 but also repealed Orderly Liquidation Authority under Title II.

2. Statement of Thomas Jackson before the Subcommittee on Regulatory Reform, Commercial and Antitrust Law, House Judiciary Committee, March 26, 2014.

describes the living will provisions of the Dodd-Frank Act; notes the very early methodology the Federal Reserve and the FDIC appear to be using, at least to date, in applying those statutory provisions in their preliminary assessments communicated (only in early August 2014, after a considerable delay) to the eleven first-wave US filers on their second round of filings; indicates the extensive potential for remedial use of these provisions in the event any of the living wills (continue to) fall short in providing for credible and orderly bankruptcy resolution; and shows how Chapter 14 2.0 will modify the bankruptcy law in ways that facilitate resolution plans and determinations by the Federal Reserve and the FDIC of the "credibility" of such plans.

Chapter 14 2.0

As revised, Chapter 14 2.0 is intended to make the US bankruptcy laws work more effectively for large financial companies, addressing directly some of the problems arising during the Lehman Brothers bankruptcy and also providing an alternative structure that in appropriate circumstances will facilitate a single point of entry (SPOE) type of resolution. The changes to US bankruptcy law, set out in greater detail by Tom Jackson in chapter 2 in this volume, would also alter the operation of existing US law that references and incorporates US bankruptcy law, notably (for present purposes) the "living will" provisions in Title I of the Dodd-Frank Act. Those provisions, section 165(d) of the Dodd-Frank Act, require all covered financial intermediaries with assets equal to or in excess of $50 billion to periodically (annually, now that staggered regular submission schedules have been established) submit resolution plans (generally referred to as living wills) to the Federal Reserve and the FDIC.

The resolution plans are required to demonstrate in detail how the entire entity could be resolved in a "rapid and orderly resolution" without adverse systemic consequences under the bankruptcy (or other relevant) law in the event of material financial distress or failure. The plans as submitted may be determined by the Federal Reserve or the FDIC to be "not credible or not facilitating an orderly resolution under Title 11 [the bankruptcy laws]," in which case the statute further provides for successive rounds of resubmission. If these standards for credibility and facilitation ultimately remain unsatisfied after multiple successive submissions, then the Fed and the FDIC may require modification of operations and divestitures by the covered financial company. To date the agencies have been critical of the submissions on which they have publically commented. The FDIC (but not the Fed) in fact has found that *every* resolution plan from the largest eleven financial companies submitted in the second round of plan filings would fail the statutory test of credibility and facilitating resolution.[3]

Part of the purpose of the living will provision in Title I is to identify and address in advance the significant problems, now well-recognized, arising from the fact that US bankruptcy law as it now exists may not be well-suited for large financial companies. In part that is because these entities are organized juridically for regulatory, tax, geographic, and other reasons rather than by lines of business. Importantly, the judicial processes under bankruptcy operate too slowly in the often rapidly changing circumstances of a distressed and failing financial company, and the filing of bankruptcy generally allows the immediate termination and close-out of very short-term secured financial contracts. The principal example of these problems is, of course, what actually happened in the unplanned sudden Chapter 11 bankruptcy of Lehman Brothers—a serious liquidity run; gradual but untimely close-out of open financial contracts; freezing of collateral in foreign locations in a way that forestalled orderly bankruptcy proceedings in the United States, the home country of the parent entity; and a very lengthy period to evaluate and determine an appropriate (previously unplanned) resolution strategy. Thus, the difficulties of existing

---

3. Joint Board of Governors of the Federal Reserve System and Federal Deposit Insurance Corporation press release, "Agencies Provide Feedback on Second Round Resolution Plans of 'First-Wave' Filers," August 5, 2014. Since that time, there have been some more positive indications, including a statement that noted improvements in the most recent submission by Wells Fargo & Co. (joint press release, "Agencies Jointly Provide Feedback on Wells Fargo's Second Resolution Plan and Move Resolution Plan Submission Date for Three Companies," November 25, 2014) and a statement by FDIC Chairman Martin J. Gruenberg that he was expecting progress in the next round of submissions (reported in Bloomberg News, December 11, 2014).

bankruptcy law present a heightened risk that the living wills under Dodd-Frank will be ineffective and there could be the need for (over) use of Title II OLA because the bankruptcy laws do not accommodate financial companies. There is general belief that the extremely negative results in the Lehman Brothers bankruptcy can be avoided or substantially mitigated by the use of OLA under Title II of Dodd-Frank.[4] Chapter 14 2.0 is designed to address that matter directly and make the use of bankruptcy easier and more effective for covered financial companies. If the bankruptcy laws were revised as proposed in Chapter 14 2.0 to better accommodate large financial companies, more credible living wills under Title I could minimize or even avoid the need to use OLA under Title II.[5] In fact, such a change would actually provide a path for bringing Title I and Title II provisions into better coordination.

Proposed Chapter 14 2.0 addresses the shortcomings in the US bankruptcy laws for financial companies in a number of ways. First, in addition to normal reorganization provisions, there are provisions which allow a two-entity reorganization via a sale transaction with notice to relevant parties. Second, and significantly, there are provisions for this sale transaction to occur on a very accelerated basis— over a weekend, if necessary. Third, there are provisions that preserve financial contracts for a brief period, so as to avoid their immediate termination and close-out by counterparties with the consequential possible loss of value. Further, unlike OLA under Title II, there is the

---

4. An FDIC assessment of the Lehman matter contends that under Title II orderly liquidation procedures, general unsecured creditors might have received "approximately $0.97 for every claim of $1.00." See "The Orderly Liquidation of Lehman Brothers Holdings Inc. under the Dodd-Frank Act," *FDIC Quarterly* 5, no. 2 (2011): 31.

5. Jeffrey Lacker, President of the Federal Reserve Bank of Richmond, recognized this in a recent speech, "Rethinking the Unthinkable: Bankruptcy for Large Financial Institutions," National Conference of Bankruptcy Judges, Chicago, October 10, 2014: "Another provision of the Dodd-Frank Act, however, provides a much more promising strategy for ending 'too big to fail.' Section 165(d) in Title I requires large and complex financial institutions to create resolution plans, also known as 'living wills.'"

bankruptcy assurance of equal treatment of similarly situated creditors. There is a provision designed to ensure that judges with experience and expertise in financial matters preside over the Chapter 14 cases. And the proposed Chapter 14 contemplates accommodating a single-point-of-entry approach similar to what has been developed and planned by the FDIC for use in the exercise of OLA under Title II.[6]

The difficulties with existing bankruptcy law, apparent from the ongoing Lehman experience, have been recognized by the Fed and the FDIC in their comments,[7] issued after a very long period of silence, on the most recent round of living wills submitted by the largest ("first wave") financial intermediaries. The Fed public statement was highly critical of the resolution plans of the largest financial intermediaries, while the FDIC explicitly determined that *none* of the plans submitted by any of the eleven "first wave" filers would be "credible" or would "facilitate resolution." The details of these plans remain confidential and only very short summaries have been released publicly, so additional analysis and assessment here are not possible. Among the major problems identified by the agencies, according to their joint press release, were unrealistic assumptions about international cooperation and about investor and counterparty actions, including actions to terminate financial contracts, as well as possible limitations on the availability of back-office shared services and the absence of any organizational simplification. In effect, this is seen by some as an interim determination by the regulators that the problem of "too big to fail" (TBTF) may not really have been solved by Dodd-Frank, and it may be necessary to (frequently) default from ordinary bankruptcy to OLA under Title II. FDIC Vice Chairman Thomas Hoenig has even called for the repeal of Title I of the Dodd-Frank Act if bankruptcy is found to be impossible for the largest banks.[8]

---

6. Additional advantages of Chapter 14 2.0 are set out in detail in Tom Jackson's chapter in this volume.

7. Fed/FDIC press release, "Agencies Provide Feedback on Second Round Resolution Plans."

8. Thomas Hoenig, quoted in "Kill Living Wills If Banks Can't Go Through Bankruptcy," Bloomberg News, September 18, 2014.

While the FDIC and the Fed have not been explicit publicly about the possible detailed fixes to any continued shortcomings of the plans, some guidance is available from what the European Banking Authority has made public with respect to changes that might be sought in circumstances where resolution plans are deemed insufficient or unworkable.[9] These include, among others, changes to financing arrangements and operational structure and changes in business activities and divestitures. All of these are the types of changes contemplated generally by the express provisions of section 165(d), though to date the Fed and the FDIC have been far less explicit than the European Banking Authority on the matter.

Chapter 14 2.0 would directly address the difficulties that first-wave filers have encountered (and which presumably will be encountered by other financial institutions required to file living wills) because satisfaction of the statutory standard—specifically, to reorganize in a credible manner under the bankruptcy law—would be facilitated. In sum, Chapter 14 2.0 would improve pre-failure resolution planning and significantly add to the tools available to address possible contagious panic.

---

9. European Banking Authority, "Draft Guidelines on the specification of measures to reduce or remove impediments to resolvability and the circumstances in which each measure may be applied under Directive 2014/59/EU," July 9, 2014.

CHAPTER 9

The Cross-Border Challenge in Resolving Global Systemically Important Banks

Jacopo Carmassi and Richard Herring

Introduction

Just before the global 2008 financial crisis, the issue of large, complex financial institutions (LCFIs) began to catch the attention of some policymakers.[1] In general, however, officials appeared not to have anticipated the problems that would need to be addressed if one of these institutions should need to be resolved, much less considered whether the complex corporate structures of such institutions would impede or even prevent an orderly resolution.

The orderly resolution of even a purely domestic, complex financial institution presents formidable difficulties no matter whether an administrative or bankruptcy process is deployed. But the difficulties increase by an order of magnitude if the complex financial institution is international in scope. While excessive risk-taking and leverage may have caused the crisis, institutional complexity, often involving tiers of foreign affiliates, and opaque, cross-border interconnections impede effective oversight by the authorities ex ante and greatly complicate crisis management and the resolution of institutions ex post.

The second section of this chapter outlines the scope of the problem. Section three reviews some data depicting the organizational

---

1. For example, both the Bank of England and the International Monetary Fund had identified sixteen LCFIs that were crucial to the functioning of the world economy. See Herring and Carmassi (2010) for a discussion of this classification approach. It should be noted that the indications of the kinds of problems that would need to be dealt with in the resolution of an LCFI were apparent long before the crisis (Herring 2002, 2003).

complexity and the international legal structure of the twenty-nine institutions that have been designated as global systemically important banks (G-SIBs) by the Financial Stability Board (FSB) in November 2013. The fourth section discusses the implications of complexity for orderly resolution. The fifth section examines why any orderly procedure for a cross-border resolution must rely on a significant amount of cooperation among national authorities and considers why governments have great difficulty in making credible commitments to cooperate with foreign authorities and abstain from ring-fencing the portions of a foreign financial group that they control. A failure to find a way to ensure cooperation in a crisis may lead to extensive subsidiarization and a substantial amount of fragmentation in the global financial system. The sixth section explores the implications of this approach. And, the concluding section emphasizes the problems resulting from the lack of a plausible framework for the cross-border resolution of G-SIBs.

The Scope of the Problem

The financial crisis of 2008–2009 highlighted the complex, opaque, cross-border structures and interconnections among G-SIBs. As Mervyn King (2010) observed, these entities are global in life, but local in death.[2] Each of the legal entities within the group must be taken through some sort of resolution no matter whether it be bankruptcy, an administrative resolution, or, in the case of a prepackaged bankruptcy, the unwinding of contracts. During the crisis, the challenges of coordinating, much less harmonizing, scores of legal proceedings across multiple jurisdictions proved to be insuperable, particularly within the tight time constraint of a "resolution weekend" (Huertas 2014). Once the financial group has been dissolved into separate legal entities, information can become so fragmented that it is virtually impossible to preserve any going-concern value the group may have

---

2. Huertas (2009) made the point in more detail: "The Lehman bankruptcy demonstrates that financial institutions may be global in life, but they are national in death. They become a series of local legal entities when they become subject to administration and/or liquidation."

had. Indeed, in the case of Lehman Brothers, it proved difficult even to gather the data necessary to resolve many of the separate entities.[3]

When policymakers were confronted with the magnitude of the challenge of devising an orderly resolution for a large, complex, global financial institution, they appear to have believed they had no good choices. A bailout would avoid the anticipated short-term costs of a disorderly resolution which might inflict significant harm on other financial institutions, financial markets, and, most importantly, the real economy. But a bailout could impose huge fiscal costs and might increase the likelihood that even larger and more costly bailouts would be necessary in the future. Nonetheless, when faced with the choice between immediate and possibly uncontrollable damage to the economy and possible future harm and fiscal costs that could be delayed, the authorities frequently chose to organize a bailout.

The magnitude of the bailouts implemented during the recent crisis was so great[4] that they could not be convincingly justified on political or economic grounds. Leaders of the Group of Twenty, meeting in the depth of the crisis, reached a consensus neatly summarized by Huertas (2010) as "too big to fail[5] is too costly to continue." The rallying cry was that taxpayers should never again be put at risk of such substantial losses, but the authorities realized that they lacked effective tools to deal with a faltering G-SIB. This realization has led to a number of policy innovations, many of them still in the process of implementation.

---

3. The bankruptcy of Lehman Brothers provided a particularly stark illustration of this problem. The resolution of Lehman Brothers involved more than one hundred bankruptcy proceedings in multiple jurisdictions. Because crucial data centers were sold with one of the entities, other affiliates (and their resolution authorities) lost access to fundamental information about who owed what to whom. See Kapur (2015) for a remarkably detailed analysis.

4. Haldane (2009) estimated that at the height of the crisis over $14 trillion (about one-quarter of world GDP) had been committed by the United States, the United Kingdom, and the euro area to support their banking systems.

5. Although in common use, this term is regrettably imprecise. Size is one, but not the only, attribute of such institutions. It should be interpreted as a proxy for institutions that are also too interconnected, too complex, too international in scope or too important to be resolved in an orderly fashion. A cynic might also add that many of these institutions appear to have been too big to manage.

The Extent of Organizational and Geographic Complexity among G-SIBs

Several of the G-SIBs have developed remarkably complex corporate structures and a vast global reach. These trends can be documented for the largest bank holding companies in the United States. Figure 9.1a shows the number of subsidiaries controlled by the largest US bank holding companies. Six bank holding companies now control well over one thousand subsidiaries. Relative to 1990, corporate complexity for several of these bank holding companies had increased markedly. Figure 9.1b depicts the international expansion of these firms. Seven of them are now active in more than forty countries and one is active in more than eighty countries.

Figure 9.2 shifts the focus to the G-SIBs identified by the FSB (which include eight US bank holding companies). This chart shows the evolution of the average number of subsidiaries and total assets for the twenty-nine G-SIBs from 2002 through 2013. Note that despite all of the regulatory and supervisory measures adopted to encourage banks to simplify their corporate structures since the crisis, the average number of subsidiaries continued to grow after the crisis, peaking in 2011. The average number of subsidiaries has begun to decrease a bit, but has still not returned to pre-crisis levels, when many of these firms were implicitly deemed too complex to fail.

Figure 9.2 also shows the growth in average total assets for these firms. Average total assets increased by more than 2.6 times from 2002 to 2008. This fell a bit during 2009 and 2010, when several of these firms were obliged to deleverage, but by 2011 average total assets had once again risen to their pre-crisis highs and remained very close to that level through 2013. The data on total assets and the total number of subsidiaries reveal a fairly robust correlation.[6] This probably reflects the influence of the mergers and acquisitions through which most of the G-SIBs grew. Although most made efforts to reduce the resulting

---

6. Carmassi and Herring (2015) present evidence suggesting this correlation may be spurious and disappear when the M&A history of G-SIBs and time effects are taken into account.

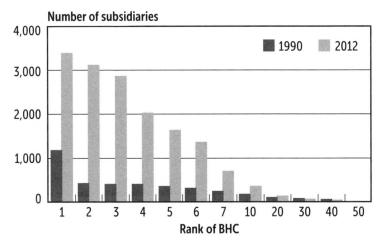

Figure 9.1a. Number of Subsidiaries of the Largest US Bank Holding Companies

Source: D. Avraham, P. Selvaggi, and J. I. Vickery, "A Structural View of U.S. Bank Holding Companies," *Economic Policy Review* 18, no. 2 (July 16, 2012), on National Information Center data and FR Y-10. Data as of February 20, 2012, and December 31, 1990.

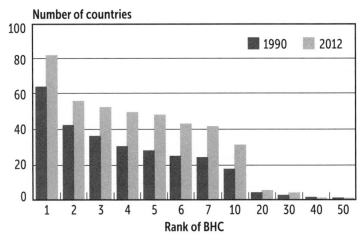

Figure 9.1b. Number of Countries in Which US Bank Holding Companies Have Subsidiaries

Source: D. Avraham, P. Selvaggi, and J. I. Vickery, "A Structural View of U.S. Bank Holding Companies," *Economic Policy Review* 18, no. 2 (July 16, 2012), on National Information Center data and FR Y-10. Data as of February 20, 2012, and December 31, 1990.

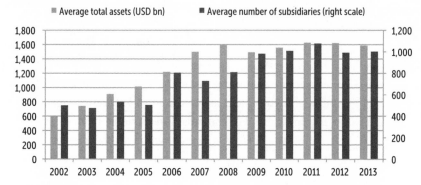

Figure 9.2. Evolution of Average Number of Subsidiaries and Total Assets for G-SIBs

Source: Based on Bankscope data.

Note: Majority-owned subsidiaries for which G-SIBs are the ultimate owners with a minimum control path of 50.01% at all steps of the control chain.

Table 9.1. Profile of G-SIBs

	Assets	% foreign assets	Total subsidiaries	Number of countries	% foreign subsidiaries	% subs in offshore centers
Average	$1.587 trillion	42%	1,002	44	60%	12%
High	$3.100 trillion	87%	2,460	95	95%	28%

Source: Based on Bankscope data and banks' annual reports.

Note: Assets and total subsidiaries as of year-end 2013; number of countries, percentage of foreign subsidiaries, and percentage of subsidiaries in offshore financial centers as of May 2013; percentage of foreign assets as of year-end 2012.

legal complexity, the number of subsidiaries tended to ratchet up significantly.

Table 9.1 provides additional details about the universe of the G-SIBs in 2013. The largest bank in the group had more than $3 trillion in assets, while the average across G-SIBs was $1.6 trillion in assets. International involvement as measured by the percentage of foreign assets is remarkable. For the most international bank in this group, 87 percent of its assets were foreign, while for the average of G-SIBs it was 42 percent. Complexity, as measured by the total number of subsidiaries in the banking group, ranges from a high of 2,460[7] to an average of 1,002. On average, 60 percent of these subsidiaries are incorporated in countries other than the home country; for one of the G-SIBs, 95 percent of its subsidiaries are incorporated abroad. A rough (and very minimal) indication of the role that tax incentives play in this corporate complexity can be inferred from the proportion of subsidiaries incorporated in offshore tax havens. On average, 12 percent of the subsidiaries are incorporated in such offshore banking centers, while one G-SIB incorporated 28 percent of its subsidiaries in tax havens.

On average, G-SIBs are active in forty-four countries, while one G-SIB has a presence in ninety-five countries. This is a minimal estimate of the coordination challenge that must be met over a resolution weekend if the authorities hoped to continue most of the operations of the G-SIB on Monday morning. This should be regarded as a lower bound for two important reasons. First, the count ignores foreign branches. Although a domestic branch is an integral part of the head office and would be subject to whatever resolution procedure is applied to the parent, the outcome may be different if the branch is

---

7. Note that the number of subsidiaries indicated for the largest US bank holding company in figure 1.A is taken from a different database, the National Information Center (Federal Reserve), which uses a lower threshold for determining control and a different methodology. Disclosure practices are so ineffectual that an unfortunate degree of uncertainty remains about the number of subsidiaries controlled by each G-SIB, something that should be straightforward to measure and report. See Carmassi and Herring (2014) for a broader discussion of sources of data.

Table 9.2. Disaggregation of Subsidiaries of 13 G-SIBs by Industry Classification (May 2013)

Banks	4%
Insurance companies	1%
Mutual & pension funds, nominees, trusts & trustees	22%
Other financial subsidiaries	25%
Non-financial subsidiaries	47%

Source: Based on data from Bankscope. Majority-owned subsidiaries. Totals do not add up to 100 percent due to rounding.
Note: "Other financial subsidiaries" include, among others, hedge funds, private equity, and venture capital subsidiaries. "Non-financial subsidiaries" include all companies that are neither banks nor insurance companies nor financial companies. They can be involved in manufacturing activities but also in trading activities (wholesalers, retailers, brokers, etc.). We have allocated foundations and research institutes to this category as well.

located overseas. Foreign branches may be subject to ring-fencing by the host country in the event of a crisis and thus subject to a separate resolution process. Second, this count almost certainly understates the coordination challenge because several countries may have two or more specialized regulators that would need to be consulted to resolve or continue operation of an individual entity. A foreign bank operating in the United States, for example, would be required to have separately regulated subsidiaries for insurance activities (one for each state in which it operates), the broker-dealer business, commodity trading, and deposit-taking.

Table 9.2 provides an indication of the complexity that may arise because of the diverse activities conducted by a G-SIB by disaggregating the total number of subsidiaries by category of business. The banking business accounts for only 4 percent of the subsidiaries, although these subsidiaries account for the majority of assets. Only 1 percent of the total number are insurance companies. Other financial subsidiaries—including, among others, mutual funds, pension funds, hedge funds, and private equity funds—account for another 47 percent of the total number of subsidiaries. More surprising, however, is that the remaining 47 percent of subsidiaries fall into the heterogeneous category of "non-financial subsidiaries," which includes manufacturing activities, trading of non-financial products, foundations, and research institutes.

Many, perhaps most, of these entities would not pose an obstacle to an orderly resolution because they may be automatically liquidated when some specified threshold condition is crossed or they may be totally insulated from the rest of the group.[8] Given current disclosure practices, however, an external observer lacks sufficient information to evaluate what kind of activity takes place in such an entity, its scale, and its interrelationships with the rest of the group or the resolution procedure it would need to undergo in the event of failure (Carmassi and Herring 2013).

In any event, the more numerous the legal entities, the greater the likely number of regulatory entities that must be consulted in planning and implementing a resolution. Because G-SIBs conduct a wide variety of businesses beyond banking and securities activities, this may involve a broad range of specialized, functional regulatory authorities, including insurance commissioners and, in the case of energy trading units, possibly even very specialized regulators such as the Environmental Protection Agency.[9] Assuming that all of these parties have the legal ability and willingness to cooperate—and that their rules and procedures do not conflict—coordination costs will be high and will increase with the number of regulatory authorities that need to be consulted. Of equal importance, the greater the number of regulatory authorities that need to be consulted to start an orderly resolution process, the greater the likely number needing to be convinced to provide licenses and permissions in order for the bridge institution to continue

---

8. For example, Lehman Brothers had more than six thousand subsidiaries when it entered bankruptcy. During the bankruptcy proceedings it was determined that fewer than one thousand had any active relationship to the ongoing business. Although it would certainly be more difficult to resolve seven thousand entities, even one thousand present a formidable challenge (Miller and Horwitz 2013).

9. For additional details regarding the activities of US G-SIBs in physical commodity and energy markets, see Omarova (2013).

critical operations on the Monday following the resolution weekend. Moreover, these operating entities must receive authorization
to continue using critical elements of the financial infrastructure
(such as payments systems, clearing, and custody services) and to
continue trading on exchanges.

Problems That Geographic and Business Complexity Pose for an Orderly Resolution

Despite their corporate complexity, G-SIBs tend to be managed in an
integrated fashion along lines of business with only minimal regard
for legal entities, national borders, or functional regulatory authorities. Moreover, interconnections among entities within the group are
opaque and may be quite substantial. Baxter and Sommer (2005) note
that, in addition to their shared (although possibly varying) ownership
structure, the entities are likely to be linked by cross-affiliate credit,
business, and reputational relationships.

What would happen should one of these G-SIBs experience extreme
financial distress? Quite apart from the difficulty of disentangling operating subsidiaries that provide critical services and mapping an integrated firm's activities into the entities that would need to be taken
through a bankruptcy process, the corporate complexity of such institutions would present significant challenges. The fundamental problem
stems from conflicting approaches to bankruptcy and resolution across
regulators, across countries, and, sometimes, even within countries.
There are likely to be disputes over which law and which set of bankruptcy or administrative procedures should apply. Some authorities may
attempt to ring-fence the parts of the G-SIB within their reach to satisfy their regulatory objectives without necessarily taking into account
some broader objective such as the preservation of going-concern
value or financial stability. At a minimum, authorities will face formidable challenges in coordination and information-sharing across jurisdictions. Losses that spill across national borders will intensify conflicts
between home and host authorities and make it difficult to achieve a
cooperative resolution of an insolvent financial group. Experience has
shown that in times of stress information-sharing agreements are likely
to fray (Herring 2007).

When the crisis erupted, approaches to bank resolution differed substantially across countries. For example, countries differ with regard to the point at which a weak bank requires resolution and with regard to which entity initiates the resolution process. Clearly cross-border differences in regard to how and when the resolution process is initiated can cause conflicts and delays that may be costly in a crisis.

The choice of jurisdiction may also have important implications for the outcome of the insolvency proceedings. Most countries have adopted a universal approach to insolvency in which one jurisdiction conducts the main insolvency proceedings and makes the distribution of assets, while other jurisdictions collect assets to be distributed in the main proceedings. But the United States follows a more territorial approach with regard to US branches of foreign banks and will conduct its own insolvency proceedings based on local assets and liabilities. Assets are transferred to the home country only after (and if) all local claims are satisfied. The choice of jurisdiction will also determine a creditor's right to set off claims on the insolvent bank against amounts that it owes the bank. The Bank of Credit and Commerce International (BCCI) case revealed striking differences across members of the Basel Committee on Banking Supervision (BCBS 1992). Similarly, the ability to exercise close-out netting provisions under the International Swaps and Derivatives Association (ISDA) master contracts may vary from jurisdiction to jurisdiction, although ISDA has achieved a remarkable degree of international harmonization and has recently agreed to modify its close-out netting procedures for dealer banks to facilitate an orderly resolution (ISDA 2014).

The outcome of insolvency proceedings will also depend on the powers and obligations of the resolution authority, which may differ from country to country. For example, does the resolution authority have the power to impose "haircuts" on the claims of creditors without a lengthy judicial proceeding? Does the resolution authority have the ability (and access to the necessary resources) to provide access to adequate liquidity or a capital injection?[10] With regard to banks, is the

---

10. The FSB agreement on Key Attributes of Effective Resolution Regimes for Financial Institutions and the recent FSB proposed requirement for Total Loss

resolution authority constrained to choose the least costly resolution method, as in the United States? Or is the resolution authority obliged to give preference to domestic depositors, as the law requires in Australia and the United States? More fundamentally, what is the objective of the supervisory intervention and the resolution process?

In an effort to reduce these differences in resolution policies and procedures across countries, the FSB has negotiated a set of Key Attributes of Effective Resolution Regimes for Financial Institutions that each member country should implement (FSB 2011, 2012, 2013a, 2013b, 2013c, 2014). The FSB has concluded that an effective resolution regime should:

1. Ensure continuity of systemically important functions
2. Protect insured depositors and ensure rapid return of segregated client assets
3. Allocate losses to shareholders and to unsecured and uninsured creditors in a way that respects payment priorities in bankruptcy
4. Deter reliance on public support for solvency and discourage any expectation that it will be available
5. Avoid unnecessary destruction of value
6. Provide for speed, transparency, and as much predictability as possible based on legal and procedural clarity and advanced planning for orderly resolution
7. Establish a legal mandate for cooperation, information exchange, and coordination with foreign resolution authorities
8. Ensure that nonviable firms can exit the market in an orderly fashion
9. Achieve and maintain credibility to enhance market discipline and provide incentives for market solutions

Many of these attributes can be read as attempts to establish a new regime that would prevent another disorderly, Lehman-like bankruptcy. The emphasis is on planning, sharing of information,

---

Absorbing Capacity attempt to minimize the likelihood that such interventions might be necessary.

cross-border cooperation, the protection of systemically important functions, and avoidance of any unnecessary destruction of value. All of these goals will be difficult to achieve, especially because some of the G20 countries have not yet established special resolution regimes for complex, international financial institutions.

Perhaps the greatest challenge, however, is to achieve credibility. The authorities tend to be judged by what they do, not by what they say, and most of the interventions and resolutions that occurred during the crisis were chaotic, without the benefit of careful planning for an orderly liquidation or restructuring process. They failed to allocate losses to unsecured and uninsured creditors, involved major commitments of public funds, and showed little evidence of substantial cross-border cooperation. None of these interventions could be described as speedy, transparent, or predictable.

The FSB's effort to enhance credibility, however, is not advanced by the vague way in which it describes the point at which resolution should take place (FSB 2011, p. 7): "Resolution should be initiated when a firm is no longer viable or likely to be no longer viable, and has no reasonable prospect of becoming so." Although the clear intent is for the authorities to intervene before equity is wiped out, the clause "has no reasonable prospect of becoming so" can be very permissive. Given the demonstrated tendency of managers, accountants, and supervisors to take an overly optimistic view of a firm's prospects for recovery, this clause seems to provide scope for delaying intervention until long after a firm's equity has been destroyed. Deep insolvencies increase the likelihood of an ad hoc improvised resolution to offset the market reaction to the realization that early intervention has not worked. The remainder of this chapter focuses on one aspect of credibility: the prospects for cross-border cooperation, the essential foundations for which are addressed by the seventh goal listed above.

The Crucial Role of International Cooperation

The fundamental challenge to a cooperative resolution is that national authorities will inevitably place a heavier weight on domestic objectives in the event of a conflict between home and host authorities.

Three asymmetries between the home and host country may create problems even if procedures could be harmonized to conform to the Key Attributes. First is asymmetry of resources: supervisory and resolution authorities may differ greatly in terms of human capital and financial resources, implying that the home supervisory authority may not be able to rely on the host supervisory authority (or vice versa) simply because it may lack the capacity to conduct effective supervisory oversight and an effective resolution. Second, asymmetries of financial infrastructure may give rise to discrepancies in the quality of supervision across countries. Weaknesses in accounting standards and the quality of external audits may impede the efforts of supervisors just as informed, institutional creditors and an aggressive and responsible financial press may aid them. The legal infrastructure matters as well. Inefficient or corrupt judicial procedures may undermine even the highest quality supervisory efforts.

Perhaps the most important conflict, however, arises from asymmetries of exposures: what are the consequences for the host country and the home country if the entity should fail? Perspectives may differ with regard to whether a specific entity jeopardizes financial stability. This will depend on whether the entity is systemically important in either or both countries and whether the foreign entity is economically significant within the parent group.

In order to enhance prospects for a cooperative resolution, the leading resolution authorities have been actively engaged in supervisory colleges and crisis management groups organized by the Basel Committee on Banking Supervision and FSB and have signed several memoranda of understanding with their counterparts. But it remains to be seen how effective these measures will be under the stress of an actual crisis.

One solution might be to harmonize resolution regimes across the world. The Key Attributes approach is, in fact, a modest step in that direction,[11] but when the question of allocating losses arises

---

11. The step is only a modest one because the document leaves considerable room for variation across countries to accommodate differences in institutional structure and regulatory traditions.

few people have confidence that this approach would hold up. Countries are understandably reluctant to allocate losses ex ante— no country is willing to make an open-ended fiscal commitment. And cross-border losses will be even more difficult to allocate ex post since it will always be possible to argue that the losses would not have occurred if home country supervision had been more effective.[12]

Even if the Key Attributes were implemented in all of the major banking centers, the FSB document does not have the status (or enforceability) of a multilateral international treaty. The Key Attributes cannot solve the basic problem: if the top-tier entity in a group were to go into default, its branches, subsidiaries, and affiliates in host jurisdictions around the world might all be called into default, either immediately or upon a consequent run by creditors and counterparties.[13] Courts in these host countries might be asked to ring-fence assets, freeze payments, and set aside rulings by the home country authorities. The problem, of course, is that legal procedures—and, indeed, the objectives of an insolvency system—differ across countries. Moreover, it would not be possible for the authorities in such

---

12. There is probably no better example of this problem than the reluctance of the European Union to adopt a common deposit insurance fund even though it is widely recognized that the link between the safety of bank deposits and country risk can pose a major threat to the integrity of the euro area. So long as the safety of a deposit in the eurozone depends on the strength of the deposit insurance system and the creditworthiness of the country where the deposit was placed, the lethal link between bank risk and country risk cannot be broken (Herring 2013).

13. This may be precipitated by ipso facto clauses that permit contracts to be terminated based on a change of control, bankruptcy proceedings, or a change in agency credit ratings. Under pressure from the authorities, ISDA has adopted a protocol to permit a limited stay in implementing the close-out netting clauses with the eighteen major dealer banks (ISDA 2014). This brief stay provides additional time for the authorities to arrange an orderly transfer of these contracts. Until this agreement takes effect, however, counterparties may liquidate, terminate, or accelerate qualified financial contracts of the debtor and offset or net them under a variety of circumstances. This can result in a sudden loss of liquidity and, potentially, the forced sale of illiquid assets in illiquid markets that might drive down prices and transmit the shock to other institutions holding the same assets.

proceedings to be bound by ex ante commitments between the home and host countries because, in many cases, it may not be possible to know in advance which authority will be asked to rule.

A more fundamental solution would be to harmonize national insolvency laws and deal with any G-SIB failure in a unified global proceeding that would treat all creditors equally, strictly according to contractual priorities and without discrimination in favor of local claimants. Although various groups have worked on proposals to harmonize insolvency laws for decades, scant progress has been made. Indeed, the obstacles under current circumstances seem insuperable.

Even though a global solution is not possible, some progress could be made with bilateral agreements. Indeed, the FDIC and the Bank of England published a memorandum of understanding in 2012 agreeing to consult, cooperate, and exchange information relevant to the conditions and possible resolution of financial service firms with cross-border operations (FDIC and BoE 2012). Since most US cross-border transactions involve entities chartered in the United Kingdom, this agreement could enhance the prospects for an orderly resolution of G-SIBs headquartered in the United States. But the memorandum does not create any legally binding obligations and, in the past, close relations between the authorities in the United States and the United Kingdom have not been sufficient to ensure a cooperative solution to cross-border banking problems.[14]

Scott (2015) has advanced a novel proposal to add greater certainty about how a resolution involving the United States might proceed and provide an incentive for other countries to cooperate. The approach would avoid the enormous obstacles to negotiating a multilateral treaty by substituting a provision in Chapter 15 providing for US enforcement of foreign country stay orders and barring domestic ring-fencing actions against local assets, provided that the foreign country adopts similar provisions for US proceedings. Such an agreement with the United Kingdom might reduce a considerable amount of uncertainty regarding the resolution of a G-SIB based in the United States. But, as

---

14. See, for example, the case of BCCI (Herring, 1993) and the more recent Lehman Brothers bankruptcy (Kapur 2015).

a member of the European Union, the United Kingdom would find it difficult to make a separate agreement with the United States.[15]

Paul Tucker (2014) has suggested an alternative, contractual approach by "hard-wiring" how a cross-border resolution would proceed in the structure of a group's liabilities. Any losses in a foreign subsidiary exceeding the equity in that subsidiary would be transferred to a higher level entity[16] within the group by writing down (converting into equity) a super-subordinated debt instrument held by that higher level entity. The host authorities could trigger the intra-group debt conversion if conditions to put the subsidiary into local liquidation or resolution were met.[17] The merit of this approach is that it would force home and host authorities to agree upfront about how they will coordinate the resolution of a global group. Tucker emphasizes this would mean nations "find out ex ante whether they can co-operate on that hard-wiring, rather than, as in the recent crisis, finding out ex post whether they can cooperate in a more ad hoc resolution."[18] In the absence of trust between the home and host authorities, the home authority will be unwilling to permit the host authority to trigger an intra-group conversion of debt into equity.

---

15. Moreover, the usual measures of the importance of cross-border transactions with the United Kingdom may overstate its importance in resolution. Many US G-SIBs have chosen to form subsidiaries in the United Kingdom because under EU rules they may then branch into any other member of the European Union. Thus US subsidiaries headquartered in the United Kingdom may have significant assets in the rest of the European Union that could be ring-fenced by the host authorities.

16. This is the basic mechanism through which the single-point-of-entry approach to resolution would work. Tucker (2014) argues, however, that the same principle applies to bail-in debt in a multiple-point-of-entry strategy.

17. As Tucker (2014) notes, "The host authority for a key subsidiary must have a hand on the trigger for converting intra-group debt into equity. If the home country alone controlled the trigger, host authorities would likely be worried that the home authorities might not, in fact, pull the trigger."

18. If the home authorities will not require that the responsible higher level entity issue a minimum amount of bail-in debt or if they will not agree to a trigger in the hand of host authorities that would allow excess losses to be transferred to the higher level entity, the host authority will conclude that the home authority is either unable or unwilling to implement a whole-group resolution.

Without a robust cross-border agreement for resolving G-SIBs, countries are taking precautions that will enable them to ring-fence the parts of a banking group that are within their borders. The United States, for example, has required that foreign banks with substantial operations in the United States establish a US holding company that would be subject to prudential rules there, including capital adequacy requirements, and could, in principle, be resolved in the United States if the home country's resolution procedures did not seem to treat US interests fairly. Other countries are requiring that G-SIBs "pre-position" capital and liquidity in the entities operating within their borders (often including branches). This has the effect of providing an additional buffer against losses in the host country and facilitates a host country resolution if necessary.

Implications of Ring-Fencing for the Corporate Structure of G-SIBs

If the home country resolution authority has the legal power and resources to resolve an entire G-SIB, it might prefer that the G-SIB operate through a single legal entity if only to minimize the costs of coordinating actions with scores of other resolution authorities.[19] Of course, this approach will succeed only if all host country regulatory authorities expect that their national interests will be treated equitably vis-à-vis residents of the home country and residents of other countries. If not, they have the right (and possibly the legal obligation) to intervene to protect local interests.

G-SIBs, particularly those that specialize in wholesale activities, tend to prefer the flexibility of a more centralized organizational structure even though they will want to establish a number of subsidiaries to take advantage of particular regulatory and tax incentives and to facilitate internal managerial goals. The advantages of conducting all banking business through a single entity are compelling.[20]

---

19. Cumming and Eisenbeis (2010) propose that G-SIBs be required to operate as a single legal entity.

20. And they may include the benefits of an implicit government subsidy if a G-SIB continues to be viewed as too complex to fail.

Unconstrained by the legal lending limits in individual countries, the G-SIB would have a larger capacity to serve the needs of its customers in any location. Moreover, the ability to exercise central control over capital and liquidity will enable the G-SIB to respond more flexibly to the changing environment. It will reduce the resources that need to be allocated to liquidity so long as the needs of various offices are not perfectly correlated. To the extent that it achieves diversification benefits across its branch offices, the G-SIB may be able to operate safely with less capital and liquidity than if it were required to allocate capital separately to each entity to achieve the same degree of safety.

The possibility of ring-fencing by the host country, however, means that this flexibility may disappear in a crisis, when it is most needed.[21] Since neither the home country nor host countries can guarantee that ring-fencing will not occur, the single entity model is not prudent.

Although operation through a single legal entity is neither feasible nor prudent, one model of corporate structure attempts to capture many of the benefits even though the G-SIB would operate through several separately incorporated subsidiaries. This "centralized" model emphasizes management of liquidity, capital, and risk exposures as well as information technology and processing from the top-tier entity. So far as local regulations will permit, subsidiaries would be managed as if they were branches and lines of business would be managed to maximize profits without regard for the legal entities in which the activities are conducted.

The anticipated benefit is not only enhanced flexibility, but also the belief that the top-tier entity can manage an internal capital market that will fund the activities of G-SIBs at lower cost than if each operating entity were obliged to raise funds in each local market. In addition, centralized management of technology and operational resources should enable the group to achieve greater economies of scale than if these resources were dispersed to the various operating units in which the services are needed. This approach results, of course, in

---

21. This is one of the major flaws in the Basel approach to consolidated bank capital regulation. If resources cannot be moved from one entity to another affiliate when needed, then a regulatory focus on consolidated capital can be misleading.

a mismatch between legal structures and operating structures that is likely to cause serious difficulties if the G-SIB needs to be resolved.

If ring-fencing is expected to be the rule, not the exception, then each national resolution authority would be responsible for resolving banks that reside in its jurisdiction. Under this assumption, foreign branches would be treated as if they were subsidiaries (which, in fact, is the case in some jurisdictions) and G-SIBs would be obliged to operate through "decentralized" or "subsidiarized" models. In this approach, the top-tier institution manages a network of local subsidiaries that operate under a common brand. Each subsidiary, however, is funded locally and governed (within constraints) by local directors. Shares in the subsidiary may be listed on the local stock exchange although, of course, the parent entity will maintain a controlling interest.

Among G-SIBs, BBVA, HSBC, and Santander have endorsed this organizational model. They regard this as a source of strength and stability as well as a way of enhancing the resolvability of the group. Each significant foreign subsidiary not only meets local capital requirements, but also maintains excess capital to meet local growth objectives and provide a buffer against most losses. In addition, each subsidiary manages its liquidity needs without relying on funds or guarantees from the parent. Consistent with the emphasis on local funding, exposure to credit risk is focused on local borrowers and is usually denominated in local currency so that cross-border credit risk exposures are relatively small. From the perspective of the host country resolution authorities, the subsidiary should be autonomous and able to stand alone in the event the rest of the group experiences financial distress.

Although the parent will have an ownership position and may provide bail-in debt, the subsidiary should not rely on the parent or on access to the parent country central bank for its liquidity needs. But even this degree of financial autonomy may not be sufficient to accomplish the main objective of a policy of subsidiarization: to ensure that a legal entity can continue to operate even though its parent may be insolvent. Or, if the legal entity itself should become non-viable, to ensure that it may be resolved at relatively low cost and its systemically important services continued. This requires limits on inter-affiliate interdependencies of all sorts. The host authority must be assured that the subsidiary will continue to have access to services that may be supplied by other entities in the group or outsourced.[22]

One can debate whether constraints put on interactions between the parent and affiliates provide useful firewalls or, in times of crisis, ignite walls of fire. Certainly control over an autonomous subsidiary gives the host country the ability to preserve the assets of the local subsidiary for the benefit of local creditors and to implement an orderly resolution if necessary. But it may reduce the likelihood that the subsidiary will receive support from the parent, if it should encounter difficulties.

The appropriate degree of insulation involves striking a balance between the benefits of capital market mobility in normal times, versus insulation from external shocks in a crisis. In general, a subsidiary that is free to engage in transactions with affiliates can fund itself more cheaply in normal times if only because the parent treasury function will be able to draw its funding from a broader array of markets. But in times of crisis involving the rest of the group, the ability of the subsidiary to fund itself may be the key to its survival. Unfortunately, it is unlikely that a subsidiary could make a rapid transition from one mode of funding to another as circumstances dictate. Access to local funding usually requires the cultivation of local relationships and access to local market infrastructure.

The issue of shared services is a bit different because it appears that institutions can avoid making a trade-off between autonomy and efficiency. A subsidiary that is constrained to develop its own back office, information technology, risk management systems, and other operational infrastructure is likely to face unnecessarily high costs because it cannot achieve scale economies. Since the host country's interest should be in ensuring that the subsidiary has uninterrupted access to such services, not in who owns the infrastructure, it is possible to address this issue in other ways. If the parent houses technology-intensive services in bankruptcy-remote entities, then the

---

22. Of course, the host country authorities must take care not to require insulation so extreme that it would undermine any economic rationale for operating a G-SIB and minimize any benefit to the host country.

host country can have some degree of comfort that the subsidiary will be able to continue its access to essential services even if the parent experiences financial distress. The credibility of this arrangement is greater if the service subsidiary adopts a business model that will enable it to reduce costs rapidly whenever its revenues fall.

Subsidiarization does improve the alignment between legal entities and the way in which the business is conducted. Moreover, provided that the subsidiary is largely autonomous from the rest of the group, it could be readily spun off to facilitate an orderly resolution. Relative to the centralized model, the decentralized approach appears to better facilitate an orderly resolution, if only because it should be easier to recapitalize and privatize an autonomous subsidiary.

Concluding Comment

In the absence of an official consensus on the appropriate model for cross-border resolution, G-SIBs continue to operate under both centralized and subsidiarized models depending on their strategic preferences and the scope for choice provided by host and home regulatory authorities. Corresponding to these differing organizational models, two approaches to cross-border resolution have been endorsed by the FSB: a single-point-of-entry strategy (SPE) and a multiple-point-of-entry strategy (MPE).

The SPE model was proposed in a joint paper by the Bank of England and the Federal Deposit Insurance Corporation (FDIC and BoE 2012). It tries to finesse the complexities of dealing with a welter of intermediate holding companies and subsidiaries by focusing the resolution process on the top-level holding company. Whenever a foreign subsidiary fails to meet its regulatory capital requirements, the top-level holding company will be responsible for recapitalizing the subsidiary. If the loss at the subsidiary is so large that it exceeds the holding company's debt claims on the subsidiary and its ability to provide additional resources, the top-level holding company will be placed into receivership.[23] The aim is to financially restructure

---

23. Note that Scott (2015) raises the pertinent question of how the decision would be made to recapitalize the failed subsidiary.

the holding company while keeping the operating subsidiaries of the holding company open. The assets of the failed holding company are transferred to a newly created bridge financial company, with most of the liabilities left behind in the bankruptcy proceedings. Temporary liquidity support can be provided if necessary, but taxpayers must be insulated from any potential loss. In principle this will permit the G-SIB's operating subsidiaries to continue without interruption and provide time for the resolution authorities to restructure the bridge bank and spin it off to the public.

The SPE depends on three critical assumptions: (1) the bank holding company will have sufficient debt at the top tier to be able to recapitalize a faltering subsidiary;[24] (2) host country authorities will permit the home country resolution authority to control the process; and (3) the resolution authority will have access to sufficient liquidity to maintain the critical operations of subsidiaries in the group while the restructuring of the top-level institution takes place. The latter may be an issue in several countries that are home to institutions with liabilities that are a substantial multiple of their gross domestic products.

This approach faces a tricky problem in a scenario in which a foreign subsidiary is the major source of losses and should be liquidated, as noted by Scott (2015). The authorities, of course, do not want to be in the position of propping up an institution that has no going-concern value. But once they admit the possibility that some foreign subsidiaries may not be protected, creditors have reason to be concerned about all of the foreign subsidiaries and it may not be possible to implement the resolution without creating spillovers as creditors engage in a flight to quality.

In addition to the hope that foreign authorities can be convinced to forbear and leave the resolution to the headquarters authority, the laws underlying many financial contracts will need to be changed or the single resolution authority will need to have the ability to impose a stay. Otherwise the initiation of resolution proceedings with regard to

---

24. Of course, the host country authority must have confidence that the parent holding company will be willing (or will be compelled by the home country authority) to sustain the operations of a local subsidiary in financial distress.

the top-level entity could be interpreted as an event of default that permits counterparties to terminate their financial contracts. This could destabilize markets and frustrate the attempt of the single resolution authority to ensure the continuity of operations.

The multiple-point-of-entry strategy relies on three critical assumptions: (1) that the failing subsidiary will have sufficient bail-in debt to recapitalize the viable part of the institution without relying on taxpayer assistance;[25] (2) that the remaining subsidiaries of the group will not suffer a loss of market confidence because of the resolution of an affiliate institution; and (3) that other countries will not use the initiation of the resolution process in one country as a rationale for intervening in affiliates of the group in their jurisdictions. Although this approach has obvious appeal for G-SIBs that are not organized within a holding company structure, based on the past behavior of market participants it appears to make a very optimistic assumption that creditors and counterparties of affiliates will not regard the resolution of one subsidiary as a signal that the entire group is in jeopardy. And if markets do not have confidence that the problem can be isolated to one subsidiary, the authorities may feel obliged to provide a bailout to preserve financial stability.

Neither strategy is certain to succeed, but maintaining the possibility that either might be employed (as envisaged for example by the new European legislation on bank crisis resolution) does not help the market to price and monitor the risk of default. In fact, if the market is surprised by the resolution strategy the authorities employ, confidence in the system may be undermined, leading to panicky reactions that will impede an orderly resolution.[26] If creditors and investors cannot anticipate the endgame, they cannot price risk efficiently. Ultimately, this uncertainty is likely to be destructive to markets and to the banks themselves, and to exacerbate the risk of disorderly resolution.

Despite an enormous amount of effort, one must conclude that we do not yet have a reliable framework to undertake the orderly

---

25. See Huertas (2014) for a lucid description of how a subsidiarized bank should be resolved in an orderly manner.

26. Gracie (2014) emphasizes the point that transparency regarding the resolution process is essential to creditors and investors.

resolution of a G-SIB. More effective bankruptcy procedures like the proposed Chapter 15 reform would certainly help provide a stronger anchor to market expectations about how the resolution of a G-SIB may unfold. Greater clarity of corporate and business structures and a greater degree of subsidiarization would facilitate any resolution process. Although too-big-to-fail is too-costly-to-continue, a solution to the problem remains elusive.

References

Avraham, D., P. Selvaggi, and J. I. Vickery. 2012. "A Structural View of U.S. Bank Holding Companies," *Economic Policy Review* 18, no. 2 (July 16): 65–81.

Basel Committee on Banking Supervision (BCBS). 1992. *The Insolvency Liquidation of a Multinational Bank*, BCBS Compendium of Documents, International Supervisory Issues III (May 2001).

Baxter, T., and J. Sommer. 2005. "Breaking Up Is Hard to Do: An Essay on Cross-Border Challenges in Resolving Financial Groups," in *Systemic Financial Crises: Resolving Large Bank Insolvencies,* ed. D. Evanoff and G. Kaufman (Singapore: World Scientific), 175–91.

Carmassi, J., and R. J. Herring. 2013. "Living Wills and Cross-Border Resolution of Systemically Important Banks," *Journal of Financial Economic Policy* 5, no. 4: 361–87.

Carmassi, J., and R. J. Herring. 2014. *Corporate Structures, Transparency and Resolvability of Global Systemically Important Banks,* Systemic Risk Council, Washington, DC.

Carmassi, J., and R. J. Herring. 2015. *The Corporate Complexity of Global Systemically Important Banks,* working paper, Wharton Financial Institutions Center.

Cumming, C., and R. Eisenbeis. 2010. *Resolving Troubled Systemically Important Cross-Border Financial Institutions: Is a New Corporate Organizational Form Required?,* working paper, Wharton Financial Institutions Center, February.

Federal Deposit Insurance Corporation (FDIC) and Bank of England (BoE). 2012. *Resolving Globally Active, Systemically Important Financial Institutions,* a joint paper by the Federal Deposit Insurance Corporation and the Bank of England, December 10.

Financial Stability Board. 2011. *Key Attributes of Effective Resolution Regimes for Financial Institutions*, October.

Financial Stability Board. 2012. *Resolution of Systemically Important Financial Institutions— Progress Report*, November.

Financial Stability Board. 2013a. *Recovery and Resolution Planning for Systemically Important Financial Institutions: Guidance on Developing Effective Resolution Strategies,* July 16.

Financial Stability Board. 2013b. *Recovery and Resolution Planning for Systemically Important Financial Institutions: Guidance on Identification of Critical Functions and Critical Shared Services,* July 16.

Financial Stability Board. 2013c. *Recovery and Resolution Planning for Systemically Important Financial Institutions: Guidance on Recovery Triggers and Stress Scenarios,* July 16.

Financial Stability Board. 2014. *Key Attributes of Effective Resolution Regimes for Financial Institutions,* October.

Gracie, A. 2014. "Making Resolution Work in Europe and Beyond—the Case for Gone Concern Loss Absorbing Capacity." Speech given at a Bruegel Breakfast Panel Event, Brussels, July 17.

Haldane, A. 2009. *Banking on the State,* paper based on presentation to the Federal Reserve Bank of Chicago, September 25.

Herring, R. J. 1993. "BCCI: Lessons for International Bank Supervision," *Contemporary Policy Issues* 11 (April).

Herring, R. J. 2002. "International Financial Conglomerates: Implications for Bank Insolvency Regimes," in *Policy Challenges for the Financial Sector in the Context of Globalization,* Proceedings of the Second Annual Policy Seminar for Deputy Central Bank Governors, Federal Reserve Bank/IMF/World Bank.

Herring, R. J. 2003. "International Financial Conglomerates: Implications for National Insolvency Regimes," in *Market Discipline in Banking: Theory and Evidence,* ed. G. Kaufman (Elsevier), 99–130.

Herring, R. J. 2007. "Conflicts between Home and Host Country Prudential Supervisors," in *International Financial Instability: Global Banking and National Regulation,* ed. D. Evanoff, G. Kaufman, and J. LaBrosse (World Scientific), 201–19.

Herring, R. J. 2013. "The Danger of Building a Banking Union of a One-Legged Stool," in *Political, Fiscal and Banking Union in the Eurozone,* ed. F. A. Allen, E. Carletti, and J. Gray (FIC Press).

Herring, R. J., and J. Carmassi. 2010. "The Corporate Structure of International Financial Conglomerates: Complexity and Its Implications for Safety & Soundness," in *Oxford Handbook of Banking,* ed. A. N. Berger, P. Molyneux, and J. O. S. Wilson (Oxford University Press).

Huertas, T. F. 2009. "The Rationale and Limits of Bank Supervision," unpublished manuscript.

Huertas, T. F. 2010. "Too Big to Fail Is Too Costly to Continue," *Financial Times,* March 22, http://www.ft.com/intl/cms/s/0/62e80b1a-35d8-11df-aa43 -00144feabdc0.html .

Huertas, T. F. 2014. *Safe to Fail: How Resolution Will Revolutionise Banking* (London: Palgrave Macmillan).

International Swaps and Derivatives Association (ISDA). 2014. *Major Banks Agree to Sign ISDA Resolution Stay Protocol,* October 11, http://assets.isda .org/media/de778136/58b5618f.pdf.

Kapur, E. 2015. "The Next Lehman Bankruptcy," chapter 7 in this volume.

King, M. 2010. *Banking from Bagehot to Basel, and Back Again,* Second Bagehot Lecture, Second Buttonwood Gathering, New York, October 25.

Mayes, D. 2013. "Achieving Plausible Separability for the Resolution of Cross-Border Banks," *Journal of Financial Economic Policy* 5, no. 4: 388–404.

Miller, H. R., and M. Horwitz. 2013. *Resolution Authority: Lessons from the Lehman Experience.* Weil, April 11.

Omarova, S. 2013. *Large U.S. Banking Organizations' Activities in Physical Commodity and Energy Markets: Legal and Policy Considerations,* Written Testimony before the Senate Committee on Banking, Housing, and Urban Affairs, Subcommittee on Financial Institutions and Consumer Protection, July 23.

Scott, K. 2015. "The Context for Bankruptcy Resolutions," chapter 1 in this volume.

Tucker, P. (2014). "The Resolution of Financial Institutions without Taxpayer Solvency Support: Seven Retrospective Clarifications and Elaborations," speech delivered to the European Summer Symposium in Economic Theory, Gerzensee, Switzerland, July 3.

About the Contributors

Jacopo Carmassi is a research fellow at CASMEF, the Arcelli Center for Monetary and Financial Studies, University LUISS Guido Carli, and a fellow of the Wharton Financial Institutions Center, University of Pennsylvania. He was previously an economist at Assonime, the Association of Joint Stock Companies incorporated in Italy, and a researcher at the Italian Banking Association. His research and work activities have focused on banking regulation and supervision and financial crises, including the 2008 global financial crisis, bank capital rules, deposit insurance, the structure of financial supervision, derivatives, bank crisis management and resolution, bank recovery and resolution plans, corporate structures of global systemically important banks, and the banking union in Europe.

Darrell Duffie is the Dean Witter Distinguished Professor in Finance at the Graduate School of Business, Stanford University; a member of the Financial Advisory Roundtable of the Federal Reserve Bank of New York; and a member of the Board of Directors of Moody's Corporation. He serves on the boards of scholarly journals in finance, economics, and mathematics, and was elected president of the American Finance Association for 2009. He is a fellow and member of the Council of the Econometric Society, a fellow of the American Academy of Arts and Sciences, and a research associate of the National Bureau of Economic Research. He recently chaired the Financial Stability Board's Market Participants Group on Reference Rate Reform. He is a coauthor of *The Squam Lake Report: Fixing the Financial System* (2010). Other recent books include *How Big Banks Fail* (2010), *Measuring Corporate Default Risk* (2011), and *Dark Markets* (2012).

Simon Gleeson is a partner in Clifford Chance's financial services and markets group in London, specializing in financial markets and banking law and regulation, clearing, settlement, and derivatives. His experience includes advising governments, regulators, and public bodies as well as banks, investment firms, fund managers, and other financial institutions on regulatory issues. He is a member of the Financial Stability Board's Legal Advisory Panel on Legal Issues in Cross-Border Resolution; member of the Institute for International Finance's Special Committee on Effective Regulation and chair of its working group on cross-border resolution issues; former member of the UK Financial Markets Law Committee; and adviser to the World Economic Forum on its 2009 report on the New Global Financial Architecture. He has given evidence on financial regulation and bank resolution to parliamentary committees of both the House of Lords and the House of Commons. He is a visiting professor at the University of Edinburgh.

Richard J. Herring is Jacob Safra Professor of International Banking and Professor of Finance at The Wharton School, University of Pennsylvania, where he is also founding director of the Wharton Financial Institutions Center. He is the author of more than 150 articles, monographs, and books and has pursued research funded by grants from the National Science Foundation, Ford Foundation, Brookings Institution, Sloan Foundation, Council on Foreign Relations, and Royal Swedish Commission on Productivity. He served as vice dean and director of the Wharton Undergraduate Division from 1995–2000; from 2000–2006, he was director of the Lauder Institute, a dual-degree program that combines an MBA, an MA in international studies, and foreign-language proficiency. Outside the university, he is cochair of the US Shadow Financial Regulatory Committee and executive director of the Financial Economist's Roundtable. He is also a member of the FDIC Systemic Resolution Advisory Committee, the Systemic Risk Council, and the Hoover Institution Working Group on Resolution Policy.

Dr. Thomas F. Huertas is a partner in the financial services risk practice at EY Global Limited and chairs the firm's global regulatory network of former senior supervisors. He advises major financial firms on regulatory and strategic issues. Before joining EY, he was a member of the executive committee at the UK Financial Services Authority, alternate chair of the European Banking Authority, and a member of the Basel Committee on Banking Supervision. He also held a number of senior positions at Citigroup, including chairman and chief executive, Citibank AG (Germany). He has published extensively on banking and regulatory issues, including his most recent book *Safe to Fail: How Resolution Will Revolutionise Banking*. He is an adjunct professor at the Institute of Law and Finance at the Johann Wolfgang von Goethe University in Frankfurt, Germany.

Thomas H. Jackson, a professor at the University of Rochester, served as president of the university from 1994 to 2005. Before that, he was vice president and provost of the University of Virginia, which he first joined in 1988 as dean of Virginia's School of Law. He was a professor of law at Harvard from 1986 to 1988 and served on the Stanford University faculty from 1977 to 1986. He clerked for US District Court judge Marvin E. Frankel in New York in 1975–76, and then for Supreme Court Justice (later Chief Justice) William H. Rehnquist in 1976–77. The author of bankruptcy and commercial law texts used in law schools across the country, he served as special master for the US Supreme Court in a dispute involving every state in the country over the disposition of unclaimed dividends held by brokerage houses.

Emily C. Kapur is an attorney working on financial sector litigation and a doctoral candidate in Stanford University's Department of Economics. Her research focuses on legal and economic issues connected to efforts to reform global financial markets. Before graduate school, she spent three years leading the Hewlett Foundation's Nuclear Security Initiative. She received a bachelor's degree in economics from Stanford University, a master's degree from the London School of Economics, where she studied as a Marshall Scholar, and a juris doctorate from Stanford Law School.

William F. Kroener III is counsel at Sullivan & Cromwell LLP. He served as general counsel of the Federal Deposit Insurance Corporation from

1995 to 2006. His law practice focuses on the supervision and regulation of banks and other regulated financial institutions and their advisers. Kroener served as cochair of the American Bar Association Presidential Task Force on Financial Markets Regulatory Reform (2008–12) and chair of the Banking Law Committee of the American Bar Association Business Law Section (2011–14). He currently serves as an advisory member of the Financial Institutions Committee of the Business Law Section of the State Bar of California. He speaks and writes regularly on financial regulatory topics and has taught as an adjunct professor at Stanford, George Washington, and American University law schools.

Kenneth E. Scott, the Ralph M. Parsons Professor Emeritus of Law and Business at Stanford Law School and a Hoover Institution senior research fellow, is a leading scholar in the fields of corporate finance reform and corporate governance who has written extensively on federal banking regulation. He chairs the Resolution Project on Economic Policy. His current research concentrates on legislative and policy developments related to the current financial crisis, comparative corporate governance, and financial regulation. He is editor (with George Shultz and John Taylor) of *Ending Government Bailouts* (2010). His consulting experience includes the World Bank, Federal Deposit Insurance Corporation, Resolution Trust Corporation, and National Association of Securities Dealers (now FINRA). He is also a member of the Shadow Financial Regulatory Committee, the Financial Economists Roundtable, and the State Bar of California's Financial Institutions Committee. Before joining the Stanford Law School faculty in 1968, he served as general counsel to the Federal Home Loan Bank Board and as chief deputy savings and loan commissioner of California and worked in private practice in New York with Sullivan & Cromwell.

David A. Skeel Jr. is the S. Samuel Arsht Professor of Corporate Law at the University of Pennsylvania Law School. He is the author of *The New Financial Deal: Understanding the Dodd-Frank Act and Its (Unintended) Consequences* (2011), *Icarus in the Boardroom: The*

Fundamental Flaws in Corporate America and Where They Came From (2005), *Debt's Dominion: A History of Bankruptcy Law in America* (2001), and numerous articles on bankruptcy, corporate law, Christianity and law, and other topics. Skeel has also written commentaries for the *New York Times, Wall Street Journal, Books & Culture, Weekly Standard*, and other publications.

John B. Taylor is the George P. Shultz Senior Fellow in Economics at the Hoover Institution and the Mary and Robert Raymond Professor of Economics at Stanford University. He chairs the Hoover Working Group on Economic Policy. An award-winning teacher and researcher specializing in macroeconomics, international economics, and monetary policy, he has served as a senior economist (1976–77) and member (1989–91) of the President's Council of Economic Advisers and as undersecretary of the treasury for international affairs (2001–2005). Taylor's book *Getting Off Track: How Government Actions and Interventions Caused, Prolonged, and Worsened the Financial Crisis* was one of the first on the financial crisis; he has since followed up with two books on preventing future crises, coediting *The Road Ahead for the Fed* and *Ending Government Bailouts as We Know Them*. Before joining the Stanford faculty in 1984, Taylor held positions as a professor of economics at Princeton University and Columbia University.

About the Hoover Institution's Working Group on Economic Policy

The Working Group on Economic Policy conducts research on current financial conditions as well as prevailing economic policies and issues, including domestic and global monetary, fiscal, and regulatory policies. Ideas that examine market and government dimensions of solutions are promoted, with the goal of increasing the extent and breadth of national and global prosperity.

For 25 years starting in the early 1980s, the U.S. economy experienced an unprecedented economic boom. Economic expansions were stronger and longer than in the past. Recessions were shorter, shallower, and less frequent. Gross domestic product (GDP) doubled and household net worth increased by 250 percent in real terms. Forty-seven million jobs were created.

This quarter-century boom strengthened as its length increased. Productivity growth surged by one full percentage point per year in the United States, creating an additional $9 trillion of goods and services that would never have existed. And the long boom went global, with emerging-market countries from Asia to Latin America to Africa experiencing the enormous improvements in both economic growth and economic stability.

Economic policies that place greater reliance on the principles of free markets, price stability, and flexibility have been the key to these successes. Recently, however, several powerful new economic forces have begun to change the economic landscape, and these principles are being challenged with far-reaching implications for U.S. economic policy, both domestic and international. A financial crisis flared up in 2007 and turned into a severe panic in 2008, leading to the Great Recession. How we interpret and react to these forces—and in particular whether proven policy principles prevail going forward—will determine whether strong economic growth and stability returns and again continues to spread and improve more people's lives or whether the economy stalls and stagnates.

Our Working Group organizes seminars and conferences, prepares policy papers and other publications, and serves as a resource for policy makers and interested members of the public.

THE RESOLUTION PROJECT

When in 2009 Congress began considering financial reforms proposed by the US Treasury, a "resolution project" group was established, under the auspices of the Working Group on Economic Policy at the Hoover Institution at Stanford University, to focus on alternative ways to deal with failing financial institutions. The group's original members were Andrew Crockett, Darrell Duffie, Richard Herring, Thomas H. Jackson, William F. Kroener III, Kenneth E. Scott, George P. Shultz, David A. Skeel Jr., Kimberly Anne Summe, and John B. Taylor.

The group held a number of meetings in the fall of 2009, which led to several papers and a conference in December 2009, the results of which were published in 2010 as *Ending Government Bailouts As We Know Them,* edited by Kenneth E. Scott, George P. Shultz, and John B. Taylor. The group continued to meet and work further on members' analyses and proposals, and new members joined, including Simon Gleeson, Thomas F. Huertas, and Emily Kapur. A proposal for modified bankruptcy procedures to better handle the failure of large, nonbank financial institutions, called Chapter 14, was the result, and a second book, *Bankruptcy Not Bailout: A Special Chapter 14,* edited by Kenneth E. Scott and John B. Taylor, was published in 2012. This third book centers around a revised version of the proposal, called Chapter 14 2.0.

Index

absolute priority rule, 21
accounting standards, 262
ad hoc financing, 76–77
Adams v. National Bank of Greece, 114
additional tier 1 (AT1), 130, 132
additional tier 2 (AT2), 130, 132
adequate-assurance standard, 181, 206–8
adverse-effects standard, 181
aggregate loss-absorbing capacity
    (ALAC), 132, 132n4, 135f, 149
  parent company solvency and, 154n21
  requirements in resolution, 135–36
AIG, 12, 75
ALAC. *See* aggregate loss-absorbing
  capacity
AmericanWest Bancorporation, 68–69
American-West Bank, 68
Anchor Bancorp Wisconsin, 73n35
ancillary insolvency proceedings,
  116–17
anti-assignment provisions, 42
Article 60a, 204, 212, 221
Article III judges, 9, 17, 36, 206
assets
  devaluations of, 225f
  executory contracts as, 39
  financing through sales of, 68–69
  high quality, liquid, 71
  of holding company, 69–70
  risk-weighted, 134
  sale of, 68–69
  of subsidiaries, 69–70
  unencumbered, 169, 169n33
AT1. *See* additional tier 1

AT2. *See* additional tier 2
automatic liquidation, 257
automatic stay, 29, 52–53, 68, 210
avoiding power provisions, 42, 56

Bagehot, Walter, 83
bail-in, 137
  constructive certainty in, 161
  holding company balance sheet and,
    144, 145t, 147
  liquidity provision and, 169
  recapitalization and, 144, 144n16,
    145t, 146–47, 148t, 156–57
  reserve capital and, 144, 147, 156–57,
    158t
  subsidiaries balance sheet and, 144,
    145t, 147
bail-in debt (BID), 2, 20, 22
  capital requirements, 3–4
  CCP failure resolution, 99
  defining, 4
  in subsidiarized organizational struc-
    ture, 268
bail-in fund, 78
bailout, 176, 178
  costs of, 251
  social welfare cost, 182
balance sheet
  bail-in and, 144, 145t, 147
  CCP, 88
  Chapter 14 reorganization, 180
  insolvency, 17, 149
  Lehman Brothers, 191–94, 196t–197t
  liabilities, 194

Bank of America, 12, 208
Bank of Credit and Commerce International (BCCI), 259
Bank of England, 10–11, 80, 103, 106, 123
  FDIC cooperation agreement with, 264
  SPE proposal, 270
Bank Recovery and Resolution Directive (BRRD), 120, 124, 177–78, 183, 220
  Article 60a, 204
Banking Act of 1989, 123
Banking Act of 2009, 118
bankruptcy
  conflicting approaches of regulators, 258
  financial companies and, 245–46
  financing in, 62–63, 64
  liquidity sources in, 67–71
  prearranged funding alternatives, 75–81
  pre-bankruptcy planning, 12, 16, 18, 73, 81
  prepackaged, 73, 73n35, 151, 154n21
  SIFI liquidity needs in, 73
  SIFI viability for, 18
  universality in, 111
  See also Chapter 7 liquidation; Chapter 11 bankruptcy; Chapter 14 bankruptcy
Bankruptcy Appellate Panel, 37
Bankruptcy Code, 1–3
  Chapter 14 case termination and, 235
  Chapter 14 proposal, 15
  clearing agreement stays and, 101
  section 106, 10
  section 303, 34, 36
  section 362, 210
  section 363, 22, 27, 69
  section 364, 65, 67
  section 365, 39–40
  section 1112, 34
  section 1125, 44
  section 1145, 44–45
  section 1411, 42
  section 1412, 45
  UK recognition of, 124–26

bankruptcy judges, 36–37
Bankruptcy Not Bailout proposal, 37
bankruptcy process
  living wills addressing problems in, 245
  problems with, 16
Banque Indosuez v. Ferroment Resources, 117
Barclays, 74, 76, 207n113, 208, 217
Basel Committee on Banking Supervision (BCBS), 259, 262
Basel III, 132, 267n21
  capital requirements, 61n4
  CET1 requirement, 134
  liquidity requirements, 71–72
BBVA, 268
BCBS. *See* Basel Committee on Banking Supervision
BCCI. *See* Bank of Credit and Commerce International
Bear Stearns, 73, 75, 77, 220, 224n172
Bernanke, Ben, 176
BID. *See* bail-in debt
BlackRock, 95
branches
  domestic, 255
  foreign, 138, 255–56
  group complexity and, 255
  resolution and, 138–40
  ring-fencing of, 256
  territorial approach to, 259
bridge companies, 2, 5, 20, 52
  adequate-assurance standard and, 206
  capital requirements, 55–56
  CCP failure resolution, 97–98, 101
  defining, 49
  due process, 9–10
  FDIC control of, 21
  long-term unsecured debt, 44
  principles, 39
  as private company, 45
  recapitalization, 39
  residual equity value, 43–44
  section 1405 transfer, 32–33, 44–45
  securities distribution by, 44–45

subsidiary holdings transferred to, 42–43

territorial approach to resolution and, 139

bridge transfers, 2

broad universalism, 124–25

BRRD. *See* Bank Recovery and Resolution Directive

capital

raising, 146

regulatory, 36

T2, 132

See also recapitalization; reserve capital

capital conservation buffer, 134, 167

capital debt, 2

in Chapter 14 resolutions, 4

coverage, 5–6

definition, 3–5

in FDIC SIFI failure proposal, 3–5

capital markets, 191

capital ratio

consolidated, 224

gone concern, 154n21

capital requirements

bail-in debt and, 3–4

Basel III, 61n4

bridge companies, 55–56

Chapter 14 2.0 exemption window, 44

stress tests, 72

See also reserve capital

capital structure debt, 30n51, 32, 44

defining, 49, 203n96

left behind in transfer, 39

Lehman Brothers Chapter 14 and, 208, 215

regulatory floor for, 203, 203n97

section 1405 transfer objections and, 218

cascading run, 200

CCAR. *See* Comprehensive Capital Analysis and Review

central counterparty (CCP), 87

alternatives to liquidation, 98

balance sheet, 88

BID in failure resolution, 99

bridge companies in failure resolution, 97–98, 101

clearing members, 90–91

contractual recovery approach, 91

cross-border issues, 106–7

cross-border issues in failure resolution, 106–7

Dodd-Frank Act Title II and, 97–98, 103, 106–7

failure of, 89

failure resolution, 96–100

failure resolution process, 105–6

FDIC and failure resolution, 97–98, 106

Federal Reserve and, 103

J. P. Morgan proposal for failure resolution, 96, 99, 101

liquidity sources in failure resolution, 102–4

loss allocation, 90

no-creditor-worse-off principle, 104

OLF and failure resolution for, 103–4

recovery versus resolution, 90–96

replenishment payments, 91–92

risk managed by, 88–89

stays on clearing agreements, 100–102

tear-up, 93

waterfall recovery, 91f, 92

centrally cleared derivatives contracts, 88

CET1. *See* common equity tier 1

change-of-control provisions, 40, 42, 43, 171, 171n36, 210, 220

Chapter 7 liquidation, 42

Chapter 11 bankruptcy, 2, 22

cross-border issues, 117

funding options, 65–75

Lehman Brothers Holdings entering, 200

liquidity sources in, 67–71

runs and, 176–77

UK ancillary proceedings and, 117

Chapter 14 1.0, 25
  2.0 differences, 1, 23–25
  Article III judges instead of bank-
    ruptcy judges, 36
  commencement of case, 27, 33
  creation of new Chapter 14, 26
  debtor-in-possession financing, 28,
    207n113
  primary regulator role, 27–28
  QFCs, 29–30, 41, 210
  section 364 amendment, 67
  trustee in, 46
  venue rules, 36
Chapter 14 2.0, 244–48
  1.0 differences, 1, 23–25
  avoiding power provisions, 56
  capital requirement exemption
    window, 44
  commencement of case, 33–37, 50
  defining covered financial corpora-
    tions, 48
  designated judges, 36–37
  Dodd-Frank amendment proposals,
    57–58
  Dodd-Frank Title II and, 47–48
  Federal Reserve Board standing, 38
  QFCs and, 40, 53–54
  recapitalization in, 25, 69
  regulator roles, 37–38, 50–51
  rule sets in, 25
  section 1405 transfer provisions, 39–43
  section 1405 transfer transitional
    provisions, 43–47
  subsidiary contracts in, 54–55
  text of, 48–58
  Title 28 amendments, 57
  trustee in, 46, 52, 56–57
  two-entity recapitalization and resolu-
    tion of, 47
  venue rules, 36
Chapter 14 bankruptcy, 1, 177, 179–87,
    202
  1.0 differences from 2.0, 1, 23–25
  adequate-assurance standard, 181
  adverse-effects standard, 181
  automatic stays in, 210
  balance sheet reorganization under,
    180
  business after, 219–40
  change-of-control provisions and,
    210, 220
  commencement, 33–37
  covered financial corporations, 34–35
  creditor notification, 214
  cross-border insolvency recognition
    and, 112
  derivatives in, 8
  due process, 9–10
  European-law contracts and, 212
  Federal Reserve consultation for, 206
  financing after, 222–31
  foreign jurisdictions and, 212
  as insolvency regime, 119
  Lehman Brothers counterfactual,
    202–19
  Lehman Brothers Holdings filing,
    209–12
  liquidity and, 7–8
  liquidity stress test after, 228t–229t
  managing business after, 219–22
  meeting standards for, 205–9
  moral hazard and, 182–83, 184
  notification requirements, 214
  outcomes, 235, 237, 240
  QFEs, 8
  recapitalizing subsidiaries after, 219–22
  reorganization after, 231–33
  Resolution Project proposal, 1–2, 15
  run prevention, 186–87
  runs after, 224
  social welfare outcomes, 182–83, 235,
    237, 240
  SPOE as backstop to, 202
  SPOE in parallel to, 23
  stay orders in, 210
  terminating case, 233, 234f, 235
  timeline of Lehman Brothers counter-
    factual, 213f
Chicago Mercantile Exchange, 89
choice of jurisdiction, 259

choice of law, 112–13
Chrysler, 74
CIT Group, 74
clearing agreements, stays on, 100–102
clearing members, 90
    contractual recovery approach and, 91
    failure of, 90
    loss absorption by, 90
clients, Chapter 14 outcomes, 235, 237, 240
close-out netting provisions, 259, 263n13
CoCos. *See* convertible debt instruments (CoCos)
collateral budget, 169n33
collateral calls, 198
collateral liquidation, 137, 198
comity, 116
commercial paper, 199, 201, 230
Commission Bancaire, 214
Commission de Surveillance de Secteur Financier, 214
Committee on Payment and Settlement Systems-International Organization of Securities Commissions (CPSS-IOSCO), 89, 94. *See* Committee on Payments and Market Infrastructure.
Committee on Payments and Market Infrastructure (CPMI), 89, 102, 107
Commodity Futures Trading Commission, 27, 214
common equity tier 1 (CET1), 130, 132
    options on, 146
    parent holding company, 141
    recapitalization targets, 134–36
    reserve capital requirements, 134
    SPE-MPE hybrid resolution and, 166–67
common shocks, 12–13
complexity
    of financial institutions, 249–50
    of G-SIBs, extent of, 252–57
    number of subsidiaries, 255

resolution problems from, 258–61
    scope of problems, 250–51
Comprehensive Capital Analysis and Review (CCAR), 72
consolidated capital ratio, 224
constructive ambiguity, 161
constructive certainty, 161, 166–68
contracting out of insolvency, 122, 122n18
contractual recovery approach, 91, 93
convertible debt instruments (CoCos), 2
convexity effect, 94
cooperative resolution, 262
counterparties
    Chapter 14 outcomes, 235, 237, 240
    close-out netting clauses agreement and, 263n13
    QFC exemptions, 29
covered financial corporations, 34–35, 47
    commencement of Chapter 14 2.0 cases and, 50
    defining, 34, 48
    voluntary and involuntary petitions, 35
CPMI. *See* Committee on Payments and Market Infrastructure
CPSS-IOSCO. *See* Committee on Payment and Settlement Systems-International Organization of Securities Commissions
credibility, 261
credit default swaps, 195
credit downgrade threats, 195
credit support providers, 221
creditors
    Chapter 14 outcomes, 235, 237, 240
    equal treatment of, 117, 122
    involuntary petition by, 35
    standing committee, 155
creditors' bargain, 90
creditors' rights
    bail-in of reserve capital and, 157, 158t
    section 1405 transfer objections and, 218
critical undercapitalization, 192

cross-border credit risk, 268
Cross-Border Insolvency Regulations
    2006, 119
cross-border issues, 111
    ancillary insolvency proceedings,
        116–17
    bank resolution recognition, 112
    branches and bank resolution, 138–40
    in CCP failure resolution, 106–7
    Chapter 11 and, 117
    Chapter 14 and, 112
    choice of law, 112–13
    equal treatment of creditors, 117, 122
    foreign laws effect on English law
        contracts, 113–14
    insolvency measures, 111, 112
    regimes of mutual recognition,
        204n102
    reorganization, 114
    resolutions, 264–66, 270
    statutory powers in UK, 122–24
    variation of debts, 115–17
cross-default provisions, 43, 53, 212

DCO. See designated clearing
    organization
debt
    bail-in, 2–4, 20, 22, 99, 268
    bridge company, 44
    capital, 2–6
    convertible instruments, 2
    intermediate, 134, 134n5
    left behind, 20, 21, 39, 44
    long-term unsecured, 44
    recapitalization options, 69–70
    in section 1405 transfer, 39–40
    senior, 133–34
    statutory variation of, 115–17
    subordinated, 203
    unsecured, 20
    variation of, 115–17
    See also capital structure debt
debtor in possession (DIP), 8, 27
    in Chapter 14 1.0, 28, 207n113
    management as, 45

debtor-in-possession financing (DIP
    financing), 28, 56, 64, 65–67
    CCP failure resolution and, 103
    liens, 66
    private markets for, 74
    section 364, 65
decentralized organizational structure,
    268–70
default guarantee funds, 90–92
default-management waterfall, 91f,
    92–94
deposit insurance, 263n12
depository banks, 27
derivatives
    automatic stay and, 29
    centrally cleared, 88
    in Chapter 14, 8
    as executory contracts, 8, 29
    international regulatory agreements, 88
    Lehman Brothers holdings, 224n172
    margin increases on, 199
    market value of, 88
    resolution and, 170, 170n35
designated clearing organization
    (DCO), 106
designated judges, 36–37
DIP. See debtor in possession
DIP financing. See debtor-in-possession
    financing
discount window, 8, 82
Discount Window Facility, 103
Dodd-Frank Wall Street Reform and
    Consumer Protection Act of 2010,
    1–3, 11, 17, 202
    CCP failure resolution, 97–98, 103,
        106–7
    Chapter 14 proposal and, 47–48,
        57–58
    clearing agreement stays and, 101
    due process, 9
    financing arrangements of Title II, 63
    government as financer and, 74–75
    holding company obligations, 156n23
    living will provisions, 243–46
    Orderly Liquidation Fund, 7

pre-seizure judicial hearing, 9
resolution plans required by, 243–46
section 165, 12
Section 202, 9
section 616, 156n23
SPOE and Chapter 14 in parallel under, 23
"too big to fail" banks and, 247
See also Title I; Title II
double leverage, 159
Drexel Burnham, 220
due process, 218
Chapter 14, 9–10
Title II of Dodd-Frank Act, 9
Duffie, Darrell, 88

Eastman Kodak, 66
EEA. *See* European Economic Area
emergency lending powers, 82, 84–85
end-of-waterfall loss sharing, 93, 95
energy trading units, 257
Environmental Protection Agency, 257
equity receivership, 59–60
essential services, 170
EU. *See* European Union
European Central Bank, 224n172
European Convention on Human Rights, 121
European Court of Human Rights, 122
European Economic Area (EEA), 124
European Union (EU), 120
deposit insurance in, 263n12
executory contracts
derivatives as, 8, 29
as net assets, 39
section 1405 transfer and, 39

Fannie Mae, 12
FBOs. *See See* foreign banking organizations
FDIC. *See* Federal Deposit Insurance Corp.
Federal Banking Commission (Switzerland), 214

Federal Deposit Insurance Corp. (FDIC), 1, 2, 10–11
Bank of England cooperation agreement with, 264
CCP failure resolution, 97–98, 106
Federal Reserve consultation with, for Chapter 14, 206
living wills and, 80, 244–45, 247–48
OLA and, 162n29
resolution plan submission to, 244–45, 247–48
section 1405 standing, 38
SIFI failure proposal, 2–5
Title II resolution by, 18
Washington Mutual seizure, 201
See also single point of entry
Federal Reserve, 1, 16, 176
CCP failure resolution and, 103
Chapter 14 2.0 and standing of, 38
Chapter 14 filing by, 206
Chapter 14 notification requirements, 214
discount window, 8, 82
emergency lending powers, 82, 84–85
as financer, 74–75
liquidity requirements by, 71–72
living wills and, 80, 244–45, 247–48
Primary Dealer Credit Facility, 224n172, 227
quick sale bankruptcy financing and, 67
resolution plan submission to, 244–45, 247–48
section 13(3) authority, 8, 75, 84–85, 203
voluntary petition filing by, 35
Federal Reserve Act, 75
section 13(3), 8, 75, 84–85, 203
Federal Supervisory Authority for the Financial Services Industry (Germany), 214
Felixstowe Docks and Railways v. US Lines, 116–17
financial contagion, 21, 151
Financial Institution Bankruptcy Act of 2014, subchapter V, 86

financial market infrastructure (FMI), 102, 107
asymmetries of, 262
Financial Services Act of 2012 (United Kingdom), 106
resolution standard recommendations, 260–61
Financial Services Agency (Japan), 214
Financial Services Authority (United Kingdom), 214
Financial Stability Board (FSB), 10, 61n4, 118, 134n5, 161, 204, 250
credibility enhancement efforts, 261
Key Attributes of Effective Resolution Regimes for Financial Institutions, 118, 260–63
MPE and, 270
on point of resolution, 261
SPE and, 270
Financial Stability Oversight Council, 89
financing
ad hoc, 76–77
alternatives, 75–81
asset sales, 68–69
automatic stay and, 68
in bankruptcy, 62–63, 64
in Chapter 11, 65–75
after Chapter 14, 222–31
in crisis, 74
debtor-in-possession, 28, 56, 64, 65–67, 74, 103
Federal Reserve and, 67, 74–75
government, 74–75
guaranteed funding, 82, 83–84
lender-of-last-resort, 66
prearranged, 64–65, 75–81
private markets, 74
in quick sale recapitalization, 67
repo, 198, 199, 207, 224n172, 226
in SIFI bankruptcy, 62–63, 64
Title II and, 63
Fletcher, Ian, 114–15
FMI. *See* financial market infrastructure
foreclosure law, 59–60

foreign banking organizations (FBOs), 165n30
foreign branches, 138, 255–56
foreign home country stay orders, 49
Freddie Mac, 12
FSB. *See* Financial Stability Board

General Motors, 74
GLAC. *See* gone-concern loss-absorbing capacity
Gleeson, Simon, 111
Global Distressed Alpha Fund 1 v. P. T. Bakrie, 114
Global Financial Markets Association, 107
global systemically important banking groups (G-SIBs), 61n4, 163
complexity of, 252–57
constructive certainty in resolution of, 166–68
countries active in, 255
cross-border resolutions and, 264–66
decentralized or subsidiarized, 268–70
FDIC–Bank of England cooperation agreement and, 264
interconnections among, 250
liquidity needs in resolution, 168
regulator territorial disputes over, 259
resolution of, 171–72
ring-fencing and structure of, 266–70
SPE-MPE hybrid resolution, 166–68
subsidiaries, number of, 252–53, 254f, 255
global systemically important financial institutions (G-SIFIs), 129
Goldman Sachs, 201
gone concern capital ratio, 154n21
gone-concern loss-absorbing capacity (GLAC), 132f4, 181n17, 241
government funding, 81–85
Government of India v. Taylor, 121
Group of Twenty, 251
G-SIBs. *See* global systemically important banking groups

G-SIFIs. *See* global systemically important financial institutions
guarantee funds, 90–92
guaranteed funding, 82, 83–84

haircuts, power to impose, 259
HanMag Investment Securities, 92
high quality, liquid assets (HQLA), 71
Hoenig, Thomas, 247
holding company
    assets of, 69–70
    bail-in and balance sheet of, 144, 145t, 147
    balance sheet insolvency, 149
    change in control, 153
    creditors' rights and subsidiary conditions, 157, 158t
    with domestic and foreign subsidiaries, 159–68, 160f
    double leverage and, 159
    numbers of subsidiaries, 252, 253f
    obligations of, 156n23
    recapitalizing subsidiaries, 146, 148t
    resolution of, 149–59, 152f
    ring-fencing and structure of, 266–70
    SIFIs, 20
    subsidiary in resolution and resolution of, 155–59
    subsidiary losses causing insolvency of, 149
    subsidiary reserve capital and solvency of, 154n21
    unit bank with parent, 141, 142f, 143–44, 146–47, 149
Holdings. *See* Lehman Brothers Holdings Inc.
HQLA. *See* high quality, liquid assets
HSBC, 268
Huertas, Thomas, 129
Human Rights Act, 121

ICE Trust, 89
implied term theory, 114–15
information-sharing agreements, 258

insolvency
    ancillary proceedings, 116–17
    asset devaluations short of, 225f
    balance sheet, 17, 149
    CCP liquidation alternatives, 98
    contracting out of, 122, 122n18
    cross-border issues, 111, 112
    harmonizing laws for, 262–63
    jurisdiction choice and, 259
    Lehman Brothers operating entities entering, 200
    runs driven by, 184–86, 194–99
    subsidiary losses causing, 149
Insolvency in Private International Law (Fletcher), 115
insolvency regimes, 118–20, 124–26
insurance commissioners, 257
insurance companies, 27, 256
intercompany liabilities, 20
intermediate debt, 134, 134n5
international cooperation, 261–66
international coordination, 10–11
International Monetary Fund, 76
International Swaps and Derivatives Association (ISDA), 8, 16, 42n100, 95
    close-out netting clauses and, 263n13
    Master Agreements, 221
    master contracts, 259
    Resolution Stay Protocol, 8, 10, 42n100, 204, 220, 221
Investment Management Division, 232–33
involuntary petitions
    by creditors of covered financial corporations, 35
    regulators filing, 17, 27
IOSCO. *See* Committee on Payment and Settlement Systems-International Organization of Securities Commissions
"ipso facto" clauses, 39
ISDA. *See* International Swaps and Derivatives Association

J. P. Morgan, 73, 176–77, 224n172
  CCP failure resolution proposal, 96, 99, 101
  Washington Mutual acquisition, 201
Jackson, Thomas, 15, 243, 244
jurisdiction, choice of, 259

Kapur, Emily, 176
Key Attributes of Effective Resolution Regimes for Financial Institutions, 118, 260–63
King, Mervyn, 250
knock-on chains, 11–12
Korea Exchange (KRX), 92

large, complex financial institutions (LCFIs), 249
  scope of problem, 250–51
LBI. *See* Lehman Brothers Inc.
LBIE. *See* Lehman Brothers International (Europe)
LBSF. *See* Lehman Brothers Special Financing Inc.
LCFIs. *See* large, complex financial institutions
LCH, 89
LCH.Clearnet, 97
LCR. *See* liquidity coverage ratio
left behind debt, 20, 21, 39, 44
Lehman Brothers, 11–12, 15, 74–76, 176–79, 187, 244
  adequate-assurance finding for, 206–8
  asset devaluations short of insolvency, 225f
  balance sheet, 191–94, 196t–197t
  balance sheet liabilities, 194
  business after Chapter 14, 219–40
  capital ratio after Chapter14, 224
  capital structure debt, 208, 215
  cash drains, 198–99
  Chapter 14 counterfactual, 202–19
  collateral liquidation, 198
  counterfactual timeline of Chapter 14, 213f
  credit downgrade threats, 195
  data gathering for, 251, 251n3
  derivatives holdings, 224n172
  financing after recapitalization, 222–31
  insolvent operating entities, 200
  Investment Management Division, 232–33
  liquidity and collapse of, 195
  living wills and problems in collapse of, 245–46
  mortgage-backed securities holdings, 191n29
  overfunding policy, 198, 198n65
  prime broker operations, 199
  Q3 losses, 195
  real estate holdings, 191n29, 224
  reorganization options, 231–33
  repo financing, 198, 224n172, 226
  run on, 194–99, 226
  section 1405 transfer, 212–19
  solvency after Chapter 14, 222–31
  solvency equity value, 192, 193f
  structure at time of failure, 188–94, 190f
  structure of section 1405 transfer, 216f
  subsidiaries, 188–89, 190f, 191, 200, 214, 251, 251n3
  systemic effects after collapse of, 199–202
  terminating Chapter 14 case, 233, 234f, 235
Lehman Brothers Holdings Inc. (Holdings), 188
  balance-sheet liabilities, 194
  Chapter 11 bankruptcy filing, 200
  Chapter 14 filing, 209–12
  section 1405 transfer, 212–19
Lehman Brothers Inc. (LBI), 188, 210
  Barclays buying, 217
  Chapter 14 change of control, 220
Lehman Brothers International (Europe) (LBIE), 188, 199, 230
  entering administration, 199–200
  prime brokerage losses, 199

Lehman Brothers Special Financing Inc.
  (LBSF), 210
Lehman Estate, 176, 200, 232, 235
lender-of-last-resort funding, 66, 83
liabilities
  balance sheet, 194
  intercompany, 20
  See also debt
liens, DIP financing, 66
liquidation, 47
  alternatives in CCP insolvency, 98
  automatic, 257
  bail-in and, 169
  Basel III liquidity requirements for
    SIFIs, 71–72
  Chapter 7, 42
  collateral, 137, 198
  reserve capital conversion and, 169
  territorial approach to resolution as,
    139–40
  Title II, 18–19, 21, 61
  See also Orderly Liquidation Author-
    ity; Orderly Liquidation Fund
liquidity
  Basel III and, 71–72
  in CCP failure resolution, 102–4
  Chapter 14, 7–8
  Federal Reserve requirements, 71–72
  financing and, 63
  in Lehman Brothers collapse, 195
  in MPE approach, 169
  in new regulatory environment, 71–74
  provision to bank in resolution, 168–70
  QFCs and, 8
  quick sale strategies and, 64
  reserve capital and, 169
  in resolution, 137
  ring-fencing and allocation of, 266–67
  SIFI bankruptcy cases and, 73
  significance, 7
  sources under current bankruptcy
    law, 67–71
  in SPE approach, 169–70
  SPOE proposal, 7, 20
  stress tests, 72, 228t–229t

of subsidiaries, 70
  trapped liquidity pools, 224n172
liquidity coverage ratio (LCR), 72
liquidity crisis, 224, 224n172
liquidity runs, 245
living wills, 80, 205–6, 217
  bankruptcy law shortcomings and, 245
  Dodd-Frank provisions, 243–46
  Lehman Brothers collapse problems
    and, 245–46
  submitted to Federal Reserve and
    FDIC, 80, 244–45, 247–48
Long-Term Capital Management
  (LTCM), 76, 77, 220
loss allocation, 90
loss sharing, 93, 94
  widening, 99
LTCM. *See* Long-Term Capital
  Management
Lyondell Chemical Co., 74

market-implied losses, 224
Master Agreements, 221
master contracts, 259
master repo agreements, 212
Matthews v. Eldridge, 218
Merrill Lynch, 12
modified universalism, 124–25
Monetary Authority of Singapore, 214
money markets, 200, 201, 231
moral hazard
  Chapter 14 and, 182–83, 184
  prearranged financing and, 78–79
  SPOE and, 183
moral suasion, 77
Morgan Stanley, 201
multiple-point-of-entry (MPE), 160–62,
  164–65, 166–68, 270
  assumptions for, 272
  liquidity facilities in, 169

National Bank of Greece and Athens SA
  v. Metliss, 113
NCWOL. *See* no creditor worse off than
  under liquidation

Neuberger Bermann, 232
New York Fed, 76
no creditor worse off than under liquidation (NCWOL), 156
no-creditor-worse-off principle, 104
non-financial subsidiaries, 257

Office of the Comptroller of the Currency, 214
Office of Thrift Supervision, 214
OLA. *See* Orderly Liquidation Authority
OLF. *See* Orderly Liquidation Fund
one-entity recapitalization, 20
options, recapitalization with, 146
Orderly Liquidation Authority (OLA),
18, 19, 120, 162n29, 243, 246
Orderly Liquidation Fund (OLF), 7, 65,
82, 83–84, 183, 227
CCP failure resolution and, 103–4
organizational structure, 266–70
decentralized or subsidiarized,
268–70
overfunding policy, 198

PDCF. See Primary Dealer Credit
Facility
Peck, James, 217
point of nonviability (PONV), 130, 132,
133
prearranged financing, 64–65
advantages, 77
alternatives, 75–81
costs of, 78–79
escrowed, 78
moral hazard and, 78–79
obstacles, 77–78
pre-bankruptcy loan commitments, 81
pre-bankruptcy planning, 16
financing requirements and, 73
Lehman Brothers lacking, 12
Title I resolution plans, 18, 22
preference law, 29, 42
prefunded recapitalization funds, 99
prepackaged bankruptcy cases, 73,
73n35, 151, 154n21

pre-seizure judicial hearing, 9
Primary Dealer Credit Facility (PDCF),
224n172, 227
prime broker operations, 199, 201
priming liens, 66
private international law, 115
private markets
DIP financing, 74
stress absorption, 220

qualified financial contracts (QFCs), 1,
16, 263n13
in Chapter 14 1.0, 29–30, 41, 210
in Chapter 14 2.0, 40, 53–54
defining, 50
exemptions for counterparties, 29
liquidity, 8
resolution and, 137, 170, 170n35
section 1405 transfer and, 39, 40, 54
quick sale recapitalization, 24, 30–48
financing in, 67
House approval of, 86
liquidity needs and, 64
section 1405 transfer, 31–33, 39–47
Title II and, 47–48

railroad receivership, 59
rapid resolution plans, 80
ratings agencies, 195
Rattner, Steven, 74
*Re HIH Casualty and General Insurance
Ltd.,* 115, 117
recap gap, 136
recapitalization, 37, 47
adequate-assurance standard and,
206–8
avoiding powers and, 42
bail-in and, 144, 144n16, 145t,
146–47, 148t, 156–57
borrowing options in, 69–70
bridge companies, 39
CET1 targets, 134–36
in Chapter 14 2.0, 25, 69
new mechanisms for, 177–78
one-entity, 20

with options, 146
prefunded trusts for, 99
quick sale, 24, 30–48, 64, 86
of subsidiaries after Chapter 14,
    219–22, 223f
Title I resolution plans and, 22
two-entity, 20, 23, 39, 42–43, 47
of unit bank by parent holding com-
    pany, 146, 148t
receiver's certificate, 60
receivership
    equity, 59–60
    government, 11–12
    railroad, 59
recovery
    CCP, 90–96
    contractual, 91, 93
    default-management waterfall, 91f,
        92–94
    VMGH, 92–96
regimes of mutual recognition, 204n102
regulators
    asymmetries in, 262
    capital structure debt floor, 203,
        203n97
    centrally cleared derivatives, 88
    in Chapter 14 1.0, 27–28
    Chapter 14 2.0 and role of, 37–38,
        50–51
    conflicting resolution and bankruptcy
        approaches, 258
    involuntary petition filing by, 17, 27
    liquidity needs and changes in, 71–74
    section 1405 transfer objections and,
        218
    separate subsidiaries for different, 256
    specialized, 257
    territorial disputes in G-SIB distress,
        258
regulatory capital, 36
rehypothecation, 199
reload capability, 134
reorganization, 23, 38
    after Chapter 14, 231–33
    Chapter 14 2.0 and, 41

Chapter 14 and, 180
cross-border issues, 114
equity distribution and, 44–45, 47
two-entity, 246
repo financing, 198, 199, 207, 224n172,
    226
repurchase contracts, 29
reserve capital, 132–34, 132f4, 135f
    bail-in and, 147, 156–57, 158t
    conversion of, 169
    liquidity provision and, 169
    regulatory requirements for, 154n21
    requirements for, 134
    senior debt and, 133–34
    unit bank with parent holding com-
        pany, 141, 143, 147, 154n21
Reserve Primary Fund, 176, 200, 230
resolution
    bilateral agreements on international
        cases, 264
    branches and, 138–40
    CCP, 90–96, 102–4, 105–6
    CCP failure, 96–100, 106–7
    complexity problems for, 258–61
    constructive certainty in, 166–68
    cooperative, 262
    cross-border agreements on, 264–66,
        270
    cross-border issues, 106–7, 138–40,
        264–66, 270
    cross-border recognition of, 112
    derivatives and, 170, 170n35
    Dodd-Frank requiring plans for,
        243–46
    domestic and foreign subsidiaries,
        159–68
    explicit contractual terms recogniz-
        ing, 120–22
    FSB standards for, 260–63
    of G-SIB, 166–68, 171–72
    of holding company, 149–59, 152f
    home country statutes, 162–63
    Human Rights Act and, 121
    international cooperation in, 261–66
    MPE approach, 164–65

resolution (*continued*)
  no-creditor-worse-off principle, 104
  plans for rapid, 80
  provision of liquidity in, 168–70
  QFCs and, 137, 170, 170n35
  recapitalization targets, 134–36
  regulator conflicting approaches, 258
  service agreements and, 170, 170n34
  SPE approach, 162–63
  stages of, 130, 131f
  statutory powers in UK, 122–24
  territorial approach to, 138–40, 259
  Title I plans, 18, 22, 80
  Title II, 18
  two-entity recapitalization and, 47
  UK standards recommendations,
    260–61
  of unit bank, 132–37
  unit bank with parent holding com-
    pany, 141, 143–44, 146–47, 149
  unitary approach to, 138, 138n11, 140
  See also Key Attributes of Effective
    Resolution Regimes for Financial
    Institutions
Resolution Project, 1, 11
  Chapter 14 proposal, 1–2, 15
  expanded Chapter 14 proposal, 1, 23
Resolution Stay Protocol of 2014, 8, 10,
    42n100, 204, 220, 221
resolution weekend, 250
resolvability
  foreign branches and, 138–40
  recapitalization capital targets for,
    134–36
  standards for, 130, 132
  unit bank with parent holding com-
    pany, 141, 143–44, 146–47, 149
resolvable banks, 129
ring-fencing, 49, 212, 250
  corporate structure implications of,
    266–70
  of foreign branches, 256
  individual regulatory objectives and,
    258
risk-weighted assets (RWAs), 134

Rome I Regulation, 112–13
runs, 184–87
  cascading, 200
  Chapter 11 and, 176–77
  after Chapter 14, 224
  insolvency driven, 184–86, 194–99
  on Lehman Brothers, 194–99, 226
  after Lehman Brothers collapse, 200
  liquidity, 245
Russian financial crisis, 76
RWAs. *See* risk-weighted assets

Salomon Brothers, 220
Santander, 268
Scott, Kenneth D., 1
section 13(3) authority, 8, 75, 84–85,
    203
section 303, 34, 36
section 362 stay, 210
section 363, 22, 27, 62, 69
section 364, 65, 67
section 365, 39–40
section 1112, 34
section 1125, 44
section 1145, 44–45
section 1405 transfer, 24–25, 30n51,
    31–33, 180
  avoiding powers and, 42
  bridge companies, 32–33, 44–45
  capital requirement exemption
    window, 44
  Chapter 14 2.0 provisions, 39–43
  Chapter 14 2.0 transitional provisions,
    43–47
  Chapter 14 commencement and, 33
  conditions for, 32–33
  FDIC standing in, 38
  hearings, 217
  Lehman Brothers counterfactual,
    212–19
  management status in, 45
  notification period, 32
  objections to, 218–19
  proposed text for, 51–52
  QFCs and, 39, 40, 54

quick sale recapitalization, 31–33,
    39–47
  securities distribution following,
    44–45
  structure of, 216f
  subsidiary contracts and, 55
  time constraints, 32, 35, 40–41, 217
section 1411, 42
section 1412, 45
Securities and Exchange Commission,
    214
Securities and Investments Commission
    (Australia), 214
Securities Investor Protection Corpora-
    tion, 27
senior debt, 133–34
service level agreements, 170n34
shared services, 269–70
SIFI. *See* systemically important finan-
    cial institution
single point of entry (SPOE/SPE), 2, 5,
    60–61, 62, 244
  assumptions for, 271
  Bank of England and, 270
  Chapter 11 problems addressed by,
    177–78
  as Chapter 14 backstop, 202
  Chapter 14 in parallel to, 23
  constructive certainty and, 161
  as default process, 22
  FSB and, 270
  home country resolution statutes,
    162–63
  liquidity and, 7, 20
  liquidity facilities in, 169–70
  moral hazard and, 183
  MPE hybrid approach, 166–68
  problems with proposal, 21–22
  subsidiaries and, 159–62
  subsidiaries in multiple countries,
    162–63
Skeel, David A., Jr., 60
social welfare, 182–83, 235, 237, 240
solvency equity, 192
South Korea, 76

sovereign immunity, 49
SPE. *See* single point of entry
SPOE. *See* single point of entry
standing creditors' committee, 155
statutory variation of debts, 115–17
stay orders
  automatic, 29, 52–53, 68, 210
  on change-of-control provisions, 210
  Chapter 14, 210
  on clearing agreements, 100–102
  on close-out netting clauses, 263n13
  financing sources and, 68
  foreign home country, 49
  foreign jurisdictions and, 212
  section 362, 210
  See also Resolution Stay Protocol of
    2014
stress tests, 72, 226, 228t–229t
subchapter V, 86
subordinated debt, 203
subprime mortgages, 12
subsidiaries
  assets of, 69–70
  bail-in and balance sheet of, 144,
    145t, 147
  bail-in recapitalization of, 148t,
    156–57
  balance sheets of, 141, 142f, 143
  changing parent of, 153
  Chapter 14 stays on creditors to, 210
  constructive certainty and resolution
    of, 166–68
  creditors' rights in parent company
    bankruptcy, 157, 158t
  cross-border resolutions and, 265
  customer obligations of, 147
  disaggregation of, 256, 256t
  domestic and foreign subsidiaries,
    159–68, 160f
  double leverage and, 159
  holdings transferred to bridge compa-
    nies, 42–43
  insulated from group, 257, 257n8,
    269
  insurance, 256

subsidiaries (*continued*)
Lehman Brothers, 188–89, 190f, 191, 200, 214
liquidity of, 70
losses causing parent company insolvency, 149
as measure of group complexity, 255
MPE approach for resolution, 162–63
MPE assumptions about, 272
non-financial, 257
numbers of, in G-SIBs, 252–53, 254f, 255
numbers of, in US bank companies, 252, 253f
organizational structure and, 268
parent holding company and resolution of, 155–59
parent holding company recapitalizing, 146, 148t
as primary asset of holding company, 69–70
recapitalizing after Chapter 14, 219–22, 223f
reserve capital requirements, 143, 156–57
ring-fencing and structure of, 266–70
self-funding, 269
separate, for different regulatory jurisdictions, 256
shared services, 269–70
SPE assumptions about, 271
unit banks, 141, 142f, 143–44, 146–47, 149
subsidiarized organizational structure, 268–70
subsidiary contracts, Chapter 14 2.0 and, 54–55
SwapClear, 88
systemically important financial institution (SIFI), 1, 2
assessment under Title II, 84
bankruptcy viability of, 18
Basel III liquidity requirements, 71–72
capital requirements, 3
FDIC proposal for failure of, 2–5
financing in bankruptcy, 62–63, 64
government receivership of, 11–12
holding companies, 20
international, 10–11
liquidity needs and bankruptcy, 73
living wills, 80
two-entity recapitalization, 23
See also global systemically important banking groups
systemic harm requirement, 85
systemic risk, 11–13
common shocks, 12–13
knock-on chains, 11–12

T2 capital, 132
TBTF. *See* too big to fail
tear-up, 93, 100
territorial approach to resolution, 138–40, 259
Title 28, amendments to, 57
Title I
living will provisions, 243–46
rapid resolution plans, 80
recapitalization and, 22
resolution plans, 18, 22
too big to fail banks and, 247
Title II, 61, 183
CCP failure resolution, 97–98, 103, 106–7
due process and, 9
financing arrangements, 63
as insolvency regime, 118–20
liquidation and, 18–19, 21, 61
Orderly Liquidation Authority, 19, 120, 243, 246
Orderly Liquidation Fund, 65
quick sale recapitalization and, 47–48
resolution by FDIC, 18
SIFIs assessment under, 84
SPOE and Chapter 14 in parallel under, 23
UK and, 116, 118–20
TLAC. *See* total loss absorbing capacity
"too big to fail" (TBTF), 247
Group of Twenty consensus on, 251

total loss absorbing capacity (TLAC), 3, 61n4, 132f4, 134n5
trapped liquidity pools, 224n172
tri-party lenders, 198, 199
Troubled Asset Relief Program, 201
trust-preferred securities, 68
Tucker, Paul, 265
two-entity recapitalization, 20
  avoiding powers and, 42
  Chapter 14 resolution, 47
  principles, 39
  SIFIs using, 23
  subsidiary holdings and, 42–43
  venue rules, 37
two-entity reorganization, 246

UNCITRAL. See United Nations Commission on International Trade Law
unencumbered assets, 169, 169n33
unit bank with parent holding company, balance sheet, 141, 142f
unitary approach to resolution, 138, 138n11, 140
United Kingdom
  ancillary proceedings, 116–17
  choice of law, 112–13
  debt variation consequences, 115–17
  equal treatment of creditors, 117, 122
  explicit contractual terms recognizing resolution and, 120–22
  implied contract terms, 114–15
  insolvency regimes and, 118–20, 124–26

overseas insolvency regime recognition in, 124–26
overseas resolution statutory regime in, 123–24
statutory powers in resolution, 122–24
Title II and, 116, 118–20
US Bankruptcy Code and, 124–26
variation of liabilities by foreign statute, 113–14
United Nations Commission on International Trade Law (UNCITRAL), 119–20
universalism, 124–25
universality, 111
unsecured debt, 20
US Treasury, 76

variation margin gains haircutting (VMGH), 92–96, 98, 100, 102
variation of debts, 115–17
venue rules, 36, 37
VMGH. See variation margin gains haircutting
voluntary petition, by Federal Reserve Board, 35

Wachovia, 201
Washington Mutual, 201
waterfall recovery, 91f, 92–94
Wells Fargo, 201
workouts, 220